Facets

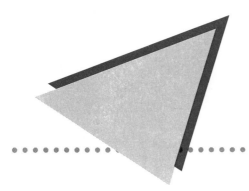

Facets
Writing Skills in Context

Sara M. Blake
EL CAMINO COLLEGE

Janet Madden
EL CAMINO COLLEGE

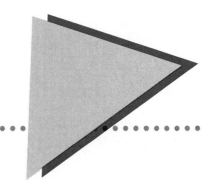

MACMILLAN COLLEGE PUBLISHING COMPANY
NEW YORK

EDITOR: Timothy Julet
PRODUCTION SUPERVISOR: P.M. Gordon Associates, Inc.
PRODUCTION MANAGER: Aliza Greenblatt
TEXT AND COVER DESIGNER: Sheree Goodman
COVER ART: Clinton Hill, Blue Seep HMP 1991

This book was set in 10.5/13 Bookman Light by Compset, Inc., and was printed and bound by Semline.
The cover was printed by Phoenix Color Corp.

Macmillan College Publishing Company
866 Third Avenue, New York, New York 10022

Macmillan College Publishing Company is part of
the Maxwell Communication Group of Companies.

Maxwell Macmillan Canada, Inc.
1200 Eglinton Avenue East
Suite 200
Don Mills, Ontario M3C 3N1

Library of Congress Cataloging-in-Publication Data

Blake, Sara M.
    Facets : writing skills in context / Sara M. Blake, Janet Madden.
      p. cm.
    Includes index.
    ISBN 0–02–310841–X (main text)
    ISBN 0–02–310842–8 (instructor's—annotated ed.)
    1. English Language—Rhetoric. 2. English language—Grammar.
I. Madden, Janet. II. Title.
PE1408.B523 1994
808'.042—dc20   93–43228
                                                              CIP

Printing: 1 2 3 4 5 6 7   Year: 4 5 6 7 8 9 0

To the Instructor

Designed for the developmental student, *Facets* takes a multicultural approach to integrating instruction in reading, writing, critical thinking, and grammar in order to prepare students for freshman-level writing. It also aims to enliven the developmental writing course by encouraging students to make connections between their cultural experiences, the situations presented in the exercises, and the work of professional writers of diverse backgrounds. Because we believe that many developmental writers are also developmental readers, this text pays particular attention to the importance of reading comprehension. We provide short reading selections of high student interest and supplement these readings with extensive guidance and comprehension exercises to encourage students to draw inferences about how writers incorporate grammatical concepts in their writing. We also provide bio-bibliographical notes about the writers and their work so that developmental students are encouraged to see writing as a viable activity for people of all ethnic and cultural backgrounds. We also hope that these selections will encourage students to read for pleasure, beyond requirements for their courses; the notes direct interested students to the works in their entirety.

Our motivation in writing this text was to produce a book that addresses basic skills in a fresh, new way; we have also endeavored to provide students with a topical and lively approach to material that has been presented to them, unsuccessfully, in the past. In hopes of helping students to bcome successful college writers and therefore successful college students, we have constructed a text that:

- provides a self-contained guide to grammar skills and to the writing process, and stresses links between the two;
- accommodates the skill levels of developmental students while validating the richness of their life experiences;
- recognizes and celebrates the diversity of the developmental classroom, which incorporates differences in age, life experience, social and educational backgrounds, learning abilities, and educational goals;

- stresses the multicultural nature of the American experience through readings and exercises that draw upon "real-life" situations;
- presents excerpts from works of professional writers to serve as models for student writing, to help students to use inference in recognizing how grammatical concepts are used in writing, and to entice students to read beyond the confines of reading assigned for course work;
- provides developmental students with real-life student essays by developmental-level student writers;
- emphasizes process in its discussion of writing—student examples are narratives, not restricted to an imposed formula—to give students an opportunity to find and explore their own voices;
- presents clear explanations of grammatical concepts and opportunities for students to practice applying these concepts;
- provides clearly articulated sequenced writing prompts, suggestions for the composing process, and guidelines for revising student writing;
- presents the concept of writing effective paragraphs in terms of paragraph pattern and development—not as an isolated skill, such as writing a one-paragraph essay, but rather in terms of the paragraph's use in developing essays and responding to assignments across the curriculum;
- recognizes the reality of the makeup of the developmental class by providing a unit that addresses issues of special concern to ESL students;
- incorporates instruction and practice material that has been classroom-tested by developmental writing students;
- provides instruction in prewriting;
- allows instructors to incorporate the concept of a writer's notebook.

While developing this book, we benefited from the thoughtful comments of colleagues who reviewed the manuscript: Hilda Barrow, Pitt Community College; Don Barshis, Wright College, City Colleges of Chicago; Elaine Hage, Forsyth Technical Community College; Joan Mauldin, San Jacinto College (South); Meritt W. Stark, Jr., Henderson State University.

We wish to extend special thanks to Barbara Heinssen, Senior Editor at Macmillan, who suggested that we undertake this project.

S.M.B.
J.M.

To the Student

The units in this text reflect the major elements of effective writing: composing complete sentences, using words correctly, joining ideas, adding information, expressing ideas clearly, punctuating sentences, spelling correctly, and developing paragraphs. In addition, a separate unit has been included to address the special concerns of ESL students. Each unit is followed by a section highlighting the information it presents and by a comprehensive practice exercise to test your mastery of the material you have studied.

Each unit is divided into chapters that will give you a chance to work with a particular aspect of the unit topic. As you work through the various chapters, you will encounter the following features:

- A *Chapter Preview* that describes what you can expect to find in the chapter
- A brief selection from *a professional writer* that illustrates the concept being discussed in the chapter. The writers, whose works have appeared in magazines and books, are from all ethnic and cultural backgrounds.
- Essays written by *students* in response to an assignment
- A series of *explanations* that break down the subject of the chapter into manageable chunks
- Exercises, called *Applications*, after each explanation to practice what you have learned
- A *Chapter Review* that recaps the information in the explanations and gives you a chance to practice what you have learned.

In writing this text, we have attempted to present the skills you need in order to write effectively and to complete college-level writing assignments successfully. We hope that this book will help you do just that.

S.M.B.
J.M.

Brief Contents

Contents

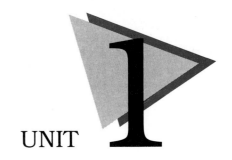

UNIT 1

Writing Sentences

CHAPTER 1

Identifying Sentences

▼ CHAPTER PREVIEW

This chapter focuses on **sentences**—the way that people arrange thoughts into words in order to express themselves. Because sentences express thoughts, they serve as the basis of all writing.

A Professional Writer Uses Sentences

About the Reading: The passage that follows comes from an early chapter of *Lacota Woman*, the life story of Mary Crow Dog. In this 1990 autobiography, Mary Crow Dog tells of her personal experiences growing up in poverty on a South Dakota Sioux Indian reservation in the 1960s and 1970s. In addition, her book records the movement for Indian tribal pride and identity that emerged at that time.

As You Read: Look carefully at the sentences in the passage that follows. As you notice the different sentences in this piece of writing, try to figure out what they have in common. Look at such features as length, punctuation, capitalization, and content.

From *Lacota Woman*

[1]We had no shoes and went barefoot most of the time. [2]I never had a new dress. [3]Once a year we would persuade somebody to drive us to the Catholic mission for a basement rummage sale. [4]Sometimes we found something there to put on our feet before it got cold, and maybe a secondhand blouse or skirt. [5]That was all we could afford. [6]We did not celebrate Christmas, at least not the kind of feast white people are used to. [7]Grandma would save a little money and when the time came she bought some crystal sugar—it looked like

small rocks of glass put on a string—some peanuts, apples, and oranges. [8]And she got some kind of cotton material, sewing it together, making little pouches for us, and in each put one apple, one orange, a handful of peanuts, and some of that crystal sugar which took forever to melt in one's mouth. [9]I loved it. [10]That was Christmas and it never changed.

After You Read: Refer to the reading selection to complete the following items.

1. What differences do you observe among the sentences in the passage? List these differences on the following lines:

_____

_____

_____

_____

2. How are the sentences in the passage similar? List these similarities here:

_____

_____

_____

_____

3. Based on the similarities you listed, try to come up with your own definition of a sentence.

_____

_____

_____

_____

Defining a Sentence

In looking at differences between the sentences in the passage from *Lacota Woman*, you may have noticed that some sentences are longer than others. In addition, some sentences have internal marks of punctuation like commas and dashes while others do not. And some sentences describe only one action while others describe several. In this chapter, however, we will be focusing on the basic elements that all sentences have in common.

As you were noting the differences between the various sentences in the passage, you may also have noticed that certain features appear in all of them:

All of the sentences begin with a capital letter and end with a punctuation mark.

Each sentence expresses at least one complete thought about a thing, a person, a place, or an idea.

Each sentence has at least one subject (word that tells *who* or *what* the sentence is about) and at least one verb (word that tells what the subject *does* or *is*).

All of these features set a sentence apart from any other group of words. If your definition does not include all of these items, go back and revise it.

APPLICATION

Read each item carefully and decide whether or not it is a complete sentence. If you think the item is a complete sentence, write **S** in the blank. If the item is not a complete sentence, write **NS** in the blank. You may wish to refer to your definition of a sentence.

EXAMPLE: _____**S**_____ Maria ran to catch the bus.
(The sentence begins with a capital **M,** ends with a period, contains the verb **ran** and the subject **Maria,** and expresses a complete thought.)

_____ 1. Leo looked stunned by the news.

_____ 2. Keisha smiled.

_____ 3. To the movies.

_____ 4. Rashid and Philip—best friends since the age of four—along with Jorge and Roger.

_____ 5. The van cruised down the dimly lit avenue

_____ 6. The sun blazed on the sunbathers, and the music blared from hundreds of boom boxes as the lifeguard watchfully eyed the inexperienced swimmers.

_____ 7. The bank teller plucked at the bills with her long pink acrylic nails.

_____ 8. Miles, who is my best friend, works afternoons in a video store.

_____ 9. Driven to the dance.

_____ 10. Which seemed like the right thing to do at the time.

▼ CHAPTER REVIEW

A **sentence** is a group of words that

1. expresses at least one complete thought about a person, thing, or idea
2. contains at least one subject and one verb
3. begins with a capital letter
4. ends with a punctuation mark

PRACTICE

In the paragraph that follows, all of the initial capital letters and end marks have been removed. Test your sentence sense by dividing the words into sentences and adding capitals and periods wherever necessary. You may wish to check your work against that of a classmate. If you have difficulty with this practice, you should go back and reread the information in this chapter.

The Harlem Renaissance

the Harlem Renaissance is the name given to an enormous outpouring of creative energy from the African-American community in the 1920s during this period African-American writers, artists, and musicians from all parts of the United States flocked to the Harlem area of New York even though the Harlem Renaissance lasted only ten years, it produced an immense body of artistic work Zora Neale Hurston and Langston Hughes are two writers who first won recognition for their work during this time today there has been a renewed interest in the works of these writers and in the Harlem Renaissance

CHAPTER 2

Recognizing Basic Sentence Elements

▼ CHAPTER PREVIEW

As you learned in the last chapter, sentences contain two basic elements—**verbs** and **subjects.** In this chapter, you will practice identifying and writing verbs and subjects.

A Professional Writer Uses Verbs and Subjects

About the Reading: Mexican-American author Arturo Islas writes about life on the border between the United States and Mexico. In this excerpt from his 1984 novel *The Rain God,* Islas describes a photograph that is important to the novel's main character, Miguel Chico. The photograph of Miguel Chico and his grandmother, which was taken when Miguel was a child, not only captures a moment of his past, but also suggests that the move from Mexico to the United States was the central event in the lives of Islas' characters.

As You Read: While you read this paragraph, pay special attention to the marked words in each sentence. Subjects are italicized, and verbs are printed in bold type.

From *The Rain God*

¹A *photograph* of Mama Chona and her grandson Miguel Angel—Miguel Chico or Mickie to his family—**hovers** above his head on the study wall beside the glass doors *that* **open** out into the garden. ²When *Miguel Chico* **sits** at his desk, *he* **glances** up at it occasionally without noticing it, looking through it rather than at it. ³*It* **was taken** in the early years of World War II by an old

Mexican photographer *who* **wandered** up and down the border town's main street on the American side. [4]*No one* **knows** how *it* **found** its way back to them, for Miguel Chico's *grandmother* never **spoke** to strangers. [5]*She* and the *child* **are walking** hand in hand. [6]*Mama Chona* **is wearing** a black ankle-length dress with a white lace collar and *he* **is** in a short-sleeved light-colored summer suit with short pants. [7]In the middle of the street life around them, *they* **are looking** straight ahead, intensely preoccupied, almost worried. [8]*They* **seem** in a great hurry. [9]*Each* **has** a foot off the ground, and Mama Chona's black *hat* with the three white daisies, their yellow centers like eyes *that* always **out-stared** him, **is tilting** backward just enough to be noticeable. [10]Because of the look on his face, the *child* **seems** as old as the woman. [11]The *camera* **has captured** them in flight from this world to the next.

After You Read: Refer to the reading selection to complete the following items.

1. In the space provided, list the verbs and subjects in the Islas paragraph.

           VERBS   *SUBJECTS*

2. Look over the list carefully; then reread the selection, paying special attention to the verbs. What, if anything, do the different verbs in your list have in common? How are they different? How do verbs function in a sentence?

_____

_____

_____

_____

3. Read the selection one more time, this time focusing on the subject words. Then look over your list of subjects. What kinds of words act as subjects? How do subjects function in a sentence?

_____

_____

_____

_____

_____

In looking closely at the subjects and verbs in the Islas passage, you may have noticed some of the following features:

VERBS

Verbs tell something about the subject.

Verbs can name actions (**wandered, sits, glances**), but they are not always action words (**seem, is**).

Sometimes verbs can be more than one word (**is tilting, are looking**).

Verbs have different endings (**-ing, -ed, -s**).

SUBJECTS

Subjects tell who or what the sentence is about.

Subjects can be people's names (**Mama Chona, Miguel Chico**), things (**hat, camera**), or words like **he, they,** and **each.**

Sometimes there can be more than one subject in a single sentence (**She** and the **child**).

You probably already know a lot more about verbs and subjects than you think though you may not know all of the rules that they follow. See if you can apply what you have observed about verbs and subjects and what you already know about them.

APPLICATION ONE

In each of these sentences, the verb (the action word) is missing. Fill in your own verb to make the sentence complete.

  EXAMPLE: The boy ___**chomped**___ his bubble gum.

1. Raj _____ at the sight of the history exam.

2. The vicious dog _____ at the frightened mail carrier.

3. Talitha and Janice _____ at the canceled class sign.

4. Delighted with her birthday check, Jasmine _____ all the way to the bank.

5. Fremont _____ as the cherry red Porsche sped by.

6. Anisha _____ at a shelter for the homeless.

7. Marvin's beeper _____ just as the chemistry instructor asked him a difficult question.

8. The subway train _____ through the underground tunnel.

9. At the end of the concert, the fans _____ and _____.

10. The commencement speaker _____ for two hours.

APPLICATION TWO

These sentences lack a subject. Fill in your own subject (the word that tells *who* or *what* performs the verb).

> *EXAMPLE:*   **Harvey** offended the history lecturer by arriving twenty minutes late to class.

1. The _____ careened off the icy road.

2. Because of her excellent grades, _____ was offered a scholarship.

3. John's _____ was unpaid, and his _____ was sick.

4. A _____ arrived at the front door one morning.

5. After outlining the chapters and rereading the class notes, _____ felt well prepared for the test.

6. That new _____ looked ridiculous on Rudy.

7. After the hurricane, the _____ was totally destroyed.

8. _____ and _____ decided to elope to Las Vegas.

9. The gorgeous _____ strutted across the stage.

10. _____ was Felicia's favorite song.

Looking at Verbs

Action Verbs and Linking Verbs

You may remember hearing in English classes that verbs are words that show "action or state of being." **Action verbs** are fairly easy to spot. They name an action such as **walk, yell, throw,** and **eat.**

I **walk** to school two days a week.

Fred's parents always **yell** at him to drive more carefully.

We often **throw** reusable items in the trash.

Cyndi and Fay **eat** at McDonald's every Monday morning.

Words that show "state of being" are called **linking verbs.** Instead of naming an action, these verbs link the subject with a word that describes it or renames it. Linking verbs include all forms of **be** (**am, is, are, was, were, being, been**) and words such as **appear, seem, become,** and **feel** that can be substituted for forms of *be.* Sense verbs like **look, sound,** and **smell** can also be linking verbs if they are not describing actions.

She **is** ill. (**ill** describes the subject, **she**)

She **seems** ill. (**seems** can be substituted for **is**)

She **looks** ill. (**looks** is not an action in this sentence)

He **felt** tired. (**felt** can be substituted for **was**)

He **felt** the doorknob. (**felt** is an action in this sentence)

Ralph and Orlando **were** best friends. (**best friends** renames the subjects, **Ralph and Orlando**)

Ralph and Orlando **became** best friends. (**became** can be substituted for **were**)

APPLICATION

In each of the following sentences, the verb has been printed in italics. In the blank next to each sentence, write *V* if the italicized word is an action verb, or write *LV* if it is a linking verb.

EXAMPLE: ___LV___ Fernando *was* captain of the soccer team. (**captain of the soccer team** renames **Fernando**)

_____ 1. William *rides* the bus to school.

_____ 2. Marcia *seems* quite happy with her new promotion.

_____ 3. Phil and Hernando *drove* to Mexico over spring break.

_____ 4. Sara *raised* four children and *worked* as a waitress before she *enrolled* in college.

_____ 5. Her husband *appeared* nervous during the party.

_____ 6. Manuel *sounded* quite happy with his new job.

_____ 7. Talitha *slammed* the door with a loud bang.

_____ 8. The stray cat *meowed* pitifully for some food.

_____ 9. Fahid *became* more and more upset with the rude customer.

_____ 10. Anita *sang* the national anthem before the game.

Tense and Number

When you are trying to identify the verbs in a sentence, remember that verbs change spelling to show **number** or **tense.**

Verbs are the *only* words that change their spelling to show tense. **Tense** refers to the time (present, past, or future) at which an action takes place.

They **play** today. (present)

They **played** yesterday. (past)

Present tense verbs can also change their spelling to show *how many.* A single subject (**he, it, the man**) takes a **singular** verb. A subject of more than one thing or person (**they, the cars, Jan and Marta**) takes a **plural** verb.

The man **plays** in a band. (**plays** with an **-s** is a **singular** verb)

Jan and Marta **play** in a band. (**play** is the **plural** form)

If you have trouble deciding whether a verb is singular or plural, try using the verb with the subjects **he** and **they.** The form that can be used with the subject **they** (more than one person) is plural; the form that goes with **he** (one person) is singular.

He **plays** in a band.

They **play** in a band.

The two exceptions are the verbs used with **I** and the verbs used with **you** (meaning one person). Both of these subjects are singular, but the verb forms used with these subjects look the same as the plural verb forms.

I **play** in a band.

You **play** in a band.

APPLICATION

Put an **X** in the blank if the italicized word or words in the sentence are verbs. If you are unsure, ask yourself if the word changes spelling to show tense and number.

> *EXAMPLE:*   ___**X**___ The college *operates* quite efficiently. (Today it **operates.** Yesterday it **operated.** The college **operates.** The colleges **operate.**)

_____ 1. LaShawn *revised* her essay several times.

_____ 2. Natalie *was* first in line at the after-Christmas sale.

_____ 3. Before she *went* to the interview, Jean *felt* nervous.

_____ 4. English was not Tram's first *language.*

_____ 5. Lorraine and Dion *spent* an hour at the bus stop.

_____ 6. David took his stepson to a *basketball* game.

_____ 7. Ralph *adores* Chinese food.

_____ 8. Danny gave his girlfriend an expensive gold *chain.*

_____ 9. *Under* the bridge a street vendor sold ice cream.

_____ 10. Joyce *drove* her ten-year-old Toyota slowly and carefully.

Main Verbs and Helping Verbs

The verbs you have looked at up to now have been one-word verbs: **walk, run, is,** and so on. Many English verbs, however, are made up of more than one word. For example, to show an action occurring in the future you need to use two words—**will** + an action verb.

I **will go** to the library after class.

Or, to show that an action is a necessity, you might add the word **must** to the action verb.

I **must go** to the library after class.

In these two examples, the words **will** and **must** are considered **helping verbs.** The word **go** in each case is called the **main verb.** The main verb, together with any helping verbs, is called the **complete verb.**

As the previous examples illustrate, **helping verbs** are used with main verbs for two reasons:

1. To show tense:

   I **am going.** (right now)

   I **will go.** (in the future)

   I **have gone.** (at some time in the past)

2. To indicate shades of meaning that cannot be expressed by a single-word verb alone:

   I **may go** to the lecture. (possibility)

   I **must go** to the lecture. (necessity)

   I **should go** to the lecture. (advisability)

   I **can go** to the lecture. (ability)

Sentences may contain more than one helping verb.

   I **should have gone** to the lecture.

   I **will be going** to the lecture.

Notice that the main verb always comes *after* the helping verbs.

Some words are *always* helping verbs:

can	may	could
will	must	would
shall	might	should

Other words can be either main verbs or helping verbs depending on how they are used:

is	be	was	has	do
am	being	were	have	does
are	been		had	did

          MV
Roberto **had** 3,000 baseball cards.
   HV HV   MV
He **had** been collecting them for over five years.

APPLICATION

In the following sentences, write **HV** over helping verbs and write **MV** over main verbs. Remember, some sentences will have only main verbs.

               HV   MV
EXAMPLE: Sonia was enjoying her new job in the library.

1. Otto had been attending Weight Watchers meetings for a month.

2. Florence felt dizzy during the parade.

3. His history instructor was incredibly boring.

4. The harried salesperson should have been more pleasant to the customer.

5. The repetitious job could have been performed by trained monkeys.

6. The middle-aged couple was shocked by the singer's foul language.

7. Her perfume smelled terrible.

8. His study habits could be improved with a little less MTV.

9. Lola's new outfit looked sensational.

10. Mario was going to a nightclub after work.

Words Often Mistaken for Verbs

Some words seem to be verbs either because of their placement in a sentence or because of their appearance. Words like **not, ever, never, always, only, very, already,** and **often** are not verbs, but they are often placed in the middle of the verb.

      HV   MV
He had **never** driven a motorcycle before.
                                 HV   MV
The college registration process did **not** work efficiently.

Words ending in **-ing** look like verbs, but they cannot stand alone without a helping verb as the complete verb of a sentence.

                      HV MV
Studying all the time can be stressful.
                     HV
Moving quickly, the cat pounced on the unsuspecting mouse.

To + **verb** cannot be the verb of a sentence though it can be a subject.

        MV
Mark lived **to play** football.
    S   MV
To travel by air is expensive.

APPLICATION

In each sentence, underline the complete verb.

> *EXAMPLE:* My brother <u>wants</u> to buy a sports car.

1. Melvin spent all of his time sitting in front of a computer.
2. Toni was always dating someone much older.
3. I have never liked English class until now.
4. Teresa tried to keep a straight face.
5. I should never have forgotten my mother's birthday.
6. He was always giving terrible advice to others.
7. Giving driving lessons is a stressful way to make a living.
8. Moana often rode the 4:50 bus home from school.
9. Dan enjoyed watching old movies.
10. The sweating witness refused to answer the prosecutor's question.

Contractions

In conversation and in informal writing, we often use a kind of short-cut called a **contraction.** In a contraction, a word is shortened and attached to another word, with an apostrophe (') to signal where the letters have been removed. For example, in the contraction **can't,** the words **can** and **not** have been joined together, and the letters **n** and **o** have been replaced by an apostrophe.

Oftentimes verbs are part of a contraction.

MV   MV   HV   MV

I'll (I will)   **we've** (we have)   **she'd have** (she would have)

So, when you are trying to locate the verb in a sentence, keep in mind that a helping verb or even a main verb may be disguised as part of a contraction.

COMMON CONTRACTIONS

is not = isn't	there is = there's
are not = aren't	he will = he'll
does not = doesn't	they will = they'll
should not = shouldn't	I would = I'd
I am = I'm	I have = I've
you are = you're	could have = could've (*not* could of)
who is = who's	must have = must've (*not* must of)

APPLICATION

Underline the complete verb in each sentence. Remember that a helping verb or a main verb may be part of a contraction.

> *EXAMPLE:* Mr. Lopez <u>shouldn't</u> <u>have been</u> so generous.

1. She'll volunteer to chaperone.
2. You should've come to class on Thursday.
3. It's very windy outside.
4. They are planning to attend the African art exhibit.
5. The Peruvian restaurant didn't do enough business.
6. You're not ever ready on time.
7. They've been in trouble since day one.
8. I should not have enrolled in eighteen units.
9. It's been hard to keep my mouth shut.
10. Mrs. Luong's been an inspiration to the class.

More Than One Main Verb

Sentences may have more than one main verb.

Helen either **watched** the *Today Show* or **read** the morning paper.

By May, Mr. Nguyen **had moved** to Pittsburgh and **bought** a house.

On his vacation, Marty **fished, canoed,** and **hiked.**

After Julius **retired,** his wife **got** a job.

Delilah **loved** to dance, and her sister **enjoyed** singing.

Whenever you are locating the verbs in a sentence, double-check to make sure you have found *all* of the verbs.

APPLICATION

In the following sentences, underline the complete verbs. Remember to watch for more than one main verb and for helping verbs.

EXAMPLE: Rosa <u>mowed</u> the lawn and <u>weeded</u> the flower bed.

1. Curtis always rides his bike or walks to school.
2. The hockey player checked his opponent and then scored a goal.
3. The large dog jumped and slobbered on the guests whenever they entered the house.
4. The naughty toddler had smeared lipstick on the wall and had filled the drawer with dirt before his mother caught him.
5. Jack and Jody bought a new house and moved in immediately.
6. Barry was arrested, convicted, and sentenced.
7. The owners of the Chinese restaurant cooked the food and served it themselves.

8. Carla changed the oil, adjusted the carburetor, and replaced the fan belt on her car.

9. Eric left his wife of twenty years and married his young secretary.

10. Members of the Asian Pacific Islanders club built a float, and it won a prize in the homecoming parade.

Two-Word Main Verbs

A number of English verbs consist of a verb followed by an additional word. These special verbs take two words to describe a single action, and many times you can even find a single word to describe the same action.

throw up	(vomit)
get up	(arise)
come across	(find)

For those who have learned English as a second language, these verbs cause special difficulties because they can occur for no obvious reason. For example, there is no good reason to explain why you ***call up*** people on the phone instead of ***calling to*** them.

In addition, two-word main verbs often express what is called an **idiomatic meaning.** An idiomatic meaning is one that cannot be understood literally. For example, if you ***run across*** a friend, you do not trample him; instead, you happen to see him unexpectedly.

Sometimes, the two parts of this type of verb can be separated by another word.

Beatrice **cleaned up** the mess.

Beatrice **cleaned** it **up.**

COMMON TWO-WORD MAIN VERBS

ask out	get up	play around
break down	give back	point out
bring up	give in	put away
burn down	give out	put back
burn up	give up	put on
call off	go out	put out
call up	go over	quiet down
clean up	grow up	run across
come across	hand in	run into
cut up	hand out	run out
do over	hang up	see off
drop in	help out	shut off
drop off	keep on	speak to
drop out	leave out	speak up
fill in	look into	stay up
fill out	look over	take care of
fill up	look up	take off
get along	pick out	think over
get away	pick up	throw away

throw out	turn on	wake up
try on	turn up	wear out
turn down		

APPLICATION ONE

Draw a line to match each two-word main verb on the left with its one-word equivalent on the right.

EXAMPLE: cut up ——————————— chop

1. call up   awaken

2. take over   telephone

3. pick out   quit

4. keep on   distribute

5. wake up   mature

6. look into   continue

7. hand out   choose

8. grow up   omit

9. leave out   retake

10. drop out   investigate

APPLICATION TWO

Choose five two-word verbs from the following list and write a sentence using each one. If you are unsure of the meanings of the verbs, look them up in a dictionary or ask a classmate.

ask out	quiet down	hand in
came across	dropped off	pointed out
throw away	wear out	tried on

1. _____

_____

2. _____

_____

3. _____

_____

4. _____

_____

5. _____

_____

Looking at Subjects

Locating the Subject

In addition to a verb, every sentence must have a subject. The subject tells *who* or *what* the sentence is about. After you are able to locate the verb or verbs in a sentence, it is much easier to find the subject or subjects. To find a subject, first identify the verb and then ask *who* or *what* performed the verb. The answer to this question will be the subject.

Darrell lives in Ohio.

In this sentence, the verb is **lives.** Look at the rest of the sentence carefully. Which word in the sentence answers the question, "*Who* or *what* lives?"

The only word in the sentence that answers the question is **Darrell,** so Darrell is the subject of the sentence. Look at the next sentence and follow the same procedure to find the subject:

She always feels hungry at two o'clock.

First locate the verb (**feels**). Then ask yourself *who* or *what* feels. The answer, **she,** is the subject.

APPLICATION

In each of the following sentences, the subject—the *who* or *what* word—is missing. First locate and circle the verb or verbs in each sentence. Then ask yourself *who* or *what* performs the verb, and fill in a word or words that complete the meaning of the sentence.

EXAMPLE: __The mouse__ (ran) wildly through the house.

1. _____ rented the same movie three weekends in a row.

2. My _____ ate six tacos and two burritos.

3. A _____ walked up to Malcolm in the mall parking lot

and demanded his car keys.

4. After several years of taking classes for fun, _____ finally

decided to get serious about a degree.

5. Watching the sunset, _____ planned their life together.

6. _____ has been missing for several weeks.

7. Because of the tremendous tidal wave, the _____ suf-

fered considerable damage.

8. Every Saturday night, _____ goes to her favorite club in

hopes of meeting someone.

9. _____ went to look at an apartment nearer to the cam-

pus.

10. To get the rent money, _____ placed an ad in the local

paper and sold his guitar.

Simple Subjects and Complete Subjects

In working through the preceding sentences, you may have had occasional questions about exactly what a subject includes. Look at this sentence and find the subject:

My first strapless dress was a disaster.

When you have found the verb (**was**), and asked *who* or *what* **was,** you may have wondered whether the subject was **My first strapless dress** or the word **dress** by itself. **My first strapless dress** is called the **complete subject; dress,** the single-word subject, is called the **simple subject.**

Most often, the simple subject of a sentence is a **noun.** A noun names a person, a place, a thing, or even an idea, such as *liberty* or *respect. Dress* in the sample sentence is a noun. Words like *aardvark, Eldon Campbell, Yosemite,* and *telephone* are also nouns. **Pronouns,** words which take the place of nouns, can also be subjects. *I, you, she, he, it, we,* and *they* are subject pronouns. In the following sentences the simple subjects are underlined.

Felix felt excited about getting the concert tickets.

He felt excited about getting the concert tickets.

Magda Martin enrolled in a weight training class.

She enrolled in a weight training class.

The frustrated driver struggled to get the wheelchair in the van.

The man struggled to get the wheelchair in the van.

APPLICATION

In each of the following sentences, locate the simple subject of the sentence by first identifying the verb and then asking the *who* or *what* question. Underline the verb twice, and underline the simple subject once.

EXAMPLE: My uncle lives in a small town outside of Toledo.

1. Melchor lived in New York for six years.
2. I enjoy 60s sitcoms like *Bewitched*.
3. Her brother bought a new Harley-Davidson motorcycle.
4. My first blind date was a disaster.
5. Jealousy causes a lot of broken relationships.
6. Daphne had a huge fight with her English instructor yesterday.
7. Satia came to the U.S. from Cambodia in the early 1980s.
8. His son came home late again last night.
9. *Ghost* is one of the most popular love stories of recent years.
10. Her parents want to meet him.

A **complete subject** is made up of a **simple subject** and any words that describe it. (If there are no descriptive words, then the complete subject is the same as the simple subject.) In the sentences that follow, the complete subjects are underlined.

The haunting photograph caused her to cry.

A beautiful young woman smiled seductively at Jose.

Tristan's aged grandmother lives with his family.

The simple subject in the first sentence is ***photograph.*** In the second sentence, the simple subject is ***woman.*** In the third sentence, the simple subject is ***grandmother.***

APPLICATION

Underline the complete subject in each of the following sentences. Then write the simple subject on the line provided.

EXAMPLE: <u>A very small balance</u> remained in Cheung's bank

account. __balance__

1. Annika went home early. _____

2. The long, green hose stretched across the path. _____

3. Becky's sister works here. _____

4. Chi lives near us. _____

5. The vicious Doberman snapped at me. _____

6. The old man yelled at the group of boys on bicycles.

_____

7. The new puppy chewed up the carpet. _____

8. Omaha is the best place in the United States for steaks.

_____

9. Beatriz sent her father a blue shirt for his birthday.

_____

10. Once I found a ring at the park. _____

Subjects Not in Prepositional Phrases

Sometimes, in addition to subjects, other words in sentences can answer *who* or *what*. These words can usually be found in **prepositional phrases.** When you are locating subjects, it is important to remember that a word in a prepositional phrase will *never* be the subject of a sentence.

If you are able to identify prepositional phrases, then you will not become confused by them. Every prepositional phrase contains a **preposition** (a word such as *in, at, of,* or *from*) and the preposition's **object** (a noun or pronoun).

with Marika   (**with** is the preposition; **Marika** is the object)

on the bus   (**on** is the preposition; **bus** is the object) in the café   (**in** is the preposition; ***café*** is the object)

Prepositional phrases can also contain additional words describing the object. These words come between the preposition and the object.

> **from** my generous, eccentric Yugoslavian **aunt**
>   (***from*** is the preposition; ***aunt*** is the object)

When you are trying to locate the subject of a sentence, the easiest way to keep from confusing a word in a prepositional phrase with a subject is to put a line through all prepositional phrases first. Then, find the verb, and ask yourself *who* or *what* performs the action. Your answer will be the subject.

Look at the following sentence:

In the middle of the morning two of my friends witnessed a robbery at the minimart near campus.

Without eliminating prepositional phrases, it is difficult to decide "*who* or *what* witnessed." Both **two** and ***friends*** could tell who witnessed the robbery. Now look at the same sentence with a line drawn through the prepositional phrases:

~~In the middle of the morning~~ two ~~of my friends~~ witnessed a robbery ~~at the minimart near campus.~~

After the prepositional phrases have been eliminated, the subject is clearly **two.**

In order to recognize prepositional phrases, you need to be able to recognize prepositions. The list that follows contains some of the most common English prepositions.

COMMON PREPOSITIONS

about	by	over
above	during	past
across	except	since
after	for	through
against	from	throughout
along	in	to
among	inside	toward
around	into	under
as	like	underneath
at	near	up
before	of	upon
behind	off	with
below	on	within
beside	outside	without
between	outside	without

Note: Be sure that you do not mistake **to** + **verb** for a prepositional phrase. Remember that **to** + **verb** (**to go, to see, to eat,** and so on) cannot be a prepositional phrase because the object of the preposition cannot be a verb; it must be a noun or pronoun.

APPLICATION

Find the subject in each of the following sentences. First, put a line through any prepositional phrases. Then locate the verb and underline it twice. Finally, underline the simple subject once.

> *EXAMPLE:*   The boy put his bike in the garage.

1. Melissa rode two buses to go to the grocery store.
2. Two of my best friends went to the beach yesterday.
3. In only two days I will get my first paycheck.
4. I won't go to the party without you.
5. Isauro lives around the corner, at 2518 Elm Street.
6. A money order for Fahad has arrived from overseas.
7. Tuong sat beside Delia in the second row at the concert.
8. Lamont won the lottery.
9. In the middle of the morning, a bomb threat was received by the campus police.
10. During vacation I'll be working extra hours as a sales clerk.

Subjects That Come after Verbs

If you look over the sentences in the previous exercises, you will notice that in every sentence the subject comes before the verb. However, although the subject usually comes before the verb, it does not always do so. Look at these sentences:

> In the middle of the expressway stood the toddler.
> (*who* stood? ***toddler***)

> Where is my wallet?
> (*what* is? ***wallet***)

> Here comes the bride.
> (*who* comes? ***bride***)

> There are two good-looking guys in my history class.
> (*who* are? ***guys***)

As long as you follow the procedure of first finding the verb and then asking *who* or *what*, these sentences should give you no problems. It might help to remember that subjects often follow verbs in sentences that ask a question and usually follow verbs in sentences that begin with **there** or **here. There** and **here** will *never* be subjects, so you might wish to cross them out when you are looking for subjects.

APPLICATION

In each of the sentences that follow, underline the verb twice and the simple subject once. First, put a line through any prepositional phrases and cross out the words **here** or **there** whenever they appear. Then locate the verb and ask *who* or *what* to find the subject.

> *EXAMPLE:*   Where is Maria going?
> (Remember to find the *complete* verb first. In a question, the subject can come between the helping verb and the main verb.)

1. Where are the coupons from Sunday's paper?
2. Here are two different styles.
3. On the corner is a video store.
4. There are four boys in that family.
5. What time are you going to call me?
6. There are my parents' friends.
7. Here is the only good song on this album.
8. Here comes my sister now.
9. In the top left corner was a smudge mark.
10. There are too many people in this elevator.

Subjects in Requests and Commands

Not all sentences contain clearly expressed subjects. Sometimes when you command or request something, you leave out the name of the subject because the subject is identified by your tone of voice or by eye contact.

> Please hand me that hammer. (request)
>
> Give me a break! (command)
>
> Get here on time tomorrow! (command)

In these types of sentences, the subject is understood to be **you,** the person being addressed.

> (You) please hand me that hammer.
>
> (You) give me a break!
>
> (You) get here on time tomorrow!

APPLICATION

In each of the sentences that follow, underline the verb twice and write the subject in the blank. If the sentence is a command or a request, write the understood subject in parentheses on the line to the left of the sentence.

EXAMPLE: _(You)_ Give me your wallet.

1. _____ Make my day.

2. _____ Keep cool.

3. _____ Sit quietly, please.

4. _____ John waited patiently.

5. _____ Please turn off the television.

6. _____ Drop it.

7. _____ Get a life.

8. _____ Brush your teeth.

9. _____ Please finish that immediately.

10. _____ She completed the paper on time.

Singular and Plural Subjects

In addition to being able to locate subjects in sentences, you need to know whether a subject is **singular** or **plural**. *Singular* means one of something; *plural* means more than one.

David was furious.

The subject of the sentence is **David.** Because **David** is one person, this subject is singular.

The men went to the basketball game.

The subject of the sentence is **men.** Because **men** refers to more than one person, the subject of the sentence is plural.

Joe and Peter went to the basketball game.

The subject of the sentence is **Joe** and **Peter.** Because **Joe** and **Peter** are more than one person, the subject of the sentence is plural.

APPLICATION ONE

The list that follows contains possible subjects for sentences. If the subject is singular, put an **X** in the singular column. If the subject is plural, put an **X** in the plural column.

SUBJECTS	SINGULAR	PLURAL
EXAMPLES:		
tortillas		X
Sergio and Phoung		X
an egg roll	X	
1. a slice of angel food cake		
2. engagement ring		
3. my sisters		
4. Connor and Shane		
5. quizzes		
6. cassette tape		
7. blackboard		
8. explicit lyrics		
9. my three sons		
10. cellular phone		

APPLICATION TWO

Locate and circle the complete subject in each of the following sentences. Then, in the space provided, indicate whether the subject is singular (**S**) or plural (**P**).

EXAMPLE: ___S___   (My friend Danny) is learning American Sign Language.

_____ 1. Pro basketball players earn a lot of money.

_____ 2. Here is my all-time favorite video game.

_____ 3. I went to the Guns n' Roses concert with him.

_____ 4. My cousin Shelina is always hungry.

_____   5. I can't find the cursor on this computer.

_____   6. Where is my wallet?

_____   7. The radio is too loud.

_____   8. Ana and Sam love this place.

_____   9. The cats ate my mother's fern.

_____   10. He never calls me.

▼CHAPTER REVIEW

Verbs

1. Verbs tell what the subject is doing or link the subject with a word that describes or renames the subject.
2. The complete verb of a sentence includes the main verb and all helping verbs.

Subjects

1. Subjects tell who or what the sentence is about.
2. The complete subject includes the simple subject and all of the words that describe it.
3. Subjects are never in prepositional phrases.

PRACTICE

Test your understanding of subjects and verbs by locating all of the subjects and verbs in the following passage. First, cross out any prepositional phrases. Then, locate the verbs in each sentence and underline them. Finally, circle the simple subject. If you have difficulty locating subjects and verbs, go back and review the information in this chapter.

The Japanese Internment

[1]After the bombing of Pearl Harbor in December 1941, a frightened U.S. government acted against its own citizens of Japanese ancestry. [2]Under the provisions of executive order 9066, Japanese-Americans living on the West Coast of the United States were forced to report to designated relocation centers. [3]From these

centers, men, women, and children were taken by bus and train to internment camps in remote areas of California, Arizona, Colorado, Idaho, Utah, and Arkansas. [4]In the camps, Japanese-Americans were treated like prisoners of war. [5]By the end of the war, many of the internees had lost everything, including their homes, businesses, and personal possessions. [6]Only recently has the United States government acknowledged its unfair treatment of these citizens. [7]The government has now apologized and has offered some monetary compensation to internees.

CHAPTER 3

Writing Complete Sentences

▼ CHAPTER PREVIEW

You probably use partial sentences many times when speaking to your friends:

"You going?"

"Yeah."

"Me too."

"See you then."

In college writing, you will be expected to use **complete sentences.** In complete sentences, the same conversation would look like this:

"Are you going?"

"Yes, I am going."

"I am going too."

"I will see you then."

The incomplete sentences used in conversation are used on purpose, but many student writers use incomplete sentences without meaning to. In fact, writing incomplete sentences is one of the most common errors of student writers. An incomplete sentence is called a sentence **fragment.** In this chapter, you will practice identifying and correcting sentence fragments.

A Professional Writer Uses Complete Sentences

About the Reading: Mike Rose, the son of immigrant parents from Southern Italy, was born in Pennsylvania in 1944 and grew up in south Los Angeles. After spending the first part of high school on the voca-

31

tional track, he pursued an academic career. Rose earned a number of degrees, including a doctorate in educational psychology from UCLA, where he is the associate director of Writing Programs. He is now a nationally recognized expert on the teaching of writing. In the following passage, which comes from his 1989 book *Lives on the Boundary: The Struggles and Achievements of America's Underprepared,* Rose describes the house where he grew up in south Los Angeles.

As You Read: You have already learned that a complete sentence requires both a subject and a verb. As you read the passage that follows, look carefully at Mike Rose's sentences, paying special attention to his use of subjects and verbs in each sentence.

From *Lives on the Boundary*

¹Let me tell you about our house. ²If you entered the front door and turned right you'd see a small living room with a couch along the east wall and one along the west wall—one couch was purple, the other tan, both bought used and both well worn. ³A television set was placed at the end of the purple couch, right at arm level. ⁴An old Philco radio sat next to the TV, its speaker covered with gold lamé. ⁵There was a small coffee table in the center of the room on which sat a murky fishbowl occupied by two listless guppies. ⁶If, on entering, you turned left, you would see a green Formica dinner table with four chairs, a cedar chest given as a wedding present to my mother by her mother, a painted statue of the Blessed Virgin Mary, and a black trunk. ⁷I also had a plastic chaise lounge between the door and the table. ⁸I would lie on this and watch television.

After You Read: Refer to the selection to help you complete the following items.

1. The verb *Let* in sentence 1 appears to lack a subject. However, as you have learned, requests and commands often have understood subjects. What is the understood subject of *Let?* _____

2. In sentence 3, what is the complete verb? _____ What is the simple subject? _____

3. In sentence 4, the word *covered* looks like a verb, but it is only part of a complete verb. Fill in the helping verb that would be needed to make the following a complete sentence:

   Its speaker _____ covered with gold lamé.

4. Sentences 7 and 8 are reprinted below. In each sentence, first cross out any prepositional phrases. Then underline each verb twice and each subject once.

[7]I also had a plastic chaise lounge between the door and the table.

[8]I would lie on this and watch television.

Sentences with Subjects and Verbs

Remember that every sentence must have a subject and a verb. Any sentence that lacks a subject or a verb or both is only a **fragment,** or piece, of a complete sentence. Look at these examples:

A new color television with a remote control.

Carlos bought a new color television with a remote control.

A new color television with a remote control was delivered to Carlos' house.

Which of the three samples lacks a subject, or verb, or both? In the first sample, *television* could possibly be a subject, but the sample clearly lacks a verb. The second sample contains the verb *bought* and the subject *Carlos.* The third sample contains the verb *was delivered* and the subject *television.* Therefore, only the last two samples are complete sentences; the first one is a **fragment.**

In order to identify a complete sentence, you must look for both a subject and a verb. If you cannot find either or both, the sentence is a fragment. Remember that commands are not fragments because the subject is understood to be *you.*

APPLICATION ONE

In the spaces provided, put a check next to each complete sentence.

EXAMPLES: _____ In the middle of the afternoon.

___✓___ He searched everywhere.

_____ 1. Went to the hardware store to buy a lighting fixture.

_____ 2. Kendra reached her credit limit.

_____ 3. Pass the potatoes.

_____ 4. Minh had a dental appointment after class.

_____ 5. After lunch, Victor and Molly returned to their motel room.

_____ **6.** In the dimly lit restaurant.

_____ **7.** Sid put an elaborate stereo system on layaway.

_____ **8.** On the corner in front of the copy shop was a vandalized phone booth.

_____ **9.** Norman Bates and his mother had a lot in common.

_____ **10.** Painted her fingernails during English class.

To correct a fragment that is lacking a subject and/or a verb, you need to provide a subject, a verb, or both. You may also want to add additional words to complete the thought of your sentence.

Was getting ready to go out. (lacks a subject)

Henry was getting ready to go out. (added a subject)

The top of her head. (could be a subject, no verb)

The top of her head **was** barely visible. (added the verb **was** and the additional words **barely visible**)

The **bird perched** on the top of her head. (added a subject and a verb)

APPLICATION TWO

Correct the following fragments by supplying the missing subjects, or verbs, or both, along with any additional words needed to complete the meaning of your sentence.

EXAMPLE: Into the inner city.

Corrected: **Marion rarely ventured into the inner city.**

1. Over the river and down the turnpike to Grandmother's house.

Corrected: _____

_____

_____

2. The bumpy subway car.

Corrected: _____

_____

_____

3. Went into premature labor in the parking lot.

   Corrected: _____

   _____

   _____

4. Down the unlit alley.

   Corrected: _____

   _____

   _____

5. Lost in the shopping mall.

   Corrected: _____

   _____

   _____

6. Waited for her husband to arrive.

   Corrected: _____

   _____

   _____

7. The waiter in the Vietnamese restaurant.

   Corrected: _____

   _____

   _____

8. The elegantly dressed couple.

   Corrected: _____

   _____

   _____

9. The most talked-about movie of the year.

Corrected: _____

_____

_____

10. Dropped the aluminum cans in the recycling container.

Corrected: _____

_____

_____

Sentences with Complete Verbs

You have seen that any group of words that does not have a subject and a verb is a fragment. Many fragments contain parts of verbs.

Julia waiting for her mother.

The word **waiting** looks like a verb, but remember that an **-ing** word cannot be the verb of the sentence by itself. It must have a helping verb such as **is** or **was.**

Joe forgotten by the others.

The word **forgotten** also looks like a verb. But it is not a complete verb. This form needs a helping verb such as **was** or **has been** to be a complete verb. To identify this type of fragment, look to be sure all verbs are complete.

APPLICATION ONE

Put an **S** next to each complete sentence. Remember to check for a *complete* verb as well as a subject.

EXAMPLES: ___**S**___ He bought ice cream for all of his friends.

_____ Edward opening the door of the auditorium.

_____ 1. Gone but not forgotten.

_____ 2. Listening intently to the disc jockey on the radio.

_____ 3. He was riding a brand-new dirt bike.

_____ 4. Sandra washing her lingerie with great care.

_____ 5. Seen on Spanish-language television.

_____ 6. The visitor known to everyone in the room.

_____ 7. The Chablanis had left in a great hurry.

_____ 8. He was always giving up French cigarettes.

_____ 9. Swaying from side to side to the reggae beat.

_____ 10. Taken from her shopping bag.

To correct a fragment that is lacking a complete verb, you may use one of two methods:

1. Supply a helping verb.

Loren taken the last donut. (lacks complete verb)

Loren **had** taken the last donut. (added helping verb)

2. Change the verb to another form that is a complete verb.

Leonard running for the bus. (lacks complete verb)

Leonard **ran** for the bus. (changed to complete verb)

As you may have noticed in some of the items in Application One, fragments with incomplete verbs can also lack subjects. To make them sentences, you may either supply a subject and a helping verb or change the partial verb form to a complete verb form. Another way to fix this kind of fragment is to add it to a sentence that is already complete.

Tugging at the rope. (lacks subject and complete verb)

He was tugging at the rope. (added subject and helping verb)

He tugged at the rope. (added subject and changed verb form)

Tugging at the rope, **he tried to pull the car out of the mud.** (added fragment to a complete sentence)

APPLICATION TWO

All of the following fragments lack complete verbs. Some of them lack subjects as well. Correct them using any method of your choice. There is no single right answer.

EXAMPLE: Lavonne expecting her to phone.

Corrected: **Lavonne was expecting her to phone.**
_____

_or_

Lavonne expects her to phone.
_____

1. Willie hoping for a passing grade.

   Corrected: _____

   _____

2. Standing in line.

   Corrected: _____

   _____

3. Chosen for his fine singing voice.

   Corrected: _____

   _____

4. Isabel shaken after her close call on the highway.

   Corrected: _____

   _____

5. Frank cheating on his taxes.

   Corrected: _____

   _____

6. Eating shrimp and rice.

   Corrected: _____

   _____

7. Mercedes written a letter to the boss.

   Corrected: _____

   _____

8. Strolled leisurely down the hall.

   Corrected: _____

   _____

9. Watching his favorite soap opera.

Corrected: _____

_____

10. Kumar paying for his purchases.

Corrected: _____

_____

Sentences That Express a Complete Thought

Some fragments may have a subject and a verb, but they still do not express a complete thought.

Although he had worked hard all day.

After Coco left the room.

If she had known his reputation.

Notice that each of these examples begins with a word that leaves the reader expecting more. ***Although he had worked hard all day,*** what happened to him after work? ***After Coco left the room,*** what did she do? ***If she had known his reputation,*** would she have acted differently? All of these examples depend on information that is missing to complete their meaning. For this reason, words like ***although, after,*** and ***if*** are called **dependent words.**

COMMON DEPENDENT WORDS

after	ever since	whenever
although	since	wherever
as	so that	whether
because	unless	while
before	until	
even though	when	

Whenever a sentence begins with one of these dependent words, you should check to make sure the meaning of the sentence is complete.

Ever since Henry moved to town. (incomplete)

Ever since Henry moved to town, things have been more lively. (expresses a complete thought)

There are other dependent words, ***who, whom, which,*** and ***where,*** that rarely appear at the beginning of a sentence unless the sentence asks a question. If one of these words does appear at the beginning of a word group that is *not* a question, the word group will most likely be a fragment.

Who is at the door? (complete sentence)

Who is at the door. (fragment)

Except in rare cases, the word ***that*** does not appear at the beginning of a sentence.

That he was guilty was obvious. (complete sentence)

That he was guilty. (fragment)

Sometimes the appearance of the word ***who, whom, that, which,*** or ***where*** *near* the beginning of a sentence will result in a fragment.

The grade **that** Gary deserved. (fragment)

The meaning of this sentence is incomplete. What was the grade Gary deserved? What happened to the grade he deserved?

The grade that Gary deserved was an *A*. (complete)

The grade that Gary deserved was given to his lab partner instead. (complete)

So, whenever you find a dependent word, check to make sure the meaning of the sentence in which it appears is complete.

APPLICATION ONE

Circle the dependent word in each word group. Put an **S** in the blank next to each complete sentence, and put an **F** next to each fragment.

EXAMPLE: _____**F**_____ (After) Nanette finished her marketing.

_____**S**_____ (After) he came home from work, Mr. Phillips flipped on the television.

_____ 1. Until Carol Ann turned eighteen years old.

_____ 2. The house where I used to live.

_____ 3. Unless I quit smoking, my girlfriend refused to quit.

_____ 4. The price that he charged was outrageous.

_____ 5. Whose name shall remain a secret.

_____ 6. So that I could stop by the store on the way home.

_____ 7. Wherever Melissa goes, her little brother follows.

_____ 8. Whenever she thought of her math teacher.

_____ 9. The creepy guy who dates my older sister.

_____ 10. Which one of you is going to drive?

Fragments caused by dependent words usually occur when these word groups are cut off from the rest of a sentence to which they belong.

I will not leave the house. **Until he apologizes.**

Dale wanted to buy the car. **That he saw in the showroom.**

In the examples, the fragments belong in the sentences that come before them.

I will not leave the house until he apologizes.

Dale wanted to buy the car that he saw in the showroom.

Some dependent-word fragments can be corrected by placing them either at the beginning or at the end of a complete sentence. When these word groups occur at the beginning of a sentence, they are followed by a comma.

Until he apologizes, I will not leave the house.

I will not leave the house until he apologizes.

Another way to correct dependent-word fragments is to get rid of the dependent word.

Whenever the phone rang. (fragment)

The phone rang. (complete sentence)

APPLICATION TWO

All of the fragments that follow contain a subject and verb but begin with a dependent word. Correct the fragments using any method you choose. There is no single correct answer.

EXAMPLE: After the New Year's Eve party was over.

Corrected: **Tyrone and Gwen stayed to clean up after the New**

Year's Eve party was over.

1. Before Richard could make up his mind.

   Corrected: _____

   _____

   _____

2. The place where the accident occurred.

   Corrected: _____

   _____

   _____

3. As soon as the teacher entered the room.

   Corrected: _____

   _____

   _____

4. Melody, who owned a blue Corvette.

   Corrected: _____

   _____

   _____

5. If I give you the money.

   Corrected: _____

   _____

   _____

6. When Miranda went to the Counseling Office.

   Corrected: _____

   _____

   _____

7. The room where the test was given.

   Corrected: _____

   _____

   _____

8. The new VCR that we bought.

   Corrected: _____

   _____

   _____

9. Even though DeAnn studied for the test.

   Corrected: _____

   _____

   _____

10. After the professor explained the course requirements.

    Corrected: _____

    _____

    _____

▼ CHAPTER REVIEW

A complete sentence must contain both a subject and a verb and must make sense by itself. An incomplete sentence is called a sentence **fragment.**

1. Any word group that is punctuated as a sentence but that does not contain both a subject and a verb is a sentence fragment.
2. Any word group that does not contain a complete thought is a fragment. This type of fragment often begins with a dependent word like **unless, if,** or **after,** or it may contain a dependent word such as **who** or **which.**

PRACTICE

Test your understanding of complete sentences by identifying and correcting any sentence fragments that appear in the following paragraph. Remember to watch for dependent words that might signal an incomplete thought.

America, Land of the Immigrant

[1]Many American citizens today are descended from European ancestors. [2]Who arrived in this country during two great waves of immigration. [3]The first wave of immigration occurred between 1820 and 1860. [4]When overcrowding, hunger, and poverty in northern and western Europe forced thousands to leave their homelands in search of a better future. [5]The second wave of immigration occurred from 1880 to 1902. [6]When Jewish and Catholic immigrants from southern and eastern Europe fled not only economic and social forces, but religious persecution as well. [7]All of the immigrants lured to the United States by stories of opportunity and riches. [8]Unfortunately, the hopeful expectations of these newcomers were often quite different from the reality of prejudice and exploitation that many of them encountered. [9]As soon as they arrived in this country.

Composing
Sentences of
Your Own

▼ CHAPTER PREVIEW

In the first three chapters of this unit, you have been looking at the sentence—identifying sentence elements and distinguishing complete sentences from incomplete sentences. But, composition research has shown that if you were merely to study sentences for an entire semester, you would probably not see much improvement in your own writing. The only way to become a better writer is to practice writing. This chapter focuses on the writing process itself and asks you to do some writing of your own. At the end of the chapter, you will have the opportunity to apply what you have already learned about sentences to your own writing.

A Student Composes Sentences

About the Reading: Most students think of writing only as a structured activity that occurs in response to a formal assignment or a question on an exam. But writing takes many forms, as one student discovered when his instructor asked class members to draft essays about all of the writing they had done the previous day. The following essay was written by Mario Suarez, a nineteen-year-old freshman who works part-time at the customer service desk of a retail store.

As You Read: Mario did not begin writing by trying to compose a complete essay. Instead, he first explored his ideas about his topic by taking an inventory of all of the writing he had done the previous day. As you read the essay itself, notice how Mario uses the ideas from his inventory in the sentences that appear in the essay.

Tuesday

letter to mom
grocery list
phone message for John
freewriting
work report for merchandise return
history notes

---

[1]Even though I hate writing, I guess I do a lot of it every day. [2]Last Tuesday is a good example. [3]Before I left for school, I finally wrote a letter to my mom to say thanks for the $50 check she sent me for my birthday last month. [4]I also made up a grocery list so I would remember to get some things from the market on my way home from work. [5]While I was at school, I did even more writing. [6]In Dr. Brown's class I took three or four pages of notes about the Reconstruction period after the Civil War, and in my English class, Dr. Leu made us freewrite until my hand felt like it would drop off. [7]At work I had to fill out a report on a cordless phone some lady wanted to return. [8]Since she said it was damaged when she bought it, I had to describe every little detail about what was wrong with it. [9]When I got home after work, there was a message on the answering machine for my roommate to call some guy about a job interview, and I had to write down all the information so I wouldn't forget anything.

After You Read: In the blank next to each item on the following inventory list, put the number of the sentence in which the item is discussed.

letter to mom _____

grocery list _____

phone message for John _____

freewriting _____

work report for merchandise return _____

history notes _____

Getting Started

Though all of the items on Mario's list are examples of "writing," they differ in one important way from the type of formal writing you will be asked to do in many college courses. All of the items listed—writing a letter, taking a message, recording a complaint, taking notes, and so on—could be completed in one step. Most college writing assignments cannot be handled effectively in one step. You may find it helpful to think of writing not as a single act but as a process that includes several stages: prewriting, writing, revising, and editing. This section focuses on prewriting, the stage of writing that occurs before the writer actually begins to compose an essay or a paper.

Often the hardest task for a writer is just getting started. If, in the past, you have expected to sit down and start right in with the title or first word of your essay and continue straight through to the last period, you may have found that ideas would not come to you, or that the really good ideas started coming to you only after you had forced yourself to write most of the essay and had too much work invested to start over. **Prewriting** (*pre-* means "before") is a term used to describe various strategies that help a writer generate ideas and get them focused before actually starting on an essay. While **prewriting** can refer to anything you do to come up with ideas, from talking to friends to reading a magazine, there are three techniques that you might find particularly helpful: **listing, brainstorming,** and **freewriting.**

When Mario made an inventory of the different types of writing he had done in one day, he was using a simple prewriting technique called **listing.** Listing is a good strategy to use when you want to remember facts or actions.

APPLICATION ONE

Choose a typical day in the past week (preferably one when you were attending classes) and list all of your writing activities during that day.

_____

_____

_____

_____

_____

_____

_____

_____

Brainstorming can be used not only to remember facts or actions, but also to generate ideas. Brainstorming is similar to dumping the contents of a catchall drawer onto a table, except that in brainstorming the drawer is your brain, the contents are ideas, and the table is a piece of paper or a computer screen. The purpose of brainstorming is to get all of your ideas out where you can later look them over, choose which ones you might want to use or develop further, and discard others. When you brainstorm, you simply write down any words or phrases that pop into your head, without worrying about whether they make sense, whether they relate to one another, or whether they are spelled correctly. There is no wrong answer in brainstorming! This stage of writing is for generating ideas, not for organizing or censoring them.

If Mario had brainstormed about his day's writing, his results might have looked like this:

freewriting   sign-in for conference
phone exchange report   letter to mom
grocery list   phone messages
survey form
art drawing   history notes

Notice that not everything that appears in brainstorming will be used for writing; like the items in a cluttered drawer, some of the ideas will be useful, and others can be discarded.

APPLICATION TWO

Brainstorm to come up with as many types of writing as you can think of that you are required to do in your life. Remember that nothing you put down is incorrect—even if it seems silly or insignificant.

Like brainstorming, **freewriting** is a method for getting ideas out of your head and onto the paper without worrying about making errors. Freewriting is particularly useful for generating thoughts and exploring attitudes about a topic. This technique requires that you write for a specified amount of time, usually five to ten minutes, *without stopping.* If you cannot think of anything else to say, you can copy down your last sentence, or repeat the topic, or write, "I can't think of anything else to say." In most cases, your mind will get tired of this repetition and come up with another idea. As you might suppose, a lot of the material generated by freewriting makes little or no sense, and freewriting often contains many spelling and grammar errors. But if you go back over what you have written, you will usually be able to find several ideas worth developing or using for writing. At the very least, you will be warmed up for the task of writing.

The example of freewriting that follows was done by Mario to explore his attitudes toward writing.

I've always been afraid to write for classes teachers are so picky theyre allways looking for ways to chop you down and make you feel stupid. Especially when I have to worry about spelling and punctuation. Like this time when I wrote a report for my administration of justice class and the teacher marked me down a whole grade for grammar and spelling and stuff. I can't think of anything except how much I hate to write and how I wish that I didn't have to take a writing class. But maybe it's a good thing that I have to take this class if I learn how to get past the spelling and grammar and because I feel so frustrated when I try hard and it still gets marked down. Sometimes I feel so embarrased I want to tear up the paper and I feel bad when people are going around saying what did you get and I don't want to tell them. I hate it when people are nosey about grades. School shouldn't be about competition I had enough of that in high school and I thought college would be different.

After you finish freewriting, you can read over what you have written and underline anything you might want to use. The underlined portions of Mario's freewriting show which ideas he thought he would use to develop an essay. Notice the different feelings Mario identified, and the good specific example of the administration of justice paper. Notice also that Mario came up with some ideas, such as grade competition, that he decided not to use because they weren't really about attitudes toward writing.

APPLICATION THREE

A. On a separate sheet of paper, freewrite for seven minutes on one of the following topics. Write your topic at the top of your paper. Set a timer or have someone time you so that you don't have to worry about watching a clock. Remember not to stop writing; if you get stuck, try repeating your topic.

1. My attitude toward writing
2. My past experience with writing
3. My fears about writing
4. My strengths as a writer

B. After you have finished freewriting, read back over what you have written and underline any ideas that you might find useful if your instructor were to assign an essay on your topic.

Now that you have tried out three prewriting techniques, look back over your prewriting results and record your reactions to these strategies. For example, have you tried any of these techniques before? Did you have more success with one technique or another, or does a particular technique seem easier to work with? You may wish to share your reactions with your classmates.

_____

_____

_____

_____

_____

_____

_____

Keeping a Writer's Notebook

Many writers, both students and professionals, find it helpful to keep all of their writing and writing-related materials in a single notebook. Keeping all of these materials in one place allows you to preserve all stages of your writing from prewriting to final draft and to keep track of and correct spelling and grammatical errors. Because it contains all of your writing over a period of time, a writer's notebook also gives you a sense of your progress as a writer.

Perhaps the easiest way to create a writer's notebook is to begin with a one-inch three-ring binder (either plastic or cardboard is ideal in terms of weight and cost) and a pack of section dividers. Your instructor may specify a particular arrangement for setting up the notebook. If not, you may wish to create a section for each of the following:

1. Writing assignments: Include *all* pieces of writing, from prewriting to finished drafts of essays.
2. Spelling log: Record all spelling errors on returned papers and write each word correctly.
3. Grammar log: Record all ungrammatical sentences marked on returned papers, note the rule for correcting your error, and include a corrected version of each sentence.

4. Self-assessment: On a regular basis, perhaps once each week, use this section to record your feelings about what you are learning, your progress, and your attitudes toward writing.

Writing Assignments

Now you are ready to practice your writing skills by responding to one of the following topics. You may want to use your prewriting from this chapter as a source of ideas. If you select a topic that is different from the topics of your prewriting, use one of the techniques you have practiced to generate ideas before you actually begin to write your essay.

1. Choose one day in the past week or two and describe all of the writing that you did on that day.
2. In one sentence, describe your attitude toward writing. Then, explore the reasons for your attitude.
3. Describe in detail a memorable experience with writing, either positive or negative, that you have had.
4. Think about your career goal and explain the types of writing that you expect you will need to do in that career.
5. Describe your writing history, including the courses you have taken, the instructors you have had, the writing you have done on your own, and so on.

Revising for Complete Sentences

One of the most important elements of writing is revising. Revising means looking over your work and making any changes that will make your ideas clearer and the reader's job easier. An important element in revision is making sure that your thoughts are expressed in complete sentences that communicate your ideas to the reader.

To practice revision, read through the piece of writing that you produced in response to the writing topic you selected. Either on your own or with a classmate, use what you learned in Chapters 1–3 to check your sentences for completeness. Use the following steps to aid in your revision:

1. Remember that all sentences must have a subject and verb. Check your sentences for subjects and verbs.
2. Underline all the verbs twice, and underline the subjects once. Revise any sentences that do not have both a subject and a verb by adding the missing element or elements or by rewriting the sentences.
3. Check to make sure that the sentences that begin with dependent words make sense by themselves. If they do not, check to see whether they need to be connected to either the sentence that precedes them or the one that follows them. Revise as necessary.

▼ CHAPTER REVIEW

- Use **prewriting** techniques to help you generate ideas and remember details. Three of these techniques are **listing, brainstorming,** and **freewriting.**
- When you **revise** a piece of writing, you make changes to clarify meaning.

Highlights

- A **sentence** is a group of words that

  1. expresses a complete thought about a person, thing, or idea
  2. contains at least one subject and one verb
  3. begins with a capital letter
  4. ends with a punctuation mark

- A **verb** tells what the subject is doing or links the subject with a word that describes or renames the subject. The **complete verb** of a sentence includes the main verb and all helping verbs.
- **Subjects** tell who or what the sentence is about. The **complete subject** includes the simple subject and all the words that describe it.
- Use **prewriting** techniques to generate ideas and remember details before you begin to write an essay. Three of these techniques are **listing, brainstorming,** and **freewriting.**

    When you **revise,** you make changes in a piece of writing in order to clarify meaning.

PRACTICE

Use the sentences in this section to test your mastery of the material in Unit One. If you have difficulty, go back and look over the explanations in Chapters 1–4.

A. Decide whether each of the following items is a complete sentence. If the item is a complete sentence, put an **S** in the blank. If it is not a complete sentence, put **NS** in the blank.

    EXAMPLE: **NS**   Kelly running down the alley.
                    (This is not a sentence because it lacks a verb.
                    An **-ing** word by itself cannot be a verb.)

_____ 1. Where did you put it?

_____ 2. Ty taken my pepperoni stick.

_____ 3. Leave me alone.

_____ 4. Duc got lost at the mall.

_____ 5. Ann and Ritchie, both students in Dr. Moore's class.

B. The following sentences lack subjects or verbs or both. Put one noun, one subject pronoun, or one verb in each blank to complete each sentence.

EXAMPLE: The _____**food**_____ at the reception was unforgettable.

1. Professor Wiggins _____ his 8:00 class.

2. _____ and _____ were friends in high school.

3. Under the table lay a sick-looking _____.

4. The children _____ in the streets.

5. The suspect _____, _____, and _____ before he was subdued.

C. In each of the sentences, underline the verb twice and the simple subject once.

EXAMPLE: Tao was homesick for her family.

1. Marilyn is going to New York after graduation.
2. He felt ill.
3. The pushy woman elbowed her way in the door.
4. The thirsty flowers drooped in the vase.
5. Sasha is majoring in sociology, and her brother is majoring in dance.
6. He brushed his teeth, shaved, and combed his hair.
7. Jared and Sylvia left on Friday.
8. Martin will not be here on time.
9. Tran picked out a new sofa for his apartment.
10. She isn't my friend any longer.

D. Most, but not all, of the following items are fragments. If an item is a complete sentence, put an end mark after it. If it is a fragment, revise it so that it is a complete sentence.

EXAMPLE: Ricardo ~~standing~~ **stood** in line for hours for the tickets

1. Jeremy taken this class twice already

2. Running along the jogging path

3. Fakir enrolled in an apprenticeship program

4. Although Elena arrived late

5. On top of the building stood a life-sized statue of a horse

6. Gino looking for a job as a brick mason

7. Before he could decide what to do

8. The delicious spaghetti that she made

9. Open the door

10. In the front row of the classroom

UNIT **2**

Using Verbs

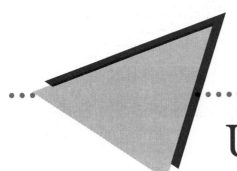

CHAPTER 5

Using Present Tense Verbs

▼ CHAPTER PREVIEW

As you learned in Chapter 2, verbs change form to show tense (time) and number (how many). This chapter focuses on the **present tense** forms of verbs and shows you how to make sure that present tense verbs and their subjects **agree** with one another in number.

A Professional Writer Uses the Present Tense

About the Reading: Born in 1940, Roger Rosenblatt is an American journalist and essayist. In addition to serving as a staff writer and editor for various publications, including *Time* and *Life* magazines, Rosenblatt has taught English and American literature at Harvard and served as director for the National Endowment for the Humanities in Washington, D.C. In order to write his prize-winning 1983 book *Children of War,* he traveled to Thailand, Hong Kong, Israel, Lebanon, Greece, and Northern Ireland. The selection that follows is taken from "Children of Cambodia," which appears in *Children of War.* In this excerpt, Rosenblatt describes his arrival in Khao I Dang, a refugee camp near the Thai-Cambodian border, where large numbers of Khmer people from Cambodia have fled to escape the war between the Khmer Rouge and the Vietnamese.

As You Read: Present tense verbs in the selection have been printed in bold type. Pay close attention to the appearance and function of verbs in the present tense.

From "Children of Cambodia"

[1]In the middle of the morning on October 13, we **arrive** in Khao I Dang, swarmed immediately by small girls calling "**Buy,** please, **buy,**" and selling wooden birds on wooden perches. [2]Socua **guides** us through the children. [3]She **points** to a huddle of Khmer adults waiting by the gate to be moved in trucks to other camps. [4]Their faces **are** lifeless. [5]At its largest Khao I Dang held over 120,000 refugees. [6]That population is reduced to 40,000 now, a number that **sounds** more manageable, given the small-town size of the camp, about seventy square acres. [7]Behind the neat rows of straw-roofed huts **rises** the mountain Khao I Dang, or "spotted bitch mountain" or simply "spotted mountain"; evidently it **translates** both ways. [8]Socua **leads** Matthew and me along Phnom Penh Road, a mud path named to recall the homeland of the Khmer. [9]Their camp **looks** like an ancient village to me. [10]Women in *sampots* **skitter** by with naked babies riding on their hips. [11]Monks in yellow gowns **sit** cross-legged on long bamboo tables, their shaved heads lowered in contemplation. [12]We **arrive** on a holiday, the last days of the Buddhist Lent. [13]Everyone **smiles** at us openly, the children tagging along. [14]Some **are** in tatters. [15]I **find** them astonishingly beautiful.

After You Read: Several present tense verbs with their subjects appear in the following list. Refer to the list to fill in the blanks.

Socua guides	camp looks
she points	we arrive
mountain rises	women skitter

A. The present tense verbs *guides, points, rises,* and *looks* all end in the letter _____.

B. Look carefully at the subjects of the verbs *guides, points, rises,* and *looks.* Are they singular (one) or plural (more than one)?

_____

C. Based on your observations in A and B, complete this sentence: Present tense verbs used with singular subjects often end in the letter _____.

D. The subjects *women* and *we* are plural. Look carefully at the verbs used with these subjects. Do they end in *s*? _____

E. Based on your answer in D, complete the following sentence: Present tense verbs used with plural subjects usually do not

_____.

F. Look at the verb in sentence 13. Is it the verb form used with a plural or a singular subject? _____. Based on your answer, do you think the subject **_everyone_** is singular or plural? _____

If you have answered A through E correctly, then you have observed two rules that can help you tell plural verbs from singular verbs. In the present tense, singular verbs usually end in **s**; plural verbs in the present tense usually do not end in **s**.

Verb Form

The present tense has two forms:

1. The **non -s** form (the form used after the word **_to_**):

      (to) **_ask_**   (to) **_walk_**   (to) **_feel_**

2. The **-s** form:

      ask**s**   walk**s**   feel**s**

The present forms of the verb can stand alone as main verbs without any helping verbs. By themselves, verbs in the present tense indicate action that is taking place right now, describe habitual actions, summarize an author's words, or make statements that are always or generally true.

Some people **ask** the stupidest questions. (general statement)

Chassidy always **walks** to campus. (habitual action)

Taking the microphone, I **feel** excited and nervous. (right now)

The author **writes** of his experiences growing up in Arkansas. (summary of author's words)

Present tense verbs may change form to indicate **number** (to show whether they are singular or plural). The **singular** verb form is the form used with a singular subject. The **plural** verb form is the form used with a plural subject.

He **runs.** (singular)

They **run.** (plural)

APPLICATION

Write a sentence of your own using one of the present verb forms in parentheses.

> EXAMPLE: (remove, removes) **My two-year-old nephew constantly removes his shoes.**

1. (growl, growls) _____

   _____

   _____

2. (admire, admires) _____

   _____

   _____

3. (want, wants) _____

   _____

   _____

4. (need, needs) _____

   _____

   _____

5. (ride, rides) _____

   _____

   _____

Present Tense with Helping Verbs

To show **future** tense or to show different shades of meaning, the **non -s present** form of the verb can also be used in combination with a helping verb like *can, could, may, might, must, shall, should, will,* or *would.*

Marcus **could ask** the most probing questions. (possibility)

Felicity and Evan **can dance** for three hours without tiring. (ability)

Karla **will feel** better in a few days. (future)

These verbs do not have different forms for singular or plural subjects.

The boys **should be** here soon.

Janet **should be** here soon.

The **non -s present** form of the verb can also be used with the helping verbs **do, does,** or **did.** Use **do** + **present form** with a plural subject and **does** + **present form** with a singular subject. **Did** can be used with either a plural or singular subject.

They **do** like to complain. (plural)

Eleanor **does find** the good in everyone. (singular)

He **did find** her address after all.

Kyle and Tracy **did get** tickets to the playoff game.

However, the present form is *never* used after the helping verbs *has, have, had, am, is, are, was, were,* or *been.*

APPLICATION

Fill in an appropriate present tense *main* verb in each of the blanks. Notice that some of the sentences already contain helping verbs.

EXAMPLE: Mr. Evans _____**looks**_____ ridiculous in that hat.

1. Delia _____ her hair five times a day.

2. Arnold will _____ to the academic decathlon.

3. Clarinda and her mother _____ at the mall.

4. The basketball team _____ every game.

5. Francis could not _____ cold pizza.

6. Joe's dad can _____ a tire in less than ten minutes.

7. Sarah's ex-husband _____ to pay his child support.

8. Chloe and Karen _____ in Atlantic City.

9. In spite of his best efforts, the teacher never _____ the class.

10. My cousin should _____ his job.

Making Subjects and Verbs Agree

Read aloud the two sentences that follow and decide which one sounds correct:

The boy goes.

The boys goes.

If you are a native speaker of standard English, your ear probably told you that the first sentence is correct and the second incorrect. **Agreement** is the grammatical term that explains why one is correct and the other is not. Because verbs change form to show number (how many), you have to be careful to use the correct form. A subject and a present tense verb **agree** if both are plural or both are singular. In the first example, the subject **boy** is singular because there is only one boy. The verb **goes** is also singular, so the subject and verb in this sentence are said to **agree** in number. The subject in the second example is plural because there is more than one boy. However, because the verb **goes** is singular, the subject and verb in this sentence do *not* agree.

The subject pronouns **I, you** (referring to one person), **he, she,** and **it** are always singular. The subject pronouns **we, you** (referring to more than one person), and **they** are always plural. Any noun that refers to one person or one thing, such as **Ms. Moreno, lamp,** or **man,** is singular, and any noun that refers to more than one person or thing, such as **pizzas, hamsters,** or **professors,** is plural. As the following chart indicates, singular nouns and pronouns take the singular verb form, and plural nouns and pronouns take the plural verb form. The **-s** form is always singular; the **non -s** form may be either singular or plural.

VERB: LOOK

Singular		Plural	
Subject	Verb Form	Subject	Verb Form
he	looks	they	look
Mr. Jones	looks	Lori and Ken	look
the dog	looks	we	look
it	looks	the players	look
she	looks	the women	look
I	look	you (more than one)	look
you (one)	look		

Notice that singular nouns and the singular pronouns **he, she,** and **it** take the singular verb form that ends in **-s.** The singular pronouns **I** and **you,** as well as all of the plural subjects, take the **non -s** verb form.

APPLICATION ONE

Write the correct present tense form of the verb **walk** next to each of the following subjects.

EXAMPLE: he _____**walks**_____

APPLICATION
....

Fill in the present tense form of **to be, to have,** or **to do** that agrees with the subject in each sentence.

EXAMPLE: Yolanda _____**has**_____ difficulty with math.

1. Wendy _____ usually late for her first class.

2. Felicia and Latoya _____ their homework together.

3. Miguel _____ gone to get the tickets.

4. Florence _____ it better than anyone else I know.

5. My mother _____ taking classes at Fairview Community

   College.

6. The sales clerk _____ not know her merchandise.

7. The police officers _____ looking for my brother.

8. Her pet python _____ an important part of her act.

9. Marty _____ walking and chewing gum at the same time.

10. One man in my art class _____ 65 years old.

Agreement in Questions

As you learned in Chapter 2, the subject often follows the verb in a question. To determine whether the subject and verb agree, be sure to locate the verb first and ask *who* or *what.* The answer to *who* or *what* should agree with the verb.

>   V
> Where is Alisha?
> (Who **is? Alisha** is. **Alisha** and **is** are both singular.)

>   V
> Who are those men on the street corner?
> (Who **are? Men** are. **Men** and **are** are both plural.)

When the subject comes between the helping verb and the main verb in a question, only the helping verb changes form to show whether it is singular or plural.

>   HV   MV
> Are Marta and Phillip still dating?
> (Who **are dating? Marta and Phillip** are dating. The plural subject is **Marta** *and* **Phillip.** The helping verb **are** is also plural. The main verb **dating** does not change.)

HV   HV

What does Tracy know about the theft?

(Who **does know? Tracy** does know. The singular subject is **Tracy.** The helping verb **does** is also singular. The main verb **know** does not change.)

APPLICATION

Put an **X** in the blank next to the correct sentence in each pair.

EXAMPLE: _____ Have the cashier gone to lunch?

_____**X**_____ Has the cashier gone to lunch?

1. _____ Are the twins going to graduate this year?

_____ Is the twins going to graduate this year?

2. _____ He have really tried my patience.

_____ He has really tried my patience.

3. _____ Why are Thom and Garrett leaving so early?

_____ Why is Thom and Garrett leaving so early?

4. _____ The dentist love to hear his patients scream.

_____ The dentist loves to hear his patients scream.

5. _____ The washing machine break down on a regular basis.

_____ The washing machine breaks down on a regular basis.

6. _____ He have a lot of problems for someone so young.

_____ He has a lot of problems for someone so young.

7. _____ Have you ever met a celebrity?

_____ Has you ever met a celebrity?

8. _____ She never have time for me!

_____ She never has time for me!

9. _____ Julisa have two boyfriends.

_____ Julisa has two boyfriends.

10. _____ Working parents is always in a hurry.

_____ Working parents are always in a hurry.

Agreement with the Correct Subject

When words come between the subject and the verb, they will not affect whether the verb is singular or plural.

> The **woman** with the three screaming children **lives** next door to me. (woman lives)

> The **bus,** running late as usual, **arrives** at the college after 8:00. (bus arrives)

> The **mayor,** along with two of his aides, **is** the guest of honor. (mayor is)

Sometimes words that come between the subject and the verb can make it difficult to identify the subject. Remember, putting a line through prepositional phrases and asking yourself *who* or *what* performed the verb can make finding the subject much easier.

Also remember that the words ***there*** and ***here*** can be confusing when you try to locate a subject because they often appear at the beginning of a sentence, right before the verb. The important thing to remember when you check for subject/verb agreement is that the words ***there*** and ***here*** cannot be subjects, so they will not affect the verb.

> There **are** several **causes** for the growing dropout rate. (causes are)

> Here **is** the **winner** of the radio contest. (winner is)

APPLICATION

In the following sentences, put an **X** over the words ***here*** and ***there,*** and put a line through any prepositional phrases. Then underline the simple subject and circle the correct verb in parentheses.

> *EXAMPLE:*   One of the colleges in our division (has, have) a championship basketball team.

1. His girlfriend's mangy dog always (tries, try) to bite him.
2. My father, along with my two uncles, (owns, own) a landscaping business.
3. There (goes, go) my chances of getting an "A" in the class.
4. Melvin (wants, want) to enter the nursing program.
5. Here (is, are) your physics notes.
6. The highway, running through the countryside (go, goes) across my father's land.
7. She (hope, hopes) to be accepted into the police academy.
8. My goals (are, is) simple.

9. Here (come, comes) the mail carrier with my check .

10. Mario and Luigi (is, are) always in trouble.

Agreement with Subjects Joined by *And, Or,* or *Nor*

As you learned in Chapter 2, subjects joined by **and** are always plural; accordingly, they always take a plural verb. When subjects are joined by **or** or **nor,** however, the word nearest the verb determines whether the verb will be singular or plural.

> Candy *and* flowers **make** a nice Mother's Day gift. (plural)
>
> Either candy *or* flowers **make** a nice Mother's Day gift. (plural)
>
> Either flowers *or* candy **makes** a nice Mother's Day gift. (singular)

In a question, the present tense helping verb changes form to agree with the subject nearest to it.

> **Is** Professor Minelli *or* his students attending the rally? (singular)
>
> **Are** the students *or* their professor attending the rally? (plural)

APPLICATION

In each sentence write **S** above the simple subject or subjects of the verbs in parentheses. Then circle the correct verb form.

>   **S**   **S**
>
> *EXAMPLE:*   Neither Japanese nor Latin (is, are) offered at the college.

1. Salsa and bean dip (goes, go) great with tortilla chips.

2. Either Sergio or Farina (has, have) my script for the play.

3. There (goes, go) Eleanor with my former boyfriend.

4. Neither my mother nor my father (has, have) a college degree.

5. Here (is, are) the cheeseburger and French fries you ordered.

6. (Do, does) you like heavy metal music?

7. Miriam and her Great Dane (walks, walk) along the beach every

   evening.

8. Susie, along with most of her family, (work, works) at the swap meet.

9. Where (is, are) the plumber and his helper?

10. (Is, are) your mother or sister able to drive you to school?

Agreement with Indefinite Pronouns and Relative Pronouns

Unlike subject pronouns, **indefinite pronouns** do not refer to a specific person or thing. The indefinite pronouns shown here are always singular and always take singular verbs:

SINGULAR INDEFINITE PRONOUNS

-one Words	*-body* Words	*-thing* Words
anyone	anybody	anything
everyone	everybody	everything
no one	nobody	nothing
someone	somebody	something
each	either	neither

Each, either, and *neither* are often followed by prepositional phrases which contain plural nouns, but the verb will still be singular.

Everyone wants to get into Dr. Meyer's sexuality course.

Nobody gets an "A" in Professor Morgan's class.

Each of the contestants **plays** a musical instrument.

Neither of the jobs **is** very appealing.

Some **indefinite pronouns,** including *most, some, part, all,* and *none,* may take either a singular or a plural verb. If these pronouns describe a noun that *can be counted,* use a plural verb. If these indefinite pronouns describe a noun that *cannot be counted,* use a singular verb.

Some of the milk **is** spoiled.
   (Milk is measured, not counted, so use a singular verb.)

Some of the children **are** throwing stones.
   (Children can be counted, so use a plural verb.)

Most of his hair **is** gray.
   (Individual strands of hair are not usually counted, so use a singular verb.)

Most of the guests **have** invitations.
(Guests can be counted, so use a plural verb.)

Sometimes verbs will have as their subject the word **which,** **who,** or **that.** These words are called **relative pronouns** because they introduce information related to a noun or another pronoun that appears in the same sentence.

There is the dog **that** is doing the damage.
(***that is doing the damage*** describes the noun ***dog***)

People **who** are squeamish should not be paramedics.
(***who are squeamish*** describes the noun ***people***)

Whether a relative pronoun is singular or plural is determined by the word it depends on for meaning. If the word is plural, the pronoun is plural. If the word is singular, the pronoun is singular. In the first example, the relative pronoun ***that*** refers to the singular noun ***dog,*** so it takes the singular verb ***is.*** In the second example, ***who*** refers to the plural noun ***people,*** so it takes the plural verb ***are.***

APPLICATION

After you put a line through the prepositional phrases, underline the subject of the verb in parentheses and circle the correct verb form.

EXAMPLE: One ~~of the most popular cartoon shows~~ today (is, are) *The Simpsons.*

1. Each of my friends (have, has) a special talent.
2. None of Enrique's instructors (pronounce, pronounces) his name correctly.
3. The man who (live, lives) across the street is a strange character.
4. Most of the ice cream (is, are) melted.
5. Some of the peanuts (is, are) stale.
6. Nobody (like, likes) a poor loser.
7. Students who (take, takes) that class are in for a difficult semester.
8. Problems that (seem, seems) overwhelming at age fourteen often seem trivial at age forty.
9. Either of the colors (suit, suits) you.
10. Coffee (smell, smells) wonderful in the morning.

Agreement in Special Cases

When the word **each, every,** or **any** is used to modify a subject, the subject it modifies will always take a singular verb.

> **Each** man, woman, and child **needs** to feel loved.

> **Every** Tom, Dick, and Harriet **wants** to be an attorney.

Collective nouns, nouns that refer to groups of people or things, usually take the singular form of the verb. Common collective nouns include **team, group, family, audience, crowd, committee,** and **government.**

> The **team travels** on a private jet.

> The **government raises** taxes every year.

A few nouns that end in **-s** may look plural, but they are considered singular and take the singular form of the verb. Some of these nouns are **measles, mumps, mathematics, economics, physics, politics,** and **news.**

> The **news** about the economy **depresses** me. (singular)

> **Politics is** an unstable career right now. (singular)

To identify one of these nouns, you might ask yourself whether you can use the word without the **-s.** If not, it probably falls into this category. For example, it is unlikely that you have ever heard of someone having the "measle" or taking a course in "mathematic."

Units of time, measurement, weight, or **money** usually take a singular verb because the entire amount is considered to be a single unit.

> One hundred **dollars seems** a bit expensive for that jacket.

> Thirty **pounds is** a lot of weight to gain in six months.

In **contractions,** it is often difficult to hear whether or not a verb agrees with its subject because the verb is not heard alone. To decide whether a contraction is singular or plural, first divide it into the two words from which it was formed and then consider only the verb.

> The shoes **don't** fit her.

> The shoes **do not** fit her. (**shoes** and **do** are plural)

> There **isn't** one thing of interest.

> There **is not** one thing of interest. (**thing** and **is** are singular)

APPLICATION

In each sentence, choose the correct form of the verb and write it in the blank.

EXAMPLE: Each of my cousins _____**plays**_____ a different sport.
(play, plays)

1. There _____ enough good jobs for people with limited ed-
(isn't, aren't)

   ucation.

2. Three million dollars _____ the street value of the drugs.
(is, are)

3. The audience _____ whenever she comes on stage.
(scream, screams)

4. Statistics _____ absolutely nothing.
(prove, proves)

5. Gymnastics _____ my favorite Olympic sport.
(is, are)

6. Every boy and girl _____ of growing up to be someone
(dream, dreams)

   special.

7. Someone _____ to take responsibility.
(has, have)

8. Our family _____ a camping trip every year.
(take, takes)

9. _____ anybody care?
(Doesn't, Don't)

10. Forty-eight hours _____ like a long time to wait.
(seem, seems)

▼ CHAPTER REVIEW

• The **present tense** has two forms:

   1. The form used after the word **to.**
   2. The **-s** form.

• Use the present tense to

   1. indicate action that is taking place right now
   2. describe habitual actions

3. summarize an author's words
4. make statements that are always or generally true.

- Present tense verbs change form to show **number** (how many).

- **Subject/verb agreement:** A subject and a present tense verb **agree** with one another when either both are singular or both are plural.

1. Singular verbs should be used with singular subjects, and plural verbs should be used with plural subjects.
2. In questions with a helping verb and a main verb, only the helping verb changes form to agree with the subject.
3. Words that come between the subject and the verb will not affect whether the verb is singular or plural.
4. In subjects joined by **or** or **nor,** the verb agrees with the nearest subject word.
5. The subjects **each, either,** and **neither** and indefinite pronouns ending in **-one, -body,** or **-thing** are always singular.
6. **Collective nouns** usually take the singular form of the verb.

PRACTICE

Test your understanding of subject/verb agreement by writing the correct present tense form of the verb in each blank.

Toni Morrison

[1]African-American author Toni Morrison _____ written six
(has, have)

novels. [2]Her fifth novel, *Beloved,* _____ a winner of the prestigious
(is, are)

Pulitzer Prize. [3]Morrison's latest novel, published in 1992 by Knopf,

_____ entitled *Jazz.* [4]Chosen as a Book-of-the-Month Club selec-
(is, are)

tion, *Jazz* _____ about Violet and Joe, who _____ their
(tells, tell)   (leaves, leave)

home in rural Virginia to travel north to New York City in 1906. [5]Nei-

ther their love for one another nor their exhilaration with city life

_____ them immune from the pain of the past and the city's
(keeps, keep)

destructive powers. [6]As she does in *Beloved,* Morrison _____
(experiments, experiment)

with style in *Jazz.* [7]Like the music of jazz, each of the individual sto-

ries in the novel _____ a variation on the larger themes of the work.
(is, are)

[8]Morrison's literary achievements, capped by this latest novel,

_____ her one of the most respected African-American
(makes, make)

women writing today, placing her foremost among the likes of Gloria

Naylor and Alice Walker. [9]Indeed, this group of contemporary African-

American women writers _____ setting the literary standard of ex-
(is, are)

cellence for all American writers.

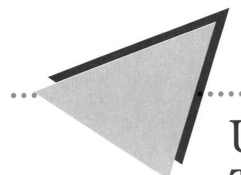

Using Past Tenses

▼ CHAPTER PREVIEW

In addition to the present tense, verbs have two other main forms: the **past** and the **past participle.** This chapter will familiarize you with the appearance and the functions of these two important forms.

A Professional Writer Uses Past Verbs

About the Reading: Jimmy Santiago Baca, a Mexican-American, was born in Santa Fe, New Mexico, and grew up on the plains near the Manzano Mountains of New Mexico. Baca was raised in an orphanage, was on the streets at eleven, and was in jail by the time he was twenty; there, he learned to read and write. Now a recognized author, Baca has published several volumes of prize-winning poetry. The selection that follows comes from *Working in the Dark: Reflections of a Poet of the Barrio* (1992), a book in which he writes about his life. This account of how Baca came to be in prison is from the chapter "Lock and Key."

As You Read: All of the verbs in bold type in the selection show actions that occurred in the writer's past. However, these verbs are not all in the same form. Notice how Baca uses these different forms in describing his past actions or experiences.

From *Working in the Dark*

¹Two years **passed.** ²I **was** twenty now, and behind bars again. ³The federal marshals **had failed** to provide convincing evidence to extradite me to Arizona on a drug charge, but still I **was being held.** ⁴They **had** ninety days to prove I **was** guilty. ⁵The only evidence

against me **was** that my girlfriend **had been** at the scene of the crime with my driver's license in her purse. ⁶They **had** to come up with something else. ⁷But there **was** nothing else. ⁸Eventually they **negotiated** a deal with the actual drug dealer, who **took** the stand against me. ⁹When the judge **hit** me with a million-dollar bail, I **emptied** my pockets on his booking desk: twenty-six cents.

After You Read: Refer to the verbs in bold type in the reading selection to answer these questions:

A. Which verbs are formed with the helping verb *had?*

_____

B. Which verbs end in *-ed?*

_____

C. Which verb forms do not end in *-ed?*

_____

Regular Past Tense

By themselves, verbs in the **past tense** indicate actions or events that occurred on a previous occasion. Past tense verbs formed by adding *-d* or *-ed* to the end of present tense verbs are called **regular verbs.**

They **waited** for the sun to rise.

She **looked** suspiciously at the man in the shadows.

The students **sided** with the teacher against the dean.

APPLICATION

Each of the following sentences is in the present tense. Change each sentence to the past tense by crossing out the present tense verb form and writing in the past tense form of the verb.

EXAMPLE: Mary ~~loves~~ her 1972 Volkswagen. _(loved)_

1. I need my French notebook to study for the test.

2. The tabouli looks delicious.

3. Mrs. Garcia owns two office buildings.

4. Todd Baylor succeeds in spite of his blindness.

5. The elderly man strokes his faithful German shepherd.

6. I watch the sunrise every morning.

7. The citizens fear another incident like the last one.

8. Jamie and her friend train for the marathon.

9. The babysitter pushes the stroller around the block.

10. The surprised woman discovers a snake in her toilet.

Have and *Had* + Regular Past Participle

Like regular past tense verbs, regular **past participles** end in *-d* or *-ed.* Unlike the past tense, however, the past participle is never used by itself as a verb. When it acts as a verb, the past participle is always used with a helping verb, usually a form of **have** or **be.** The past participle has different functions, depending on its helping verb.

When the past participle is used with **has** or **have,** it indicates an action that occurred in the past and continues to occur today.

My mother **has used** that same brand for twenty years.
   (She used that brand in the past and continues to use it today)

When the past participle is used with **had,** it indicates a past action that occurred prior to another past action.

She finally divorced her husband after they **had lived** apart for more than twenty years.
   (The living apart occurred prior to the divorce, but both took place in the past)

You may wish to refer to the time line below to decide whether to use the past tense or to use *had* + the past participle.

Michel **had lived** in three countries before he **moved** to the United States in 1982.

past _____ present

had + past participle	past tense
Michel **had lived** in three countries.	He **moved** to the United States in 1982.

APPLICATION

In each blank, put the correct past form of the verb indicated. If the action occurred on one occasion in the past, use the past tense. Use **have** + the past participle if the action occurred in the past and continues to the present, and use **had** + the past participle if the action occurred even earlier than another past action.

> EXAMPLE: (call) Marvin **has called** his mother every morning since he left home.
>
> (action continues to the present because he is presumably still calling)

1. (learn) Mr. Nguyen _____ a lot of English words since he arrived in the United States.

2. (open) The new video arcade _____ last Friday.

3. (visit) Naomi _____ her cousins in Florida before the hurricane struck.

4. (name) They _____ their new baby Leilani.

5. (watch) My parents _____ *The Today Show* every morning for as long as I can remember.

6. (cook) Angelica _____ enough egg rolls for forty people.

7. (start) Sanjay _____ smoking in his teens.

8. (imagine) When she graduated from high school, she _____ a life filled with money, men, and power.

9. (use) Lindsay and Leona _____ every talent they possess to make a success of their business.

10. (cause) The collapse of the savings and loan institution _____ my grandmother to lose her house.

Troublesome Past and Past Participle Verbs

The past and past participle verb forms you have looked at so far are called regular verbs because they follow the **-d** or **-ed** rule. However, a considerable number of English verbs do not follow this rule to form the past or past participle. Verbs that form the past and past participle in other ways are called **irregular verbs.**

He **ate** the entire pizza himself.

Lola and her date **rode** to the dance in a stretch limousine.

Fran **sent** the rent check a week late.

The following chart lists some common irregular past and past participle verb forms. As you look over the list, notice that some of these verbs seem to follow similar patterns in forming the past and past participle. For example, the verbs *run* and *come* both have past participles that look exactly like the present tense forms.

PRESENT	PAST (IRREGULAR)	PAST PARTICIPLE (IRREGULAR)
am, are, is	was, were	been
beat	beat	beaten
begin	began	begun
bend	bent	bent
blow	blew	blown
break	broke	broken
bring	brought	brought
build	built	built
buy	bought	bought
catch	caught	caught
choose	chose	chosen
come	came	come
cut	cut	cut
do	did	done
draw	drew	drawn
drink	drank	drunk
drive	drove	driven
eat	ate	eaten
fall	fell	fallen
feed	fed	fed
feel	felt	felt
find	found	found
fly	flew	flown
freeze	froze	frozen
get	got	gotten
give	gave	given
go	went	gone
grow	grew	grown
have	had	had
hear	heard	heard
hide	hid	hidden
hit	hit	hit
hurt	hurt	hurt
keep	kept	kept

PRESENT	PAST (IRREGULAR)	PAST PARTICIPLE (IRREGULAR)
know	knew	known
lay	laid	laid
leave	left	left
lend	lent	lent
lie	lay	lain
lose	lost	lost
make	made	made
mean	meant	meant
meet	met	met
pay	paid	paid
put	put	put
read	read	read
ride	rode	ridden
ring	rang	rung
rise	rose	risen
run	ran	run
see	saw	seen
sell	sold	sold
send	sent	sent
set	set	set
shake	shook	shaken
shoot	shot	shot
sing	sang	sung
sink	sank	sunk
sit	sat	sat
sleep	slept	slept
speak	spoke	spoken
speed	sped	sped
spend	spent	spent
spin	spun	spun
stand	stood	stood
stick	stuck	stuck
swear	swore	sworn
swim	swam	swum
take	took	taken
teach	taught	taught
tear	tore	torn
tell	told	told
think	thought	thought
throw	threw	thrown
wear	wore	worn
weep	wept	wept
win	won	won
write	wrote	written

APPLICATION ONE

Fill in verbs from the list of irregular past and past participle forms that follow the patterns illustrated by the first verb. Then complete the descriptions that follow each group.

	PRESENT	PAST	PAST PARTICIPLE
EXAMPLE:	cut	cut	cut
	set	**set**	set
	hit	hit	hit
	put	put	**put**
	hurt	**hurt**	hurt

In this group the present, the past, and the past participle all

have the same spelling .

	PRESENT	PAST	PAST PARTICIPLE
1.	draw	drew	drawn
	know		known
	throw	threw	
		grew	grown
	blow		

In this group all of the present tense verbs end in _____ or

_____ . These endings change to _____ to form the past tense.

The past participles are formed by adding _____ to the present

tense.

	PRESENT	PAST	PAST PARTICIPLE
2.	begin	began	begun
	swim		swum
	drink		
		sang	sung
	sink	sank	
		rang	rung

In this group the letter _____ in the present tense form changes

to _____ in the past tense and to _____ in the past participle.

PRESENT	PAST	PAST PARTICIPLE
3. break	broke	broken
choose	chose	
	spoke	spoken
freeze	froze	
	got	gotten
ride	rode	
rise		risen
drive		driven
	wrote	written

In this group the vowel _____ appears in the middle of all of the

past tense verbs. All of the past participles end in the two letters

_____ .

PRESENT	PAST	PAST PARTICIPLE
4. shake	shook	shaken
take		taken
	gave	given
eat		eaten
fall	fell	
beat	beat	beaten
see	saw	seen

In this group, the past participle is formed by adding -n or -en to

the _____ .

PRESENT	PAST	PAST PARTICIPLE
5. build	built	built
	fed	fed
feel		
win	won	
find		found
	had	had
hear		heard
meet	met	
pay		paid
	laid	

leave	left	
keep		kept
	sat	sat
lose	lost	
	made	
		sold
weep	wept	
		shot

In this group of verbs, the _____ and _____ forms

are the same.

	PRESENT	PAST	PAST PARTICIPLE
6.	lend	lent	lent
	mean	meant	
	send		sent
	bend		bent
		spent	spent

In this group of verbs, the past and past participle forms are the

same. Both of these forms end in the two letters _____.

	PRESENT	PAST	PAST PARTICIPLE
7.	buy	bought	bought
	bring		brought
	catch	caught	
		taught	
	think		thought

In this group, the _____ and _____ form are the

same; both of them end in the three letters _____.

	PRESENT	PAST	PAST PARTICIPLE
8.	tear	tore	torn
	wear		worn
		swore	sworn

In this group, all of the present tense forms end in the three letters

_____. The past tense forms end in the three letters _____,

and the past participles end in the three letters _____.

APPLICATION TWO

Circle the verb in parentheses that correctly completes the sentence.

> EXAMPLE: She has (sang, (sung)) in the Baptist choir for seven years.

1. My brother has (swam, swum) for his college team.
2. Alex (brang, brought) his older sister to the party.
3. I had (took, taken) the test once before.
4. Rudy has (gone, went) to the doctor's office.
5. Curt has (aten, eaten) four meals already today.
6. The unhappy child had (broke, broken) his new toy.
7. The deceased dog had (run, ran) after a car for the last time.
8. The woman in the dry cleaning store had (written, wrote) my name on the wrong receipt.
9. The cat (sprang, sprung) on the unsuspecting parakeet.
10. The young boy (stole, stoled) a watch from Kmart.

Be + Past Participle

As you have seen, the past participle can be combined with **have** or **had** to show tense. When it is combined with the helping verbs **am, is, are, was,** or **were,** the past participle has another function. When it is combined with one of these forms of **be,** the past participle is used to form the **passive voice.**

When the subject of a sentence performs the action of the verb, the sentence is in the **active voice.** When the subject is acted upon, the sentence is in the **passive voice.**

```
                  S    V
ACTIVE:     The dog bit the boy.
```

(The subject, **dog,** is doing the action.)

```
                  S   HV   MV
PASSIVE:     The boy was bitten by the dog.
```

(The subject, **boy,** is receiving the action, not doing it.)

In general, you should write in the active voice because active sentences are more direct and usually take fewer words. When the doer is unknown, obvious, or unimportant, however, you might want to use the passive voice.

The mail is always delivered at three o'clock.
> (We all expect that the mail is delivered by a mail carrier, so there is no need to include this information.)

My father was injured in a subway accident.
(The man and his injury are more important than the information that it occurred in a subway.)

The note was slipped under the door.
(The doer in this case is unknown.)

Notice that the passive voice can be either past tense or present tense, depending on the tense of the helping verb.

APPLICATION ONE

Underline the verb in each sentence and indicate in the blank whether the sentence is in the active (**A**) or the (**P**) passive voice.

EXAMPLE: ___P___   Everyone was satisfied by the verdict.

1. _____ Every garment is inspected by a supervisor.

2. _____ Julie's wedding dress was handmade by her grandmother.

3. _____ The minister preached a lively sermon last Sunday.

4. _____ Nadia was disappointed by her blind date.

5. _____ The creative writing class publishes a literary magazine every semester.

6. _____ The last episode of *The Cosby Show* was watched by millions of people.

7. _____ The door slammed on his foot.

8. _____ Abdul is often irritated by his neighbor's noisy parties.

9. _____ Portuguese is spoken in Brazil.

10. _____ Under the elm tree sat Alana and Katrice.

APPLICATION TWO

Change each of the passive sentences to the active voice and each of the active sentences to the passive voice.

EXAMPLE: Their argument was soon forgotten.

They soon forgot their argument.

1. The supermarket opening was attended by the mayor and his wife.

   _____

   _____

2. The Corvette was given by Marty to his fiancee as a Valentine's Day gift.

   _____

   _____

3. The post office delivered the package right at 5:00.

   _____

   _____

4. The frightened child was comforted by the elderly man.

   _____

   _____

5. The voters elected the judge despite his drunk driving arrest.

   _____

   _____

6. People had taken all of the good seats by the time I arrived.

   _____

   _____

7. The challenger was knocked out by the champ in the fifth round.

   _____

   _____

8. Someone had collected pillows, blankets, and clothing for the refugees.

   _____

   _____

9. Our shoes were stolen at gunpoint by two female impersonators.

_____

_____

10. The scruffy street person was ignored by the two well-dressed women.

_____

_____

▼ CHAPTER REVIEW

- Form **regular past** and **past participle verbs** by adding **-d** or **-ed** to the present tense verb form. All other past and past participle verbs are called **irregular verbs.**
- Use **past tense verbs** to indicate actions or events that occurred on a previous occasion.
- In order to function as a verb, the **past participle** must be used with a **helping verb:**

1. Use **have** or **has + past participle** to describe an action that occurred in the past and continues to occur today.
2. Use **had + past participle** to describe an action that occurred prior to another past action.
3. Use **am, is, are, was,** or **were + past participle** to form the **passive voice.**

PRACTICE

Test your understanding of the past and past participle verb forms by substituting these forms for the present tense verbs in the following selection. Cross out the present tense verbs and write the correct past or past participle form above them.

Puerto Rico

[1]In 1493, Christopher Columbus claims the island of Puerto Rico for Spain. [2]When Columbus arrives, the West Indian island is inhabited by the Arawak peoples. [3]During the period of Spanish rule, Puerto Rico is important to Spain because of its strategic location and its agricultural output. [4]After the Spanish-American War, the is-

land becomes a United States commonwealth, and the inhabitants become American citizens. [5]Because of high unemployment and over-population, many Puerto Ricans move to the mainland, especially in the period since World War II. [6]Seeking a better life, many of these immigrants face discrimination and unemployment. [7]In many cases, they also find themselves torn between the culture and values of their homeland and those of their new communities.

Using Progressive Tenses

▼ CHAPTER PREVIEW

So far, you have looked at present and past tenses, and verb tenses using the past participle. As you learned in Chapter 2, words ending in *-ing* can never by themselves be the complete verb of a sentence. They can, however, act as main verbs when they are combined with a helping verb. The **progressive** tenses combine an *-ing* word with a form of **be.** This chapter will focus on the formation and uses of the progressive tenses.

A Professional Writer Uses the Progressive Tenses

About the Reading: In 1967, Jonathan Kozol, an elementary school teacher in his twenties, wrote a book entitled *Death at an Early Age,* in which he described the plight of poor children in the Boston public schools. Since 1967, Kozol has written books on education, the poor, and the homeless. Kozol's 1991 book, *Savage Inequalities,* describes the shocking conditions that the author found when he visited schools in America's inner cities and lower income suburbs from 1988 to 1990. The following selection, taken from *Savage Inequalities,* describes the classroom of a Chicago teacher who uses unorthodox methods to make a difference for her students despite a lack of funds and adequate facilities.

As You Read: Look carefully at the verbs in bold type in the following selection. Some of them are in the forms you have studied so far—present, past, and helping verb + past participle. But notice that many of them are in another form. Pay close attention to the formation of this additional tense, and try to figure out how it differs in function from the other tenses you have studied.

91

From *Savage Inequalities*

[1]The room **looks** like a cheerful circus tent. [2]In the center of it all, within the rocking chair, and cradling a newborn in her arms, **is** Ms. Hawkins.

[3]The 30 children in the class **are seated** in groups of six at five of what she **calls** "departments." [4]Each department **is composed** of six desks pushed together to create a table. [5]One of the groups **is doing** math, another something that they **call** "math strategy." [6]A third **is doing** reading. [7]Of the other two groups, one **is doing** something they **describe** as "mathematics art"—painting composites of geometric shapes—and the other **is studying** "careers," which on this morning **is** a writing exercise about successful business leaders who **began** their lives in poverty. [8]Near the science learning board, a young-looking woman **is preparing** a new lesson that **involves** a lot of gadgets she **has taken** from a closet.

[9]"This woman," Ms. Hawkins **tells** me, "**is** a parent. [10]She **wanted** to help me. [11]So I **told** her, 'If you **don't have** somebody to keep your baby, **bring** the baby here. [12]I'll **be** the mother. [13]I **can do** it.'"

After You Read: Refer to the reading to complete the following items:

In the spaces provided, list the complete verbs in the Kozol piece that end in an *-ing* word.

_____   _____

_____   _____

_____

Look at the verbs you have listed. How are these verbs formed?

_____

_____

Circle the number of the explanation that you think best describes the way these verbs function in the selection:

1. To show an action that began and ended in the past
2. To show an action that is in progress
3. To show an action that will happen in the future

All of the verbs in the Kozol piece that end in an *-ing* word are formed by combining the *-ing* word with the word *is,* the present tense form of *be.* Each of the actions described by these verbs is in progress at the time the author describes it, so number 2 is the correct answer.

Describing an action in progress is only one function of the progressive tenses, but, as you have probably guessed, it is the function that gives them their name.

Present Progressive

Verbs in the **present progressive tense** are formed by adding a **present tense form of** *be* (*is, am, are*) to an *-ing* word.

I **am going** to the movies.

He **is feeling** tired lately.

They **are performing** next Saturday.

Use the present progressive tense to describe an action **in progress** or an action that will take place in the **future.**

Sheba **is looking** for a new apartment. (right now)

Farley **is throwing** himself a huge graduation celebration at the end of the semester. (in the future)

APPLICATION

Rewrite each sentence, changing the verb to the present progressive tense.

> *EXAMPLE:*   Martha will arrive on Thursday.
>
> **Martha is arriving on Thursday.**

1. Helene plays the accordion with a great deal of feeling.

   _____

   _____

2. Mr. Sanchez works for the government.

   _____

3. My mother will return to school to get a high school diploma.

   _____

   _____

4. Gish attends classes at the state university.

   _____

5. Pablo spends a lot of time with Noel lately.

_____

6. Anne acts peculiar these days.

_____

7. Bonnie expects to give birth two days after final exams end.

_____

_____

8. They will come by here after the show.

_____

9. On her way to the beach, she will pick up the food.

_____

10. The doorbell rings.

_____

Past Progressive

Verbs in the **past progressive tense** are formed by adding a **past tense form of** _be_ (_was, were_) to an _-ing_ word.

He **was planning** a surprise party for his wife.

Anita and Shirley **were working** together on a project.

Use the past progressive tense to stress the duration of an **ongoing action or condition in the past,** to emphasize that **a past action was in progress at a particular time,** or to describe **an action that was in progress when something else occurred.**

Workers **were remodeling** the science building all last term.
    (The remodeling was an ongoing activity over a period of time in the past.)

He **was washing** his car at 3:00 in the morning.
    (The washing was in progress at a particular time.)

She **was finishing** her research paper when the computer screen went blank.
    (The writing was in progress when the computer failure occurred.)

APPLICATION ONE

Change the italicized past tense verb in each sentence to the past progressive tense.

> EXAMPLE: While in Mexico, I *drank* the water every day.
>
> **While in Mexico, I was drinking the water**
>
> **every day.**

1. She *wore* Joe's letterman's jacket when she fell in love with someone else.

2. The instructor *wrote* on the board for at least ten minutes.

3. Father O'Malley *said* the rosary when the earthquake occurred.

4. Troy and Cynthia *dated* when she was only in junior high.

5. We *ate* lunch when the restaurant was robbed.

6. He *acted* like a complete idiot at the party.

7. My mother *shouted* at the other driver when the police arrived.

8. The men on the corner *played* cards every afternoon.

9. Rusty *looked* for a good used car for his sister.

_____

10. Delia *took* a nap while the other students wrote the final exam.

_____

_____

APPLICATION TWO

Circle the appropriate verb form in each sentence.

> EXAMPLE: The beekeeper (got, (was getting)) the honey when he was stung.
> (He was in the process of collecting honey when the stinging took place.)

1. The band's song (plays, is playing) on the radio right now.
2. Tricia (drove, was driving) when the accident occurred.
3. The phone rang while he (worked, was working) on his car.
4. They (serve, are serving) in the student government this year.
5. The firefighters (reached, were reaching) the child just in time.
6. She (hates, is hating) any dish made with meat.
7. The college (cancels, is canceling) three classes due to budget cuts.
8. Jessica and Janine (took, were taking) an aerobics class when they met.
9. Richard (works, is working) on a construction site this summer.
10. After he leaves the computer center this afternoon, Fritz (goes, is going) to pick up his children.

Other Progressive Tenses

Other progressive tenses can be formed by placing **helping verbs before *be*** or ***been*** + an *-ing* word.

They **will be going** to summer school in June.

Maria **has been looking** for a new job for the last three months.

Manfred **had been meaning** to get started earlier.

In general, use these progressive tenses when you want to stress that an action or condition has continued over a significant period of time or when you want to use a helping verb like ***will, would, might,*** or

could to give a particular shade of meaning or emphasize future tense.

> Olga **will be performing** at the Comedy and Magic Club next week.
>
> (The performance will take place in the future.)

> Forrest **had been working** as a movie extra before he broke his leg.
>
> (The job lasted for a considerable period of time.)

> She **would be going** to Mexico with her friends during spring break if she had not spent her money on clothes.
>
> (The word ***would*** suggests that she had hoped to go to Mexico during the upcoming vacation.)

The word ***be*** itself is used before the ***-ing*** word only when it is preceded by the helping verbs ***will*** or ***shall.*** In all other cases, the ***-ing*** word follows a form of ***be*** such as ***is, am, was,*** or ***been.***

> He **be** going. (incorrect)

> He **is** going. (correct)

> He **will be** going. (correct)

> He **has been** going. (correct)

APPLICATION

Circle the verb in parentheses that best fits the meaning of the sentence.

> *EXAMPLE:* Gabrielle (went, had been going) to college for six years before she got her degree.
>
> (***had been going*** stresses the long time period of her attendance)

1. Elissa (speeded, was speeding) when she ran into the Carl's Jr. sign.

2. That man (be asking, is asking) for you.

3. He (listened, was listening) to the radio when his name was announced as winner of the contest.

4. Aunt Madeline told me she (will be arriving, be arriving) after lunch on Saturday.

5. The clock chimed six o'clock, just as they (had sat, were sitting) down at the dinner table.

6. Next month, my brother (joins, is joining) the Marine Corps.

7. She (looking, is looking) pale tonight.

8. Every Friday night my cousin and his friend (cruised, were cruising) the main street of town.

9. Charlie (be graduating, will be graduating) in June.

10. He (had been meaning, meant) to call her for the past six months.

▼ CHAPTER REVIEW

- **Progressive tenses** combine a **form of *be*** with an ***-ing* word.**
- The **present progressive tense** combines a **present tense form of *be* (*am, is, are*)** with an ***-ing* word.** Use the present progressive tense to

  1. describe an action in progress
  2. describe an action in the future.

- The **past progressive tense** combines a **past tense form of *be* (*was, were*)** with an ***-ing* word**. Use the past progressive tense to

  1. stress the duration of a past action or condition
  2. describe an action that was in progress when something else occurred
  3. emphasize that a past action was in progress at a particular time.

- **Other progressive tenses** combine ***be*** or ***been*** + an ***-ing* word** with another **helping verb or verbs.** Use these forms to

  1. stress the duration of an action or condition
  2. give a shade of meaning not present without helping verbs such as ***could, might,*** and ***would***
  3. emphasize the future tense.

PRACTICE

Test your understanding of the progressive tenses by underlining all verbs in the following paragraph that are in a progressive tense. Be sure to underline the complete verb, with all of its helping verbs.

America—A Meal in Itself?

[1]For the last hundred years, historians, sociologists, and others have been using food imagery to describe the American population. [2]For a long time, people had been thinking of the United States as a "melting pot," with all immigrants from other lands mixing together to form a new kind of blended population. [3]This image of a sort of

soup, with its flavors blending together, seems less appropriate than it once may have. [4]Today, Americans are becoming more aware of the diversity of this country's peoples. [5]Now many Americans are beginning to see the United States as a sort of salad, with all of the different peoples tossed together but still retaining their own unique ethnic and racial heritages. [6]One can only wonder what type of food imagery people will be using in the future to describe the American population.

CHAPTER 8

Using Verbs in Your Own Writing

▼ CHAPTER PREVIEW

In the other chapters of this unit, you have learned about forming verb tenses and making verbs agree with their subjects. In this chapter, you will be looking at the way verb choice affects your writing. Then you will be given a choice of writing assignments, followed by a sample student essay on one of the topics. Finally, you will practice revising your own essay based on what you have learned in this unit.

Avoiding Overused Verbs

Most people tend to use the same verbs over and over again: **be, go,** and **say** are probably the most overused of all. Although these verbs give the reader some basic information, they are not very specific, nor are they very interesting.

>The truck **went** off the road.

While this sentence informs the reader that the truck left the roadway, the verb **went** does not indicate the manner in which the truck exited. Compare the sentence with **went** to the sentences that follow:

>The truck **plunged** off the road.

>The truck **slid** off the road.

>The truck **careened** off the road.

>The truck **turned** off the road.

By changing only the verb, each of these sentences paints a much more vivid picture of what happened to the truck.

Whenever you write about actions, try to use the most specific word you can think of to describe those actions. If you are writing

went and thinking **slid,** your reader may be reading **went** and thinking **turned.** As a result, you are not communicating as effectively as you could.

APPLICATION

Rewrite each of the sentences, changing the overused verb to a more specific verb.

> EXAMPLE: She **went** out the door.
> **She slammed out the door.**

1. He **said,** "I'll never forgive you for this!"

   _____

2. There **was** the most gorgeous woman he had ever seen.

   _____

3. Martin **got** out of the car.

   _____

4. The limousine **went** past the upscale shops.

   _____

5. They **went** downtown.

   _____

6. The mysterious woman **got** off the train.

   _____

7. At that point, Nathan **says** that his grade is unfair.

   _____

8. Professor Guerra **said** that he would lower an essay grade one letter for each day it was late.

   _____

   _____

9. The singer **went** onto the stage.

   _____

Writing Assignments

Choose *one* of the following writing assignments:

1. Think about a memorable experience. Maybe this experience was embarrassing or exciting or humorous or frightening. It may have happened when you were a child, or it may have happened last week. Focus on just that part of the experience that makes it memorable, and try to recreate that part for your reader.
2. Think about the "firsts" in your life—your first date, your first car, your first day of college, and so on. Choose one of these firsts that is particularly special to you. Describe this first in writing, focusing on the details that make it so special.

To come up with a topic, you might use one of the following strategies:

a. List all of the firsts in your life.
b. Complete one or all of the following sentences:

I can't help laughing when I think of the time I . . .

I've never been as scared as I was when . . .

I get embarrassed all over again when I think of . . .

Once you have chosen a topic, use one or more of the prewriting strategies you learned in Chapter 4 to come up with details about your topic. Once you have remembered the details of your experience, try to write about the experience so that your reader will feel like he or she has actually done and felt what you are describing. As you write, pay particular attention to the verbs you use: ask yourself if you are using the most specific word you can think of.

A Student Responds to One of the Writing Assignments

Before you begin writing about your own experience, you might find it helpful to look at the way another student responded to one of the assignments. Because the entire student essay has been included, each indented section—or paragraph—has been numbered instead of each separate sentence.

About the Reading: The student author of the essay that follows is Brenda T. Butler, a 21-year-old sociology major. When she is not at school, Butler works as production coordinator for a fashion merchandising business. When she graduates, she would like to work with children. Butler wrote this essay for an English class one level below freshman composition. In the essay, she describes going to buy her first car.

As You Read: Pay close attention to the specific details that make the essay interesting.

....

My First Car

We can all remember our first cars. We can recall the feeling of happiness and excitement of every moment. It is especially exciting and unforgettable if at a young age we independently bought our first cars. This can also leave an everlasting impression on our lives. We all have exciting, yet different, stories to tell about our first cars. I can't help laughing at myself when I remember my first car. I wasn't laughing then, but now, when I look back, I find it funny. First, I was so nervous and excited I made a complete fool of myself. Even more, I remember not being able to leave the car dealer without totally embarrassing myself.   **1**

When I think back on that day I bought my first car, the first thing that comes to mind is how nervous I was. I thought I could drive since I had gotten my driver's license two years prior to that day, although I had had very little practice driving. The thought of my inexperience never occurred to me until that day, when I got behind the wheel and frantically discovered that I was indeed inexperienced and a nervous wreck. Wreck is precisely what almost happened. I was so nervous and excited that after I started the car, I froze in panic because I had totally forgotten everything the dealer said about where things were. I finally found the brake release, lights, and shift, and put the car in reverse. Then I slammed on the accelerator, and the car went back fast, making a loud squeezing noise, toward the other cars on the lot. I slammed on the brakes within an inch of the other cars.   **2**

Now my nervousness and excitement over my car turned into fear and embarrassment. I will never forget all the car salesmen's expressions when they saw me almost back into their other cars. Well, needless to say, I was extremely embarrassed. I was so young and stupid then that I thought that they were going to change their minds and take the car back. So I immediately smiled at the salesmen, and slowly drove past them. Unfortunately, I was still there while the dealers watched me try to leave the driveway. With a loud bang and bump of the car's back end hitting the curb, I eventually left the car dealer's lot.   **3**

Finally, I was driving away in my first car. I don't remember ever being so excited, nervous, and embarrassed. But now, looking back I find it funny. This was an unforgettable experience; thus, that day felt like the first day of the rest of my life. It took months for me to calm down and stop going around showing off my first car to everyone I knew.   **4**

....

After You Read: Refer to the reading to complete the following items:

1. Writers often include a sentence that sums up their essay. Find one sentence in the essay that to you sums up this writer's experience.

   _____

   _____

2. This essay has lots of specific details: not being able to find anything in the car, almost hitting the other cars in the lot, the difficulty getting out of the driveway. Which detail do you like best? Why?

   _____

   _____

   _____

3. This essay includes a number of vivid verbs: **_slammed, froze, discovered, smiled._** In the following sentence, cross out the italicized overused verb and write above it a more specific verb:

   Then I slammed on the accelerator, and the car _went_ back fast, making a loud squeezing noise, toward the other cars on the lot.

4. Sometimes, writers include sentences that really don't give the reader any information or add to the essay in any way; these sentences are usually better off left out. Do you think that the first paragraph would be hurt or helped if it started with "We all have exciting, yet different, stories to tell about our first cars"? Explain your answer.

   _____

   _____

   _____

   _____

Revising Verbs for Tense, Agreement, and Interest

After you have written your essay, go through the essay and underline every verb. Then look over the words you have underlined, and check to see if they are grammatically correct. Make sure that each verb is in the proper tense, and that each present tense verb agrees with its subject in number. You may wish to trade papers with a classmate and have this person double-check the verbs for you.

After you are sure that your verbs are correct, look to see if they are specific. Choose at least three verbs in your essay that you think might be made more interesting or vivid. Replace these verbs with more specific words. You may need to try several words before you find just the right one to capture a particular action.

▼ CHAPTER REVIEW

- Choose **verbs** that are specific; whenever possible, avoid overused verbs like *be, go,* and *say.*

- The **present tense** form of a verb is the form used with the word **to.**
- Use the present tense to

    1. indicate an action that is taking place right now
    2. describe habitual actions
    3. summarize an author's words
    4. make statements that are always or generally true.

- Make sure a **present tense verb and its subject agree** in number.
- Form **regular past and past participle verbs** by adding **-d** or **-ed** to the present tense verb form.
- Use **past tense verbs** to indicate actions or events that occurred on a previous occasion.
- In order to function as a verb, the **past participle** must be used with a **helping verb.**

    1. Use **have** or **has** + **past participle** to describe an action that occurred in the past and continues to occur today.
    2. Use **had** + **past participle** to describe an action that occurred prior to another past action.
    3. Use **am, is, are, was,** or **were** + **past participle** to form the passive voice.

- Form **progressive tenses** by combining **a form of be** with an **-ing word**.
- The **present progressive tense** combines a **present tense form of be (am, is, are)** with an **-ing word**. Use the present progressive tense to

    1. describe an action in progress
    2. describe an action in the future.

- The **past progressive tense** combines a **past tense form of be (was, were)** with an **-ing word**. Use the past progressive tense to

    1. stress the duration of a past action or condition
    2. describe an action that was in progress when something else occurred
    3. emphasize that a past action was in progress at a particular time.

- **Other progressive tenses** combine **be** or **been** + an **-ing word** with **another helping verb or verbs.** Use these forms to

    1. stress the duration of an action or condition

2. give a shade of meaning not present without helping verbs such as *could, might,* and *would*
3. emphasize the future tense.

- In your writing, choose verbs that are **specific;** whenever possible, avoid overused verbs like *be, go,* and *say.*

PRACTICE

Use the following sentences to test your mastery of the material in Unit 2. If you have difficulty, go back and look over the explanations in Chapters 5–8.

A. In each sentence, circle the present tense verb in parentheses that agrees in number with its subject.

 EXAMPLE: Geraldo (use, uses) only the finest equipment.

1. Mrs. Berkowitz always (talk, talks) about her experiences as an army nurse in Korea.
2. Neither Ellen nor Maria (want, wants) to speak in front of the class.
3. Someone usually (forget, forgets) to let the cat out at night.
4. (Is, Are) Consuela and her parents coming tonight?
5. Either the twins or Monroe (is, are) supposed to bring the pizza.
6. Here (come, comes) the men from the exterminator company.
7. The family that (lives, live) next door must get rid of its vicious dog.
8. Each of their six children (has, have) a Super Soaker 2000 water gun.
9. Under the overpass (was, were) piles of trash.
10. Most of her days (is, are) spent in front of television talk shows.

B. In each blank, write one of these forms of the verb in parentheses: (1) past tense, (2) *have* or *had* + past participle.

 EXAMPLE: Elena thought she __had found__ her ideal mate in Henry. (find)

1. Keith thought he _____ dashing in his new hat; his date thought he _____ ridiculous. (look)
2. As long as he could remember, Trini _____ to become a fire fighter. (want)

3. Last Sunday Mrs. Lopez _____ enough tamales to feed every hungry person in the city. (make)

4. He _____ his instructor to set up a meeting. (call)

5. Mr. Yen swore that he _____ the check last week. (send)

6. Michael _____ at the restaurant several times before. (eat)

7. The Lopez family _____ before the burglar arrived. (leave)

8. Carl _____ the class when he got his first paper back. (drop)

9. Grant and Debbie _____ to take the children to the movie with them before they realized it was X-rated. (intend)

10. At one time or another during the past semester, all the students in the class _____ about the instructor. (complain)

C. Rewrite each of the sentences, changing them to the active voice.

EXAMPLE: After he won the lottery, Henry was loved by all of his neighbors.

After he won the lottery, all of Henry's neighbors

loved him.

1. The book was read by the students during the first part of the semester.

_____

_____

2. The movie *Hook* was enjoyed by everyone but the critics.

_____

_____

3. The door was opened by a mysterious, masked stranger.

_____

_____

4. The wedding dinner was catered by a local submarine sandwich shop.

_____

_____

5. A brilliant idea worth millions of dollars to the company was suggested by the mail clerk.

_____

_____

D. Circle the correct verb form in parentheses.

> *EXAMPLE:*   The third grader (drove, (was driving) his mother's car when the police pulled him over.

1. After she leaves the office tonight, she (goes, is going) to drop off the papers.
2. When he lived with me, he always (paid, was paying) his phone bill on time.
3. Sheila (runs, is running) for homecoming queen this year.
4. Carmen (had taken, was taking) the proficiency exam once before.
5. The Korean-American students (host, are hosting) a dinner every year.
6. Every time I talk to Serena, she (practices, is practicing) for another dance performance.
7. He (be going, will be going) with us tonight.
8. Pattie (looked, had been looking) for a roommate for two months before she found Charmaine.
9. Last night at 6:00 a tornado (hit, was hitting) my home town.
10. Lorraine (is interviewing, has been interviewing) for jobs since May.

E. Write a specific verb in each blank.

> *EXAMPLE:*   Imelda ____**pushed**____ her way into the club.

1. Francesca _____ money from her parents.

2. The policeman _____ the suspect.

3. Her car _____ off of the road.

4. Salitha _____ working at Kmart.

5. He _____ his mother-in-law's tuna casserole.

6. The drunken actress _____ off the stage.

7. The instructor's words _____ the students.

8. The neon sign _____ .

9. Jerome _____ a nice suit for the occasion.

10. Renalda and Scott _____ for two hours.

UNIT 3

Using Nouns and Pronouns

CHAPTER 9

Using Nouns

▼ CHAPTER PREVIEW

In Chapter 2, you learned that the simple subject of a sentence is usually a **noun.** As you may recall, a noun names a **person, place, thing,** or **idea.** In this chapter you will practice recognizing and writing singular and plural nouns. You will learn how to spot noun markers, clues that signal a noun will follow.

A Professional Writer Uses Nouns

About the Reading: James Welch is a Native American of the Blackfeet and Gros Ventre tribes. After attending schools on the Blackfeet and Fort Belknap reservations in Montana, he graduated from the University of Montana. Welch is the author of several novels; perhaps the best known is *Fool's Crow* (1986). The selection that follows is taken from his 1979 book *The Death of Jim Loney.* Set in a small town in Montana, this book explores the fate of self-destructive half-breed Jim Loney, who feels a part neither of the Native American community nor of the white community. This excerpt describes town policeman Painter Barthelme's presentation to the local high school.

As You Read: All of the nouns in the selection appear in bold print. Pay close attention to the types of things that are named by nouns.

From *The Death of Jim Loney*

¹**Painter Barthelme** pulled his **cruiser** to the **curb** and switched off the **engine.** ²He zipped up his **jacket.** ³He was feeling good. ⁴His **lecture** to the high school **students** that **afternoon** had gone off without a **hitch.** ⁵Sometimes it pays to be a **cop.** ⁶That **afternoon** it

had paid. [7]He could see just the right **amount** of **fear** in their **eyes** and he had made sure it stayed there with **stories** of high-speed **chases** and desperate **shoot-outs.** [8]Of course, it was against the department's **policy** to talk of such **things.** [9]He was supposed to be a goodwill **ambassador,** not a **messenger** of **death** and **destruction.** [10]But he had passed his **badge** around and he had handcuffed the **teacher** to the **radiator** and he had told them that he could be their **friend,** he wanted to be their **friend.** [11]But he just couldn't help **putting** a little **fear** into them. [12]And the **siren** had been a **stroke** of **genius.** [13]By the **time** he pulled up to the **school** there were twenty **people** running out the **door** to see what was up. [14]He had got their **attention.**

After You Read:

A. Some of the nouns from the selection appear in the following list. Write each word from the list after the noun category into which it fits. You may wish to compare answers with a classmate.

Painter Barthelme	fear	eyes	badge
messenger	friend	radiator	attention
destruction	school	engine	curb

Person: _____

Place: _____

Thing: _____

Idea (something that cannot be touched or seen or heard): _____

_____

B. Refer to your response in A and to the reading selection to answer the following questions:

1. What two-word noun is capitalized? _____

2. What two nouns end in *-tion*? _____

   Do these nouns name a person, a place, a thing, or an idea? _____

3. Look over the selection once again, and notice the words that come directly before each noun. List three words which appear more than once directly before a noun. _____

Types of Nouns

Nouns are **naming words.** Most often, they name a **person, place,** or **thing.** But they can also name an **idea,** an **emotion,** a **condition,** or a **quality,** such as *freedom, health,* or *love.*

> The eighty-year-old astronomy **instructor** retired. (person)
>
> We enjoy camping at the seaside **park.** (place)
>
> Myron's **backpack** was missing. (thing)
>
> He was charged with sexual **harassment.** (idea)

There are two kinds of nouns: **common nouns** and **proper nouns.** A common noun names a general thing, such as *car, man, state,* or *socialism.* Do not capitalize a common noun. A proper noun names a particular thing, individual, or place, such as *Cadillac, Mr. Perez,* or *Lake Erie.* It can also name a thing or idea that takes its name from a specific person or place, like *English* or *Marxism.* Because they include names, proper nouns may be more than one word. Be sure to capitalize proper nouns.

> We got lost on the **interstate.** (common noun)
>
> We got lost on **Highway 605.** (proper noun)
>
> That **woman** is always smiling. (common noun)
>
> **Ms. Wong** is always smiling. (proper noun)

APPLICATION ONE

In the sentences that follow, underline each noun and label it **CN** for common noun or **PN** for proper noun.

$\qquad$ PN $\qquad\qquad\qquad$ CN

EXAMPLE: <u>Johnny</u> cried when his <u>father</u> left.

1. Maureen and Ken drove to the beach.

2. The art class went to an exhibition at the Metropolitan Museum of Art.

3. Her cat was trapped on the roof.

4. What do you think of Madonna?

5. Mr. Chevarria backed his van into the driveway.

6. My father went to Seattle looking for a job.

7. You can never be too careful in matters of love.

8. My grandmother is from Latvia.

9. Happiness is great if it doesn't cost too much or ruin your health.

10. I took three years of Spanish in high school.

APPLICATION TWO

For each of the proper nouns given, write a corresponding common noun.

EXAMPLE: George Washington   __president__

PROPER NOUN	COMMON NOUN
1. Doberman	_____
2. Mrs. McCormick	_____
3. Michael Jackson	_____
4. Pepsi	_____
5. Italian	_____
6. Mexico	_____
7. Jimmy	_____
8. The Smiths	_____
9. Mr. Figueroa	_____
10. Melissa	_____

Singular and Plural Nouns

Most nouns change form to show whether they are singular or plural. A **singular** noun names **one** person, thing, place, or idea. A **plural** noun names **more than one** person, thing, place, or idea. Nouns usually add **-s** or **-es** to form the plural. Nouns that end in **y** often change the **y** to **i** before adding **-es.**

SINGULAR	PLURAL
girl	girls
tomato	tomatoes
market	markets
sandwich	sandwiches
library	libraries

Some nouns form the plural in other ways.

SINGULAR	PLURAL
child	children
man	men
woman	women
mouse	mice
tooth	teeth
foot	feet

Some nouns, usually nouns referring to animals, do not change to form the plural.

SINGULAR	PLURAL
fish	fish
deer	deer
sheep	sheep

Most nouns ending in *-f* or *-fe* change to *-ves* to form the plural.

SINGULAR	PLURAL
knife	knives
life	lives
wife	wives
leaf	leaves
shelf	shelves

Most hyphenated nouns form the plural by adding *-s* or *-es* to the first word only.

SINGULAR	PLURAL
mother-in-law	mothers-in-law
brother-in-law	brothers-in-law
father-to-be	fathers-to-be

If you are unsure how a particular noun forms the plural, look up the singular form in a dictionary. If the plural is formed in some way other than adding *-s* or *-es,* the dictionary will give the plural form as well.

APPLICATION

Write the correct plural form for each singular noun.

EXAMPLE: knife   _____**knives**_____

SINGULAR	PLURAL
1. moose	_____
2. scarf	_____
3. boy	_____

4. computer   _____

5. runner-up   _____

6. self   _____

7. woman   _____

8. half   _____

9. potato   _____

10. story   _____

Identifying Nouns

In some sentences, nouns can be difficult to identify; however, there are certain clues that you can look for that indicate the presence of a noun.

Certain **word endings** tell you that a word is a noun: **-tion, -ness, -ity,** and **-ism.** Words with these endings name ideas or other things that cannot be seen or touched.

He believed in **capitalism.**

Obesity can be unhealthy.

Her **attention** wandered.

Goodness is not always rewarded.

Words **a, an,** and **the** are often called **noun markers** because they indicate that a noun is coming up. Sometimes the noun follows immediately after the noun marker; other times, several words can come between the noun marker and the noun. If you are unsure whether a word is a noun or not, ask yourself if it could follow one of these noun markers.

       N
The boy ran away repeatedly.

             N
The troubled young boy ran away repeatedly.
    (**boy** is the only word in the sentence that could follow the word **the**)

Other words that can act as noun markers are these:

this	my	his	one
that	your	her	two
these	our	their	three
those	its		

  N
Those enchiladas look delicious.

N   N
That man ran over **our** pet rabbit.

Oftentimes noun markers combine with the word *of* to signal that a noun is coming up.

N
One **of *my*** sisters just got married.

N
Several **of *the*** men lived nearby.

N
She is one **of *a*** kind.

Certain **noun markers** can tell you if the noun that follows is likely to be **singular** or **plural.** A singular noun will *usually* follow words like ***a, an, another, a single, each, every,*** and ***one.*** A plural noun will *usually* follow words like ***all, both, few, many, most, several, some, two,*** and higher numbers.

Some men hassled my cousin Irene.

Several men hassled my cousin Irene.

Two men hassled my cousin Irene.
    (The noun ***men*** is plural.)

He disliked **every** applicant for the job.

He disliked **each** applicant for the job.

He disliked **one** applicant for the job.
    (The noun ***applicant*** is singular.)

Words ending in ***'s*** or ***s'*** cannot function as nouns themselves, but they are often followed by nouns.

N
My **brother's** car was totaled.

N
Her **parents'** television was stolen.

APPLICATION

In the following sentences, label each noun with an ***N.*** If a noun follows a noun marker, draw an arrow from the noun marker to the noun. If a noun has a common noun ending, like ***-tion, -ness, -ism,*** or ***-ity,*** circle the ending.

EXAMPLE: One of my friends has AIDS.

1. Two women in my study group brought their children with them.

2. Socialism grew in popularity in the United States during the

    1930s.

3. Those flowers need water.

4. An uncle of mine is running for the school board.

5. The Joneses' house is being remodeled.

6. The best student in my aerobics class is a retired ballet dancer.

7. These tomatoes were grown in our backyard.

8. Attractiveness is not always a reliable measure of a person's worth.

9. Latin is called a dead language because people do not speak it anymore.

10. I can't stand Lucinda's new husband.

To + Verb and *-ing* Words

To + **a verb** often acts as a noun.

N
To forgive is often difficult.

N
She hates **to fly.**

Words ending in **-ing** can act as nouns, but they can also describe nouns or act as main verbs if they have a helping verb. If you are unsure whether an **-ing** word is a noun, see if it would make sense after **the,** if it names something instead of describing something, or if it is acting as a subject.

N
I was upset by her **crying.**
   ("The crying" could be substituted for "her crying.")

N
She was crying for **hours.**
   (The complete verb of this sentence is **was crying.** The main verb is **crying.**)

N
He paused beside the crying **woman.**
   (**Crying** describes a noun rather than naming something itself.)

N
Surfing is growing more popular.
   (**Surfing** is the subject.)

N   N
Mel purchased a surfing **magazine.**
   (**Surfing** describes the noun **magazine.**)

APPLICATION

Circle the nouns in each sentence.

EXAMPLE: (Skiing) is too expensive for many (people).

1. I am the captain of my bowling team.
2. I have always wanted to skydive.
3. Riding in Arthur's car can be dangerous because he is such a bad driver.
4. Penelope is my mother's name.
5. That woman is a famous celebrity.
6. Put that knife down!
7. The name given to Charles Darwin's theory of evolution is Darwinism.
8. Humankind has always wanted to fly.
9. My sisters-in-law do not get along.
10. Most of my classmates are working while they are going to school.

▼ CHAPTER REVIEW

- **Nouns** name a **person, place,** or **thing.** They can also name an **idea,** an **emotion,** a **condition,** or a **quality.**
- There are two kinds of nouns: **common** and **proper.** Common nouns name general things or individuals, and proper nouns name specific things or individuals. Capitalize proper nouns.
- Most nouns change form to show whether they are **singular** or **plural.** Nouns usually add *-s* or *-es* to form the plural, but some nouns form the plural in other ways.
- Nouns can often be identified by certain endings, such as *-ism, -ity, -tion,* and *-ness.*
- **Noun markers** are words that are followed by nouns. The most common noun markers are *a, an,* and *the.*
- *To* + **a verb** is often a noun. Words ending in *-ing* may be nouns, if they are not preceded by helping verbs and if they are used to name something rather than to describe something.

PRACTICE

Test your knowledge of nouns by circling all the nouns in the following paragraph.

Chinese in America

[1]During the period from 1849 to 1870, the United States welcomed Chinese immigrants. [2]Even though people leaving China could be executed by the Chinese government, many risked everything for a chance at a better life. [3]The first of these immigrants came to California during the gold rush. [4]They worked in mines, cooked for the miners, and provided laundry services. [5]In 1871, a United States mining commission praised the courage and efficiency of Chinese workers. [6]After the gold rush ended, many of the Chinese were hired by the builders of the transcontinental railroad. [7]In fact, during the last years of construction, the great majority of the railroad workers were Chinese immigrants. [8]Unfortunately, the period of economic depression that followed the completion of the railroad led to increasing antiforeigner feelings, and in 1882 the federal government passed legislation that would no longer let Chinese citizens enter the United States. [9]Even though President Arthur vetoed the act, his veto was overridden. [10]The Exclusion Act remained effective until the 1940s.

CHAPTER 10

Using Pronouns

▼ CHAPTER PREVIEW

In the last chapter you studied nouns. In this chapter you will learn about **pronouns,** words (like *he, it, they*) that can be substituted for nouns. You will learn which pronouns to use as subjects and which to use for other functions. You will also practice revising to eliminate common pronoun errors.

A Professional Writer Uses Pronouns

About the Reading: Oscar Hijuelos (pronounced **ee-*hway*-los**) is a first-generation American whose parents came to the United States from Cuba in 1943. When he was four years old, Hijuelos spent a year in a Connecticut hospital recovering from a serious kidney disease. When he entered the hospital, he spoke only Spanish; when he returned home, he spoke mostly English. After growing up in a neighborhood riddled with gang violence, Hijuelos played in several rock bands, eventually quitting to attend City College of New York. His first book is the story of immigrants coming to America from Cuba. His second novel, *The Mambo Kings Play Songs of Love,* tells the story of two Cuban brothers who come to New York in 1949. Musicians, the Castillo brothers find fame briefly when the mambo craze sweeps America. The highlight of their musical career is a performance with Desi Arnaz's band on the *I Love Lucy* television show. In 1990, Hijuelos became the first American-born Latino to receive the Pulitzer Prize for fiction, which he was awarded for *Mambo Kings.* In 1992, *Mambo Kings* was made into a motion picture, with Desi Arnaz, Jr., playing the part of his father. The following selection from *Mambo Kings* describes the initial meeting of the fictional Castillo brothers with real-life Cuban-born Arnaz and his wife, Lucille Ball.

As You Read: Notice that pronouns have been printed in bold type. Pay close attention to the way each pronoun functions in the selection.

From *The Mambo Kings Play Songs of Love*

[1]Later when the brothers were drinking by the bar, Arnaz lived up to **his** reputation as a friendly man and introduced **himself,** saying, with extended hand, "Desi Arnaz." [2]**He** was wearing a sharp blue serge suit, white silk shirt, pink polka-dotted tie, and a frilly fringed handkerchief **that** bloomed like a tulip from **his** breast pocket. [3]**He** shook **their** hands and ordered a round of drinks for all the musicians, complimented the brothers on **their** performance, and then invited **them** to sit at **his** table. [4]Then **they** met Lucille Ball, **who** spoke surprisingly good Spanish. [5]**She** was dressed in a pearl-button blouse with a velvet diamond-broached vest and a long skirt. [6]**Her** hands and wrists glittered with rings and bracelets and **she** had curly red hair **that** had been done up in a bouffant, and beautiful blue eyes.

After You Read: Refer to the selection to help you circle the response that best completes each of the following sentences:

1. In sentence 1, the pronouns **his** and **himself** refer to the noun (brothers, Arnaz).

2. In sentences 3 and 4, the pronouns **their, them,** and **they** refer to (drinks, brothers).

3. In sentences 2 and 3, the pronoun **he** acts as a (subject, verb).

4. In sentences 5 and 6, the pronoun **she** acts as a (subject, verb).

5. In sentence 4, the subject of the verb **met** is (they, Lucille Ball).

6. The pronoun **her** in sentence 6 means (Lucille Ball's, singer's).

Using Pronouns to Replace Nouns

Pronouns are words that take the place of nouns. When you write or speak, you probably refer to the same thing, person, place, or idea more than once. Pronouns allow you to avoid repeating the same noun or nouns over and over.

> When Alvaro brought his silk shirts to the dry cleaner, Alvaro said the shirts needed to be cleaned carefully.
>> (The nouns **Alvaro** and **shirts** are repeated.)

> When Alvaro brought his silk shirts to the dry cleaner, **he** said **they** needed to be cleaned carefully.
>> (The pronouns **he** and **they** are used instead of repeating **Alvaro** and **shirts**.)

As you can see in these examples, most pronouns get their meaning from nouns or pronouns mentioned earlier. The words that give pronouns their meaning are called **antecedents.** *Antecedent* is from the Latin for "to go before."

> **Pablo** was standing in the back, but Marguerite didn't see **him.**
> (***Pablo*** is the antecedent of ***him.***)

> **Sonny and Naomi** have **their** hearts set on opening a business.
> (The antecedent of ***their*** is ***Sonny and Naomi.***)

Occasionally, a pronoun can come before its antecedent.

> Honking **his** horn, the **teenager** sped past the cautious elderly couple.
> (The pronoun ***his*** takes its meaning from ***teenager.***)

The pronouns *I* and *you* do not need antecedents if *I* refers to the writer and *you* refers to the reader.

> **You** surely enjoy doing the exercises in this book.
> (***You*** = you, the reader.)

Like nouns, pronouns can be either **singular** or **plural.** Pronouns that take the place of singular nouns are singular, and pronouns that take the place of plural nouns are plural.

> **Max** lost **his** temper every time **he** spent five minutes with Larry.
> (***Max*** is singular; ***his*** and ***he*** are singular)

> The **women** on the softball team won both of **their** games.
> (***Women*** is plural, and ***their*** is plural)

Here is a list of commonly used pronouns:

I, me, my, mine, myself

you, your, yours, yourself, yourselves

he, him, his, himself

she, her, hers, herself

it, its, itself

we, us, our, ours, ourselves

they, them, their, theirs, themselves

that, this, these, those

who, whose, whom, which, what

whoever, whomever, whichever, whatever

any, anyone, anybody, anything

each, either, neither

one, everyone, everybody, everything

APPLICATION

In the following sentences, circle the pronouns and draw an arrow from the pronouns to their antecedents. You may wish to refer to the preceding list to help you locate pronouns.

EXAMPLE: John found (his) wallet in the back seat.

1. When Clara signed up for Professor Popov's class, she made a big mistake.

2. Hope and Rowena saw their science instructor at a sports bar.

3. The dog hurt its paw on a sharp rock.

4. Carlos told Marianna that he never wanted to see her again.

5. Patricia gave herself a home permanent.

6. Janet lost her mind.

7. While walking down the street, Roberto saw his brother.

8. Monique and Janelle picked up their final grades.

9. Amy's pet parakeet lost its balance and fell to the bottom of the cage.

10. The women finally got their tickets for Oprah's show.

Pronoun/Antecedent Agreement

In Chapter 5, you learned that subjects and verbs should agree in number; that is, singular verbs should be used with singular subjects, and plural verbs should be used with plural subjects. **Pronouns** and their **antecedents** should also **agree in number.** If its antecedent is singular, then a pronoun should also be singular; if its antecedent is plural, then a pronoun should also be plural.

Mrs. Johanssen forgot **her** car keys again.
(Both **Mrs. Johanssen** and **her** are singular.)

The Rodriguez **twins** are celebrating **their** twenty-first birthday on Tuesday.
(Both **twins** and **their** are plural.)

In some cases, pronouns may act as antecedents of other pronouns. In these instances, you may find yourself having difficulty making pronouns and antecedents agree. Remember that the indefinite pronouns in the following list are always singular.

INDEFINITE PRONOUNS

-one Words	-body Words	
one, no one	nobody	each
anyone	anybody	either
everyone	everybody	neither
someone	somebody	

Because **indefinite pronouns** are singular, use singular pronouns to refer to them.

Incorrect: **Someone** has left **their** shaving cream in the locker room.

Correct: **Someone** has left **his** shaving cream in the locker room.

When **singular antecedents** are **joined by *and***, use a **plural pronoun** to refer to them. When **singular antecedents** are **joined by *or* or *nor***, use a **singular pronoun** to refer to them.

The **boy *and*** his **mother** watched **their** house burn to the ground.

Neither **Felicity *nor*** Sabrina had **her** own car.

When a **singular antecedent and a plural antecedent** are **joined by *or* or *nor,*** make the **pronoun agree with the closer antecedent.**

Growing up, neither my **mother *nor*** her **sisters** had **their** own room.

Growing up, neither my **aunts *nor*** my **mother** had **her** own room.

Pronouns should also agree with their antecedents in **gender.** Use *he, him,* and *his* to refer to singular **masculine antecedents** and *she, her,* and *hers* to refer to singular **feminine antecedents.** **Plural pronouns,** like *they* and *their,* can be used to refer to **plural nouns of either gender.**

The girl **scout** was awarded **her** twelfth merit badge.

The embarrassed **boy** tripped over **his** shoelace.

The **men** finished **their** golf match in record time.

The **women** organized a group to make **their** voices heard in Washington.

Often, a singular **antecedent's gender** is **unknown** or **the antecedent names a group composed of both males and females.** In the past, the masculine pronouns were used in these cases. Today, however, many writers try to avoid gender bias by using both the **masculine and feminine pronouns.**

Traditional Usage: **Everyone** turned in **his** homework.

Current Usage: **Everyone** turned in **his or her** homework.

Using ***he or she*** or ***his or her*** may be more logical, but these expressions can sometimes sound awkward, especially if you use them too much in a short piece of writing:

Awkward: **Everyone** turned in **his or her** homework and got out **his or her** textbook.

To eliminate both gender bias and awkwardness, recast your sentences whenever possible so that antecedents of unknown or mixed gender are plural.

Improved: **All** of the class members turned in **their** homework and got out **their** textbooks.

APPLICATION

Circle the correct pronoun in parentheses.

> *EXAMPLE:*   Each of the actresses had (their, (her)) own dressing room.
> (***Each*** and ***her*** are singular.)

1. Both boys had (their, his) own cars.
2. Neither student had done (her, their) assignment.
3. Either Sheryl or her sister-in-law had (their, her) wallet stolen.
4. Neither Yuhyang nor Irena has paid (their, her) fees.
5. Every one of the girls wants to have (her, their) own way.
6. Eduardo or William will be chosen to have (their, his) picture on the cover.
7. Each of the rats in the experiment got (their, its) own cage.
8. Someone had left (his, their) athletic supporter on the bus.
9. One of the cars had lost (their, its) windshield.
10. Either the landlord or the tenants broke (his, their) lease.

Choosing the Correct Pronoun

Of all the pronouns, the personal pronouns that follow create the most difficult:

SUBJECT GROUP	NONSUBJECT GROUP
I	me
he	him
she	her
we	us
they	them

Use a pronoun from the subject group only as the subject of a verb or, after a linking verb, as a word that renames the subject.

She works with my aunt.
(**She** is the subject of the verb **works.**)

The man in the sunglasses is **he.**
(**He** follows the linking verb **is** and renames the subject, **man.**)

Use a pronoun from the nonsubject group for most other purposes.

Gilbert gave **her** a cubic zirconia engagement ring.
(**Her** is not the subject and does not rename the subject.)

Doris came with **me.**
(**Me** is not the subject and does not rename the subject.)

When a pronoun appears with a noun, try eliminating the noun to decide whether to use a subject or nonsubject pronoun.

Juanita came to the party with Jim and (I, me).

Juanita came to the party with **me.**
(You probably wouldn't say, "Juanita came to the party with **I.**")

Grandpa let (us, we) boys ride on his tractor.

Grandpa let **us** ride on his tractor.

Be sure to eliminate the noun before using your ear to decide which pronoun to use. So many people use these pronouns incorrectly that your ear may not be a good judge if the noun is left in.

Can Joe and (I, me) go to the movies?

Can **I** go to the movies?

Grandmother gave the cookies to Felix and (I, me).

Grandmother gave the cookies to **me.**

Probably the most common misuse of a pronoun is the use of **I** after the preposition **between.** Always use a pronoun from the nonsubject group after **between.**

That is a secret between Francesca and **me.**

The candy is to be split between you and **her.**

Pronouns are often used in comparisons.

Jimmy is younger than **she** is.
(**She** is the subject of **is.**)

The hair stylist charged Rhonda more than **he** charged **me.**
(**He** is the subject of **charged. Me** is not a subject and does not rename a subject.)

In each of these sentences, you could probably use your ear to tell which pronouns are correct. However, people do not always write out their comparisons completely; instead they use shortened forms.

Newman gets better grades than **I.**

The dress looked nicer on Lou Ann than on **me.**

In shortened comparisons, decide which pronouns to use by mentally filling in the words that have been left out.

Newman gets better grades than **I** (do).
(**I** is the subject of **do.**)

The dress looked nicer on Lou Ann than (it looked) on **me.**
(**Me** is not a subject.)

APPLICATION

Underline the correct pronoun.

EXAMPLE: Carlos and (I , me) decided to go after all.
(I decided; **I** is the subject of the verb **decided.**)

1. Georgeann promised Mary Beth and (I, me) a ride home.
2. Mrs. Matsushita earns more than (he, him).
3. Aurora and (me, I) have plans for Saturday night.
4. The instructor allowed (us, we) students to write our own exam questions.
5. Just between you and (I, me), I can't stand him.
6. His sister spends more time on the telephone than (he, him).
7. A package arrived for Lawanda and (her, she).
8. Are Billy and (her, she) going to get married soon?
9. The waiter split the bill between Tracy and (her, she).
10. The woman in the Lycra spandex miniskirt is (she, her).

Pronouns Ending in *-self* and *-selves* and Possessive Pronouns

Pronouns that end in *-self* or *-selves* can be used in **two ways.** First, use this type of pronoun when the **subject acts upon itself.**

> I hurt **myself.**

> **Lisa** talks to **herself.**

Second, use this type of pronoun for **emphasis.**

> **He** ate the whole banana split **himself.**

> I painted my bedroom **myself.**

> **You yourself** said the same thing.

Do not use a pronoun ending in *-self* or *-selves* as the subject of a sentence or to take the place of a nonsubject pronoun.

Incorrect:	Joey and **himself** are members of the football team.
Correct:	Joey and **he** are members of the football team.

Incorrect:	The birthday gift is from Jose and **myself.**
Correct:	The birthday gift is from Jose and **me.**

Pronouns ending in *-self* and *-selves* are formed by adding these endings to the **nonsubject** form of the personal pronouns you have just studied. The singular pronouns end in *-self* and the plural pronouns end in *-selves.*

PRONOUNS ENDING IN *-SELF* AND *-SELVES*

Singular	Plural
myself	ourselves
yourself	yourselves
himself	themselves
herself	
itself	

Pronouns that show **ownership** are called **possessive pronouns.**

POSSESSIVE PRONOUNS

Singular	Plural
my, mine	**our,** ours
your, yours	**your,** yours
his, his	**their,** their
her, hers	
its, its	

The pronouns listed in bold type (***my, your, his, her, its, our,*** and ***their***) are used before a noun; the words in standard type are not.

I forgot **my** dictionary. (**dictionary** is a noun)

The dictionary I am using is **hers.**

Possessive pronouns take the place of words that end in **s'** or **'s.**

Kyle ruined **Marvella's** presentation.

Kyle ruined **her** presentation.

Have you tasted that bean pie of **Shug's?**

Have you tasted that bean pie of **hers?**

APPLICATION

Circle the correct pronoun.

> *EXAMPLE:*   Heidi and (I, myself) enrolled in weight lifting.
> (**I** is the subject of **enrolled:** I enrolled.)

1. Has the registrar mailed (you, your) transcripts?
2. He got the job by (hisself, himself).
3. My wife and (I, myself) split the child care duties.
4. The children cleaned up the playground by (theirselves, themselves).
5. I found (me, myself) a seat in the front row.
6. The college president (himself, hisself) answered the phone.
7. My wife earns more money than (myself, I).
8. Did Kim borrow that red jacket of (yours, yourn)?
9. My mother and (myself, I) went to the family reunion together.
10. I have looked everywhere for (me, my) notebook.

Avoiding Common Pronoun Errors

Make sure that a pronoun has only one possible antecedent. To correct a confusing pronoun, you can rewrite your sentence to eliminate the pronoun, or you can replace the confusing pronoun with a noun.

Confusing: Pauley told **his** father that **he** had wrecked **his** car.
(Because **he** and **his** could refer either to Pauley or to his father, you can't tell from the sentence whether the father did the wrecking or Pauley did, or even which person was the owner of the car.)

Improved: Pauley said to his father, "I wrecked your car."
(The confusing pronoun has been eliminated by using the exact words of the speaker.)

Confusing: Belinda told her math teacher that **she** had made an error.

> (**She** could refer to Belinda or to the teacher, so you can't tell which one made the error.)

Improved: Belinda told her math teacher that the teacher had made an error.

> (The confusing pronoun **she** has been replaced by ***the teacher.***)

Be sure that each pronoun has an antecedent.

Confusing: I have always been interested in teaching, and now I have decided to become **one.**

> (A person can't become a "teaching," so the pronoun **one** lacks an antecedent.)

Improved: I have always been interested in teaching, and now I have decided to become a teacher.

Be especially careful with the words ***which, they,*** and ***it.*** Be sure that they always refer to a specific antecedent. If you have used the word ***which*** carelessly, you will probably have to revise your entire sentence to eliminate confusion.

Confusing: They finally bought a new house, **which** made them very happy.

> (You can't tell whether the buying or the house itself is what made them happy.)

Improved: Finally buying a house made them very happy.

Or: They were very happy with the house they finally bought.

In the case of ***they*** and ***it,*** however, you can usually just replace the confusing pronoun.

Confusing: At the bank, **they** said I would need a cosigner.
> (The pronoun **they** has no antecedent.)

Improved: At the bank, the loan officer said I would need a cosigner.

Confusing: On the front window, it said everything was 50 percent off.
> (The pronoun **it** has no antecedent.)

Improved: On the front window, a sign said everything was 50 percent off.

Don't use a pronoun right after its antecedent; use either the pronoun or the antecedent, not both. The only exception is a pronoun ending in ***-self*** or ***-selves.***

Repetitious: My son, **he** is a doctor. (**He** unnecessarily repeats the antecedent **son** right before it.)

Improved: My son is a doctor.

Repetitious: The professor **he** missed the error.

Improved: The professor missed the error.

Acceptable: The professor **himself** missed the error. (This sentence stresses the fact that even the professor goofed.)

APPLICATION

Revise the following sentences to eliminate any pronoun errors. If a sentence is correct the way it is, put **C** on the line.

> *EXAMPLE:*   My father and I, we work at the same place.
>
> **My father and I work at the same place.**

1. I have always enjoyed helping teach elementary school children, and now I have a job as one.

---

2. Rosemarie told her mother she had ripped her blazer.

---

3. Father's estate was divided evenly between Royal and me.

---

4. On the poster, it said the circus would open on Friday.

---

5. I couldn't find the salt shaker, and I don't like my food without it.

---

6. At the cashier's office, they said I owed $50.00.

_____

7. Susan decided to take a job which her husband disapproved of.

_____

_____

8. Dwayne told his computer instructor that he didn't understand the textbook.

_____

_____

9. It says in the class schedule that freshman composition meets for four hours a week.

_____

_____

10. In Southern California they roller-skate in bathing suits along the beachside walks.

_____

_____

▼ CHAPTER REVIEW

- **Pronouns** are words that **take the place of or refer to nouns or**, in some cases, **other pronouns.**
- Words that give pronouns their meaning are called **antecedents.**
- Be sure **pronouns and their antecedents agree in number.** If its antecedent is singular, then a pronoun should also be singular; if its antecedent is plural, then a pronoun should also be plural. A pronoun that refers to an indefinite pronoun should be singular.
- Be sure that **pronouns agree with their antecedents in gender.** If you don't know the gender of a singular antecedent, or if the antecedent refers to a group of both males and females, avoid gender bias by using the pronouns **he or she, his or her,** or **him or her,** or by changing the antecedent to the plural.
- Use the **subject pronouns I, he, she, we,** and **they** in only **two ways:**

1. As the subject of a verb
2. As a word that follows a linking verb and renames the subject.

- In a **comparison, fill in the words that have been left** out to decide which pronoun to use.
- Use a **pronoun** ending in *-self* or *-selves* to provide **emphasis** or to show that a **subject acts upon itself.**
- Use **possessive pronouns** to **show ownership.**
- **Avoid common pronoun errors** by making sure of the following:

  1. Each pronoun has only one possible antecedent.
  2. Each pronoun has a clear antecedent.
  3. A pronoun does not follow right after its antecedent unless the pronoun ends in *-self* or *-selves.*

PRACTICE

Test your familiarity with pronouns by writing the correct pronoun from the following list in each blank. Some pronouns in the list may be used more than once; others may not be used at all.

their	his	her	themselves	it
they	he or she	himself	he	

The Lesson of Jack

[1]Scholars, psychologists, and sociologists have tried to make the case that the folk and fairy tales people tell to _____ children teach the youngsters important life lessons. [2]A look at the old English folktale "Jack and the Beanstalk" might make a person question just what type of lesson is being taught. [3]First of all, Jack _____ is not very bright, and second, his behavior is terrible. [4]In one version of this story, young Jack and _____ mother are living in poverty when the boy trades the family cow for some supposedly "magic" beans. [5]The mother beats Jack for _____ stupidity (introducing the idea of child abuse), the beans grow into a magic beanstalk, and Jack climbs the beanstalk to the home of a giant. [6]When the giant's wife tries to be kind to Jack, the youth lies to _____, gains entrance to the house, and steals the giant's most prized possessions. [7]Jack repeats this behavior several times, until

_____ finally chops down the beanstalk, killing the giant in the process. [8]The boy and _____ mother are now financially secure, and, presumably, _____ live happily ever after. [9]One lesson that might be learned from this story is that stupidity, treachery, and violence are the keys to success. [10]Another is that a mother should forgive a child anything if _____ brings home lots of expensive gifts.

CHAPTER 11

Using Nouns and Pronouns in Your Own Writing

▼ CHAPTER PREVIEW

In the other chapters of this unit, you have learned about words that function as namers: nouns and pronouns. In this chapter, you will learn how using specific nouns can add to your writing. Then you will be given a choice of writing assignments, followed by a sample student essay on one of the topics. Finally, you will practice revising your own writing based on what you have learned in this unit.

General and Specific Nouns

Nouns can name **abstract** ideas, like **liberty** or **love,** or they can name **concrete** things, like **pencil** or **paper.** When nouns name concrete things that you can see, hear, touch, feel, or taste, they can be either quite general or very specific—or they can be in between.

most general			**most specific**
animal	dog	collie	Lassie

As you can see, nouns that name categories or types are general in nature because they include many people or things; proper names are the most specific nouns because they refer to only one person or thing. Look at the way these different words affect a sentence.

An **animal** approached the stranger cautiously.

A **dog** approached the stranger cautiously.

A **collie** approached the stranger cautiously.

Lassie approached the stranger cautiously.

Given only the general word **animal,** someone who reads just the first sentence may be picturing a bear or a mouse. In the next sentence, the reader may be picturing a toy poodle instead of a collie. Although the word ***collie*** is pretty specific, it does not tell the reader anything about the dog's coloring or about its personality. It could still be a fang-baring, deranged collie, or it could be a sweet family pet. The name of a particular dog, ***Lassie,*** gives this type of information instantly to any reader familiar with this specific collie.

In your writing, whenever you choose a noun, be sure that it is the most specific noun you can use. In this way, you can be pretty sure that your reader is picturing the same thing that you are.

APPLICATION

For every general noun on the left, fill in a noun that is more specific, then fill in another noun that is even more specific.

	GENERAL	MORE SPECIFIC	MOST SPECIFIC
EXAMPLE:	water	**ocean**	**Atlantic Ocean**
1.	performer		
2.	educator		
3.	mail		
4.	furniture		
5.	road		

Writing Assignments

Write on one of the following topics:

1. Describe a situation in which you found yourself that either left you feeling bad about yourself or made you feel good about yourself. Perhaps you did better at something than you thought you would, maybe winning an award or feeling satisfaction at having tried your hardest. Or, you might have overestimated your ability at something and had your pride hurt.

2. Describe your initial reaction to a change in your life situation. Perhaps you moved, changed schools, began a new job, or got married or divorced. Be sure to focus on your *first* reaction, though you may wish to end by telling *briefly* how things worked themselves out.

To come up with a topic, you might use one of the following strategies:

a. Look back over your life, and make a list of any major changes that have occurred.

b. Get two pieces of blank paper. In the middle of one, write "things that made me feel good" and on the other, "things that made me feel bad." Circle each of these topics, then brainstorm on each one to come up with ideas.

Once you have decided on a topic, use a strategy like freewriting to come up with all of the details of your experience. To help you focus your essay, look over these details, and try to write a main idea statement about your experience like one of these:

My first day as a waitress at Denny's was a disaster.

Losing the 100 meter race really hit me hard.

When you have written a complete draft of your essay, read it over to make sure that you haven't added details that get off the track of the main idea in your statement. Check also to see if you have used specific nouns wherever possible.

A Student Responds to One of the Writing Assignments

About the Reading: Fernando A. Guerra, who wrote the essay that follows, is a 19-year-old math major. He currently works as a food clerk but would eventually like to be a university professor. When Guerra is not working or studying, he likes to play sports.

As You Read: Pay attention to the writer's use of nouns and pronouns, and notice how he paints a clear picture of his misery as a young child at a new school.

....

New School

I remember the first day of school in this new place. I was   **1** going to be a man. I said to myself on my way to school, "I won't be scared. I won't be scared," but I was. The gate was huge, and as far as the eye could see, there were millions of kids running, laughing, and doing lots of hair-pulling, mischievous deeds. My face cracked with a smile at the sight of their joy, but I was afraid as my mother and I made our way to the school's main office. We left the office in the direction we had come, and another crack in my face appeared, but this time it was a sad one because my mom was explaining to me that I would have to stay. She told me to be brave and go to the room directly across from the gate. I didn't want to stay, but she somehow tricked me into staying, and I almost cried when she left—but I didn't.

I made my way very nervously through the kids in the   **2** school yard early in the morning as my mom forced me to go into the room by brushing her hands against the air in an upward hand motion. As I saw the last glimpse of my mom, I walked into the room and headed towards the teacher, past the probing eyes, and introduced myself very quietly. She looked at me and said that she had been expecting me. And just as I began taking comfort by her side, she heard a message through the P.A. and left me all alone to the hungry sharks.

Time passed, and class soon began. Class time was fun because the teacher kept us entertained with all kinds of learning games, but at recess I remember being the last kid to come out of the classroom. I felt alone. Outside everyone gave me stares and whispered ear to ear unknown secrets; they pointed fingers, and giggles came like blasts from their mouths.   **3**

After weeks of giggles during recess and lunch, and other students saying, "Don't talk to him. He is the new kid," I began feeling lonely and miserable. I was starting to hate this new school. I began remembering the great times I had had with all my cousins and friends at my first school. The day my parents told me we were moving, it had been like a slap in the face. I didn't want to go anywhere, but I, of course, had no say in the matter. When we finished packing all of our necessary belongings, we were on our way west from El Paso, Texas. After years of driving (from a kid's point of view), we arrived at our new home in Los Angeles. It was a grand castle to me, but the house had only 2 bedrooms, 1 bathroom and a huge garage towards the back of the long driveway, almost hidden by a huge avocado tree creeping up the left side.   **4**

I told my mom that I wanted to go back because no one wanted to be my friend, but she said that we could not go back. She told me not to worry because here I would make lots of new friends. One day I can remember sitting in class watching the school clock 10 minutes away from recess. As the teacher spoke to the class, I began thinking about the ridicule I would get during recess. The teacher's voice faded in the background as I felt my heart beating very fast. I got a huge lump in my throat, and my hands began to sweat. I was really nervous, ready to run home crying, when I was startled by a knock on the door. I jumped up and the teacher said, "Good, open the door, Fernando." I opened the door, and in came a new kid and his mother. The teacher said, "Class, this is Jorge. Everyone say hi." The class said "hi," the mom left, everyone sat down, and the teacher said, "Jorge, sit next to Fernando." He came, he sat, but we did not speak to each other.   **5**

When the "horror" bell sounded, I knew it was time for recess. I crept out of the class and leaned on the school fence directly across from the room. A while later, the last person came out of the class. It was Jorge with a sad look on his face. I remembered what it had been like when I first came out of the classroom, and all of the ridicule I had received. I looked at him for a while and thought about talking to him, but I did not want to speak to "the new kid." Minutes later two boys from my class went up to Jorge and invited him to play. He had made friends on his first day. He played with the other kids—tag, kickball, and other neat games—but I was all alone. Jorge was having the   **6** time of his life, while I sulked on the gate. As he ran with the wind in his hair and laughed at the top of his lungs, I could not understand why he was better than me.

After days of sitting together, we became friends. I remember looking at him from the corner of my eye when we were told that we had to work together. The teacher handed me a seed, and he eventually introduced himself. We grew a beautiful plant together that won first prize in the class. Through my friendship with Jorge, I was eventually accepted by the whole class. I don't exactly know why he made friends before me. Maybe it was the fact that he sat next to someone, but I genuinely think I was alienated from the class because I had not been taken by the hand to my room by my mother and introduced by the teacher to the class.

7

After You Read: Refer to the student essay to complete the following items:

1. This writer does not have one particular sentence that states the main idea of his essay. Fill in the blank in the following sentence to compose a main idea statement for this essay:

     Going to a new school was _____.

2. Even though he doesn't directly tell you in the essay, from the title and from the focus of the material, you can tell that the writer's purpose is to describe an unhappy school experience. However, at one point in the essay, he tends to get off of this subject and on to another subject. Circle any of the following items that you think get off of the topic of this essay:
     a. The long drive from El Paso to Los Angeles.
     b. The stares and giggles at recess.
     c. The description of the new house.
     d. The anxiety of watching the clock.

3. This essay contains a lot of specific details, including the mother's hand motions to get the boy into the classroom and the stares, secrets, fingers, and giggles of the children. In paragraph 6, the children are not described merely as "playing"; instead two specific games are named. What are they? _____ _____

4. Supply a specific noun for each of the general words in bold type in the following sentences. You will have to use your imagination to come up with the noun if the writer does not give you the specific information in the essay.
     a. I remember the first day of school in **this new place.** (paragraph 1) _____
     b. Class time was fun, because **the teacher** kept us entertained with all kinds of learning games, but at recess I remember being the last kid to come out of the classroom. (paragraph 3)
     _____

5. The writer does a very good job of using pronouns. None of them are confusing, and all of them agree with their antecedents. In

fact, the only pronouns used incorrectly in the essay are pronouns used in comparisons. Look at the pronoun in bold type in the following sentence from paragraph 6:

> As he ran with the wind in his hair and laughed at the top of his lungs, I could not understand why he was better than **me.**

Remember, to test which pronoun to use in a comparison, you fill in the missing words: "I could not understand why he was better **than I was.**" So, the correct pronoun should be *I.* Use this method to correct the following sentence from paragraph 7. Cross out the incorrect pronoun and write the correct pronoun above it.

> I don't exactly know why he made friends before me.

Revising for Correct Pronoun Use and Specific Nouns

After you have completed your essay, circle all of the pronouns and find the antecedent for each one. If you cannot find an antecedent, replace the pronoun with a noun. If a pronoun has more than one possible antecedent, either replace the pronoun with a noun or rewrite the sentence.

Look for the following special cases that might signal a pronoun error, and correct any errors you identify:

1. pronouns ending in *-self* or *-selves*
2. pronouns in comparisons
3. pronouns coming right after their antecedents.

You may wish to trade essays with a classmate and double-check each other's pronouns.

After you have corrected any pronoun errors, look carefully at the nouns in your essay. Choose at least two nouns that could be more specific and change them to more specific words.

▼ CHAPTER REVIEW

- Use **nouns** that are specific; whenever possible, avoid nouns that refer to broad categories, and find nouns that name particular people, places, or things.

- **Nouns** name a **person, place,** or **thing.** They can also name an **idea,** an **emotion,** a **condition,** or a **quality.**
- There are two kinds of nouns: **common** and **proper.** Common nouns name general things or individuals, and proper nouns name specific things or individuals. Capitalize proper nouns.
- Most nouns change form to show whether they are **singular** or **plural.** Nouns usually add *-s* or *-es* to form the plural, but some nouns form the plural in other ways.
- Nouns can often be identified by certain endings, such as *-ism, -ity, -tion,* and *-ness.*
- **Noun markers** are words that are followed by nouns. The most common noun markers are *a, an,* and *the.*
- *To* + **a verb** is always a noun. Words ending in *-ing* may be nouns if they are not preceded by helping verbs and if they are used to name something rather than to describe something.
- **Pronouns** are words that **take the place of or refer to nouns** or, in some cases, **other pronouns.**
- Words that give pronouns their meaning are called **antecedents.**
- Be sure that **pronouns and their antecedents agree in number.** If its antecedent is singular, then a pronoun should also be singular; if its antecedent is plural, then a pronoun should also be plural. A pronoun that refers to an indefinite pronoun should be singular.
- Be sure that **pronouns agree** with their **antecedents in gender.** If you don't know the gender of a singular antecedent, or if the antecedent refers to a group of both males and females, avoid gender bias by using the pronouns *he or she, his or her,* or *him or her,* or by changing the antecedent to the plural.
- Use the **subject pronouns** *I, he, she, we,* and *they* in only **two ways:**

  1. As the subject of a verb
  2. As a word that follows a linking verb and renames the subject.

- In a **comparison, fill in the words that have been left out** to decide which pronoun to use.
- Use a **pronoun** ending in *-self* or *-selves* only to provide **emphasis** or to show that a **subject acts upon itself.**
- Use **possessive pronouns** to **show ownership.**
- **Avoid common pronoun errors** by making sure of the following:

  1. Each pronoun has only one possible antecedent.
  2. Each pronoun has a clear antecedent.

3. Unless it ends in *-self* or *-selves,* a pronoun does not follow right after its antecedent.

- In your writing, be sure the nouns you select are as **specific** as possible.

PRACTICE

Use the following sentences to test your mastery of the material in Unit Three. If you have difficulty, go back and look over the explanations in Chapters 9 and 10.

A. Circle each noun in the following sentences:

EXAMPLE: The (child) darted into the (street.)

1. Noelle is a talented young woman.
2. My friend called after midnight last night.
3. Freedom means different things to different people.
4. Mr. McMannis once threatened my parents with a lawsuit.
5. Ice-skating is not as easy as it looks.
6. Unfortunately for his waistline, Carmine loves to eat.
7. One of my brothers recently applied to law school.
8. The child whined for her father's attention.
9. The family donated their old sheets and blankets to a charity.
10. Several weeks passed before she got her grade report.

B. Circle each pronoun and draw an arrow from the pronoun to its antecedent.

EXAMPLE: The rabbit had hurt (its) paw.

1. Mr. Raymond could kick himself for giving away the winning lottery ticket.
2. Dawn found good homes for her dog's puppies.
3. Mr. and Mrs. Garcia are celebrating their fortieth anniversary.
4. After hanging around with his older brother, the five-year-old boy cussed out the kindergarten teacher, Miss Nguyen.
5. Marsha and Tamika got their money's worth at Chippendale's.
6. Phillip bet his last two dollars on a horse race.

7. Kim accidentally ran over his brother's new bicycle.

8. Jan's computer has a mind of its own.

9. When the Fedoras got home from vacation, they found a burned-out shell where their house had been.

10. Carolyn's pet pig escaped from its pen during the night and went in the neighbors' dog door.

C. Circle the correct pronoun in parentheses.

    EXAMPLE: Somebody has left (her, their) bra in the locker room.

1. The husband and wife argued over where to spend (its, their) anniversary.

2. Neither Gerald nor Quito wanted to drive (their, his) own car.

3. Everyone had completed (their, his or her) assignment, so the class was dismissed.

4. One of the fish had injured (their, its) tail in the move.

5. Both of the women had (her, their) AA degrees from the same community college.

6. Each of the boys brought (their, his) own bike.

7. Either Elizabeth or her sister had (their, her) own shop.

8. Everybody wants to get (their, his or her) name on the waiting list for Dr. Ruth's guest lecture.

9. Neither the parents nor the son had a brain in (their, his) head.

10. Every Boy Scout in the troop could tie (his, their) own square knot.

D. Circle the correct pronoun in parentheses.

    EXAMPLE: Pat and (I, me) attended a free concert in the park.

1. He had trouble deciding whether to propose to Celie or (I, me).

2. Are you and (he, him) coming to the party on Saturday?

3. Edgar invited my brother and (I, me) to his graduation.

4. A postcard arrived for my sister and (myself, me).

5. He spends a lot more money on clothes than (she, her).

6. (We, Us) students have a harder life than people seem to think.

7. Please keep this information just between you and (I, me).

8. Dad gave the keys to his old car to (us, we) kids.

9. Georgia and (me, I) have already made plans on that day.

10. The man in the gray suit is (him, he).

E. Revise the following sentences to eliminate pronoun errors.

   EXAMPLE: My mother and I, we both love children.

   My mother and I love children.

1. In the psychology textbook, it explains that sexy pictures are hidden in the photos in advertisements.

2. At the checkout stand, they asked for an ID.

3. They finally found a larger apartment, which made them very happy.

4. Kelly told her mother that she should have taken her advice.

5. I have always loved cooking, and now I'm going to take classes to be one.

UNIT 4

Joining Ideas

CHAPTER 12

Using Coordinating Conjunctions

▼ CHAPTER PREVIEW

Joining ideas together is an important technique in writing. It allows writers to avoid choppy and repetitious writing like the sentences that follow:

> Manuel went to Paul Laurence Dunbar High School.
>
> Harry went to Paul Laurence Dunbar High School.
>
> Olivia went to St. Francis High School.

Joining the first two subjects together would eliminate the need to repeat the name of the school.

> Manuel and Harry went to Paul Laurence Dunbar High School.
>
> Olivia went to St. Francis High School.

These two sentences would not sound so choppy if they were joined together into one sentence.

> Manuel and Harry went to Paul Laurence Dunbar High School, and Olivia went to St. Francis High School.

In English, there are several different ways to join ideas. This chapter will give you practice joining ideas together using **coordinating conjunctions** (*for, and, nor, but, or, yet, so*).

A Professional Writer Uses Coordinating Conjunctions

About the Reading: Born in Kentucky, Bobbie Ann Mason now lives in rural Pennsylvania with her writer husband. Her first published book of fiction, *Shiloh and Other Stories*, won the PEN/Hemingway

Award. Her 1985 novel *In Country* describes a girl's search for a connection with her father, who was killed in Vietnam. *In Country* was made into a movie, starring Bruce Willis. The selection that follows is taken from "Piano Fingers," a story that appears in the 1989 collection of Mason's short stories entitled *Love Life.* The main character in "Piano Fingers" finds himself facing the loss of his job at a drugstore that is closing.

As You Read: The coordinating conjunctions that appear in the following selection have been printed in bold type. Notice how they act to join words and ideas in the paragraph.

From "Piano Fingers"

[1]When he was laid off from the tire plant, Dean drew enough unemployment to keep up his house payments, **but** that may not be the case now. [2]Somehow he believes everything will be O.K., because things have worked out in the past, **but** he can feel Nancy's dread, **and** he knows she expects more of him than he has been able to give. [3]"I'm not asking for the moon," she is fond of saying. [4]He takes that as a hint for him to be a better provider. [5]Dean has a lot of ideas—including training to be an electrician, **or** a real estate agent, **or** even a travel agent—**but** she just laughs at some of his notions. [6]He can never seem to do what's expected of him. [7]It's as though he has a built-in mechanism that steers him in another direction. [8]In school, his grades weren't great. [9]He was intelligent **but** easily diverted. [10]If he had to write a report on worms for biology, he'd look up worms in the encyclopedia **but** then get distracted by something more interesting, like wombats. [11]Even now, his mother nags him about what he is going to do with his life, **and** his dad keeps saying Dean should have gone into the Army. [12]Dean is only twenty-six, **and** people still call him a kid. [13]**But** he feels suspended somewhere between childhood **and** old age, not knowing which direction he is facing.

After You Read: Refer to the reading selection to answer the following questions:

1. What three coordinating conjunctions appear in this selection?

   _____

2. In sentences 1, 2, 11, and 12, the coordinating conjunctions follow the same mark of punctuation. What is the punctuation mark? (If you do not know the name of the mark, just write in the mark itself.)

   _____

3. One sentence begins with a coordinating conjunction. What is the number of the sentence, and which coordinating conjunction is used?

_____

4. In sentence 9, the word **but** connects two characteristics of Dean. What are these characteristics?

_____

5. In sentence 13, the word **and** connects two stages of development. What are they?

_____

6. In sentence 12, **and** connects two word groups that could stand alone as complete sentences. Write these two word groups as separate sentences.

_____

_____

Coordinating Conjunctions

For, and, nor, but, or, yet, and *so* are called **coordinating conjunctions.** An easy way to remember the coordinating conjunctions is to think of them as the FANBOYS. Each letter of FANBOYS stands for the first letter of one of the coordinating conjunctions.

F	A	N	B	O	Y	S
O	N	O	U	R	E	O
R	D	R	T			T

The word **conjunction** comes from two Latin words that mean "to join with," and conjunctions are words that act as joiners. In English, there are two types of conjunctions; **coordinating conjunctions** are used to join elements that are alike, from single words to whole sentences.

Jack **and** Jill went up the hill.
(**Jack** and **Jill** are both single-word subjects.)

Looking at the final exam topic, Patricia felt faint **and** slightly nauseous.
(Both **faint** and **slightly nauseous** are elements that describe how Patricia feels.)

Juan was born in Guatemala, **but** he was raised in the United States.

("Juan was born in Guatemala" and "He was raised in the United States" could both be complete sentences on their own.)

In sentences with more than one main verb, conjunctions appear between the verbs to join the verbs and any words that might go with them.

Leslie **winked** and **smiled.**

Fernando **hit the ball** and **ran around the bases.**

Coordinating conjunctions can also join word groups called **phrases.** *Phrase* is the general term given to a word group that does not have both a subject and a verb.

She looked for her shoe *under the bed* **and** *in the closet.*
(prepositional phrases)

He liked *to swim* **and** *to body surf.* (**to** + **verb** phrases)

Feeling miserable **but** *smiling bravely,* Joyce entered the room. (-**ing** phrases)

Coordinating conjunctions can also join word groups that have both a subject and verb. These word groups are called **clauses.** A clause that can stand alone as a sentence is an **independent** or **main clause.** Word groups that have both a subject and a verb but that cannot stand alone as independent sentences are called **dependent** or **subordinate clauses.**

Burton must apply for financial aid, **or** *he must find a part-time job.* (two independent clauses)

Jackie married a man who looks like a movie star **and** *who treats her like a princess.* (two dependent **who** clauses)

When the word **nor** is used to join two independent clauses, the verb comes before the subject in the second clause.

HV   S   MV
Hector does not approve of his daughter's friends, **nor** does he like his daughter to stay out past 11:00.

APPLICATION

In each sentence, circle the coordinating conjunctions. Then underline the sentence elements joined by each conjunction.

EXAMPLE: Billie (and) Roger are best friends.
(The conjunction **and** joins the two subjects **Billie** and **Roger.**)

1. Paulette is popular, but her sister is a nerd.
2. Queens are not elected, nor are kings.
3. Aneel will earn a BA and go on to graduate school.
4. Loretta must have cheated on the test, or maybe she studied the material for a change.
5. The honor will be awarded to Keisha or to Zack.
6. I called for information, but there was no answer.
7. LeAnn does not drink or smoke.
8. Martin is a big fan of college basketball and professional hockey.
9. You've never met him, but he knows all about you.
10. Tomika hoped that she would graduate with a 4.0 grade average and that she would be offered a fellowship.

Meaning

Though all of the coordinating conjunctions are used to connect words and ideas, they cannot be used interchangeably. They have different meanings, and these meanings affect the meaning of the sentence in which they are used. Notice the different meaning in these two examples:

The woman was Rosco's boss, so he married her.

The woman was Rosco's boss, yet he married her.

The first example suggests that Rosco married his wife because of her position—perhaps in an effort to get ahead at work or in response to pressure from the woman. The second example suggests that Rosco married his wife despite—not because of—her position at work.

USING COORDINATING CONJUNCTIONS

Use	**and**	to show addition
Use	**but** or **yet**	to show contrast
Use	**for**	to mean "because"
Use	**or**	to mean "either" or to indicate a choice
Use	**nor**	after a negative word like **neither** or **not** to mean "not either"
Use	**so**	to mean "as a result"

APPLICATION

Write an appropriate coordinating conjunction in each blank.

> EXAMPLE: He tied the record, _____**but**_____ he couldn't break it.
> (His inability to break the record contrasts with his ability to tie it.)

1. My wife _____ I were invited to a dinner party.

2. Neither Mr. Smythe _____ Mr. Aliva had anything to drink.

3. She won a pair of tickets, _____ she invited a friend to the concert.

4. I admire Mrs. Vandermere, _____ she has served in the Peace Corps.

5. His son likes to read, _____ he got the boy a library card.

6. Cory is taking advantage of Wendy, _____ she can't see what he is doing.

7. Terell grabbed the loose ball _____ dunked it into the hoop.

8. She had neither written _____ telephoned her parents in three years.

9. The bubble gum ended up in the child's hair _____ all over his designer clothes.

10. He wanted only to smoke dope _____ write angry song lyrics.

Punctuation

Whenever you use coordinating conjunctions to join two words, two phrases, or two dependent clauses, you do not need any additional punctuation.

Dilsy is strict **but** caring.

He looked to the left **and** to the right before stepping off the curb.

If the students enter from the left **and** if the faculty members enter from the right, graduation should go smoothly.

But if you use a coordinating conjunction to join two independent clauses that could stand alone as sentences, always put a comma before it.

Novella enrolled at the state college, **but** her boyfriend registered at the local community college.

Both clauses can stand alone as sentences:

Novella enrolled at the state college.

Her boyfriend registered at the local community college.

Max wants to be an actor, **so** he is majoring in drama.

Both clauses can stand alone as sentences:

Max wants to be an actor.

He is majoring in drama.

Occasionally you may wish to begin a sentence with a coordinating conjunction. In this case, the period would take the place of the comma.

Mrs. Morganstein worried over her son night and day, from the time he got up until he went to bed. **And** he felt like he could not breathe.

If you wish to join more than two elements in a sentence, you can use commas to take the place of all but the last coordinating conjunction.

Gina loves fast cars **and** big dogs **and** powerful men.

Or:

Gina loves fast cars, big dogs **and** powerful men.

Although it is not required, you may wish to use both a comma and a coordinating conjunction to join the last two items in a series. This practice is especially helpful when the reader might be confused about where one item ends and another begins.

He invited his mother-in-law and his father-in-law, his ex-wife and her companion, **and** his poker buddy. (Without the last comma, it would sound like the ex-wife is bringing her companion's poker buddy.)

APPLICATION

In each blank, insert either a coordinating conjunction alone or a comma and a coordinating conjunction.

> EXAMPLE: Talitha tried out for the debating team _____**and**_____ the track team.
>
> (No comma is needed because the conjunction **and** is not joining two main clauses.)

1. My mother is from Philadelphia _____ my father is from Toledo.

2. Neither my aunt _____ my uncle graduated from high school.

3. While they were in Southern California, they visited Sea World _____ Disneyland.

4. Eliza wants to be a doctor _____ she enrolled in the premed program.

5. She asked her minister for advice _____ he was wise and kind.

6. Ralph Lauren _____ Calvin Klein attended the same junior high school.

7. Both Rudy and Mike are tall _____ their brother Kevin is not.

8. I never want to see him again _____ do I want to hear about him.

9. Phillip decided that he was tired of working from nine to five _____ that he would get a job with a more flexible schedule.

10. He joined the army to see the world _____ all he saw was Fort Hood, Texas.

Avoiding Run-ons and Comma Splices

As you have just learned, a comma and a coordinating conjunction are used to join two independent clauses. If both the comma and the coordinating conjunction are missing, the resulting sentence is called a **run-on** or **run together sentence.**

> She had a tattered jacket thrown around her shoulders she clutched a bent umbrella over her head. (run-on)

If the two independent clauses are separated by a comma without a coordinating conjunction, the resulting sentence is called a **comma splice.**

> She had a tattered jacket thrown around her shoulders, she clutched a bent umbrella over her head. (comma splice)

To avoid writing a run-on or a comma splice, be sure to use both a comma and a coordinating conjunction to join two independent clauses.

> She had a tattered jacket thrown around her shoulders, **and** she clutched a bent umbrella over her head. (correct)

The words **then, also,** and **plus** are often confused with coordinating conjunctions. However, these words cannot be used either by themselves or with a comma to join independent clauses.

> Joel attended his classes then he went to his job. (run-on)

> Joel attended his classes, then he went to his job. (comma splice)

> Joel attended his classes, **and** then he went to his job. (correct)

JOINING INDEPENDENT CLAUSES

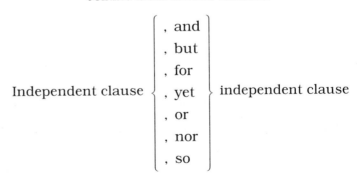

Independent clause $\left\{ \begin{array}{l} , \text{ and} \\ , \text{ but} \\ , \text{ for} \\ , \text{ yet} \\ , \text{ or} \\ , \text{ nor} \\ , \text{ so} \end{array} \right\}$ independent clause

APPLICATION

Each of the following independent clauses stands alone as a sentence. Join each of the sentence pairs into one sentence with two independent clauses, using a comma and an appropriate coordinating conjunction. Remember that the wording must be changed slightly after the word **nor.**

> *EXAMPLE:*   Charlyce did not want to be a teacher.
> She did not want to be a secretary.
>
> **Charlyce did not want to be a teacher, nor did she**
>
> **want to be a secretary.**
>
> (In the combined sentence, the coordinating conjunction **nor** has eliminated the need for the word **not,** and the helping verb **did** comes before the subject **she.**)

1. Jorge studied hard.
   He wanted to get into law school.

   _____

   _____

2. Penny was named "Employee of the Month."
   She got a plaque and a special parking place.

   _____

   _____

3. She sent away for an exercise videotape.
   She joined a fitness center.

   _____

   _____

4. My coach learned to swim at the age of two.
   She began swimming competitively the next year.

   _____

   _____

5. Ronald wanted to meet people.
   He decided to learn to dance.

   _____

   _____

6. They studied all night for the final exam.
   They were desperate.

   _____

   _____

7. Wanda dreamed of a glamorous career.
   She finally got a job as a messenger for an entertainment law firm.

   _____

   _____

8. Byron and Van worked at the same place.
   They became good friends.

   _____

   _____

9. Her grandmother does not speak English.
   Her grandfather does not speak English.

   _____

   _____

10. He entered college as a business major.
    He graduated with a degree in philosophy.

   _____

   _____

Joining Sentences with Coordinating Conjunctions

In writing, **coordinating conjunctions** provide the writer with a valuable **tool for joining two or more ideas into a single sentence.** For example, without coordinating conjunctions, if you wanted to describe more than one trait of an individual, you might have to use multiple sentences.

Alma is brilliant.

Alma is talented.

By using coordinating conjunctions, however, you can describe these two traits in one sentence.

Alma is brilliant, **and** she is talented.

Or:

Alma is brilliant **and** talented.

Notice that there is no one correct way to join ideas. In the first example, a comma and a coordinating conjunction connect two independent clauses, each one describing one trait of Alma's. Notice that the second *Alma* was changed to the pronoun *she* so that the sentence in the first example would read more smoothly. In the second example, a coordinating conjunction connects two words that each describe a different trait of Alma's.

APPLICATION

Use coordinating conjunctions to combine each of the following groups of sentences into a single sentence. You may wish to make a few changes in wording so that your resulting sentence reads smoothly. There may be several possible answers to each item, but give only one.

EXAMPLE: Mr. Martinez does not work for Hughes Aircraft anymore.
Mr. Gilman does not work for Hughes Aircraft anymore.

Neither Mr. Martinez nor Mr. Gilman works for

Hughes Aircraft anymore.

1. Nina is going to France for a semester abroad.
   Nina is spending a lot of her time studying French.

   _____

   _____

2. She swore that she would never touch alcohol.
   She swore that she would never take drugs.

   _____

   _____

3. The band finished the first song.
   The band members ducked to avoid the objects the audience threw at them.

   _____

   _____

4. Bart bought an insulting card for his sister.
To Bart's surprise, she burst into tears.

_____

_____

5. They decided to buy an old house and fix it up.
They didn't have much money.

_____

_____

6. Rowena and Angela grew up in a tough neighborhood.
Rowena and Angela were never afraid to play outside.

_____

_____

7. Jules spent hours deciding what to wear.
Jules wanted to look just right.

_____

_____

8. Tina loved to read.
She read everything, even the backs of packages.

_____

_____

9. Neil didn't like the book.
Neil didn't like the movie based on the book.

_____

_____

10. My cousin rented a tux for his high school graduation dance.
My cousin ripped the jacket while putting it on.

_____

_____

▼ CHAPTER REVIEW

• The **coordinating conjunctions** are *for, and, nor, but, or, yet,* and *so* (FANBOYS).
• Use **coordinating conjunctions** to **join words, phrases, and clauses.** A **phase** is a word group that does not have both a subject and a verb. A **clause** is a word group with both a subject and a verb. An **independent clause** can stand alone as a sentence; a **dependent clause** cannot stand alone as a sentence.
• To **avoid** writing a **run-on sentence** or a **comma splice,** be sure when you join **independent clauses** to use **both a comma and a coordinating conjunction.**
• In your writing, use **coordinating conjunctions** as a **tool for joining two or more ideas into a single sentence.**

PRACTICE

Test your familiarity with coordinating conjunctions by circling each coordinating conjunction and underlining the sentence elements it joins. The title and the first sentence have been done for you.

Television Violence (and) Our Children

[1]Many experts have looked for a connection between the violence that children see on television (and) the behavior of these children. [2]Much of the research in this area is based on the theory that children imitate what they see. [3]In one study, children were shown a televised act of aggression only once, yet they were able to repeat the action six months later. [4]Another study estimates that between the ages of five and fifteen, a child will see over 13,400 people killed on television. [5]It is thought that this repeated exposure to violence and destruction may teach children to take pride in violent behavior and to feel nothing for victims of violence. [6]If, indeed, our children are learning from television that violence is an acceptable way to get what they want, then our society is in trouble, for the Nielsen Television Index reveals that children spend more time watching television than doing any other activity except sleeping. [7]Some par-

ents suggest that television's portrayal of violence is counteracted by the values and behavior youngsters learn at home. [8]However, since neither parents nor teachers spend as much time with children as television characters do, perhaps it is time to unplug the set or at least to restrict our children's viewing.

CHAPTER 13

Using Subordinating Conjunctions

▼ CHAPTER PREVIEW

In Chapter 12, you learned about using coordinating conjunctions to join ideas. In this chapter, you will learn another method for joining ideas. Look at these two sentences:

Randy likes the outdoors.

He is majoring in forestry.

One way to join these two ideas into one sentence is to combine them using a comma and a coordinating conjunction.

Randy likes the outdoors, **so** he is majoring in forestry.

But that is not the only method for combining these two ideas. Another way to join these ideas is to put the word ***because*** before the first idea and then combine it with the second idea.

Because Randy likes the outdoors, he is majoring in forestry.

The word ***because*** is called a **subordinating conjunction.** In this chapter you will learn how to join ideas using subordinating conjunctions.

A Professional Writer Uses Subordinating Conjunctions

About the Reading: The daughter of sharecroppers, Alice Walker was born in Georgia in 1944. In 1965, she graduated with a BA from Sarah Lawrence College, where she was one of only two African-American students. Walker has published poems, essays, novels, and even a biography for children about poet Langston Hughes. She is probably best known for her Pulitzer Prize–winning novel *The Color*

Purple, which was made into a 1985 film starring Whoopi Goldberg and Oprah Winfrey. The selection that follows is taken from "Longing to Die of Old Age," an essay collected in *Living by the Word* (1988).

As You Read: Subordinating conjunctions have been printed in italics, and the clauses that they introduce have been printed in bold. Pay close attention to the types of words that act as subordinating conjunctions, and notice how clauses beginning with these words function within a sentence.

From "Longing to Die of Old Age"

[1]*When* **I was a child growing up in middle Georgia in the forties and fifties,** people still died of old age. [2]Old age was actually a common cause of death. [3]My parents inevitably visited dying persons over the long or short period of their decline; sometimes I went with them. [4]Some years ago, as an adult, I accompanied my mother to visit a very old neighbor who was dying a few doors down the street, and *though* **she was no longer living in the country,** the country style lingered. [5]People like my mother were visiting her constantly, bringing food, picking up and returning laundry, or simply stopping by to inquire how she was feeling and to chat. [6]She lay propped against pillows *so that* **by merely turning her head she could watch the postman approaching, friends and relatives arriving, and most of all, the small children playing beside the street, often in her yard, the sound of their play a lively music.**

After You Read: Refer to the selection to complete the following items:

1. List the three subordinating conjunctions in the selection.

    _____ _____ _____

2. Which clause tells *why* the dying woman was propped against pillows?

    _____

    _____

3. Which clause tells *when* people died of old age as opposed to dying of a particular disease?

    _____

    _____

4. Which clause tells *how* the neighbor's living circumstances had changed by the time she lay dying?

_____

_____

Subordinating Conjunctions

Subordinating conjunctions are words that join ideas by stressing the relationship of one idea to another. Common subordinating conjunctions are shown in the following list.

COMMON SUBORDINATING CONJUNCTIONS

after	because	since	when	whether
although	before	so that	whenever	while
as	even if	though	where	
as if	even though	unless	whereas	
as far as	if	until	wherever	
as long as				

Instead of coming between the two ideas like a coordinating conjunction, a **subordinating conjunction** attaches itself to the beginning of one idea.

I got off work at 9:00.

I drove home.

Coordinating conjunction: I got off work at 9:00, **and** I drove home.

Subordinating conjunction: **After** I got off work at 9:00, I drove home.

When a coordinating conjunction is used to join two sentences, the resulting sentence contains two independent clauses. When a subordinating conjunction is used to join two sentences, the resulting sentence contains a **dependent clause** and an **independent clause.** In the preceding example, the clause that begins with *after* can no longer stand alone as a sentence, so it is a dependent clause. The second clause can stand alone, so it is an independent clause.

Dependent clause: After I got off work at 9:00

Independent clause: I drove home.

Be careful that you do not create a sentence fragment when you use a subordinating conjunction. Be sure that every sentence containing a subordinating conjunction also contains at least one independent clause without a subordinating conjunction.

APPLICATION

Circle the subordinating conjunction in each of the sentences.

EXAMPLE: Sophia left her son with a sitter (while) she attended classes.

1. Before she met Dion, Cathy dated his brother.
2. I don't know whether I should call him or not.
3. As soon as Pat saves enough money, he will get a face-lift.
4. Since the day I met her, I have hated her.
5. Wherever you go, be sure to take your credit card!
6. He looked at her as if she reminded him of someone.
7. Even though Mary Jane had it all, she still wanted more.
8. Fast-food restaurant employees are encouraged to wash their hands before they handle the food.
9. Ferdinand took the bus because his car was in the repair shop.
10. Unless you change your ways, you will die young.

Meaning

Use subordinating conjunctions when you want to join two ideas that are related to each other in one of the following ways: one tells why, one tells where, one tells when, one tells how, or one tells how much or how little.

Mildred worked at McDonald's **so that** she could pay for a car. (why)

As far as we could see, the ocean spread in every direction. (how much)

Wherever he went, Danny ran into Sandra. (where)

Teresa paid off her charge cards **before** she applied for the loan. (when)

Some of the subordinating conjunctions can be confusing, either because they are similar in meaning or because they are often misused. Here are some guidelines to help you:

1. Use **when** to mean a specific time. Use **whenever** to mean every time.

I fell in love with her **when** I first laid eyes on her.

I want to throw up **whenever** I see blood.

2. Use **where** to mean a particular place. Use **wherever** to mean any place.

   That is the spot **where** the jacket was last seen.

   He will have to go **wherever** his job takes him.

3. Use **since** to point out the specific time or occasion that a continuous action began. Occasionally, **since** may be used like **because.**

   I have not spoken to her **since** the day she lied to me.
       (Because the action in the main clause continues, the main clause verb is usually **have** or **had** + past participle.)

   Since Vince was going, I decided to go.

4. Don't confuse **so that** with the coordinating conjunction **so.** Use **so that** to show purpose.

   He enrolled in summer school **so that** he could fulfill his English requirement.

5. **As** can be used in two ways: to show how and to show when. Use **as** to mean in the same way, or use **as** to mean at the same time.

   He tied the knot **as** he had been taught.

   She cried **as** her son boarded the train.

APPLICATION

Write an appropriate subordinating conjunction in each blank.

   EXAMPLE: They will wait to get married _____**until**_____ they fin-

   ish college.
       (The word **until** shows that the relationship between these two ideas is one of time—first one thing will happen and then the second will occur.)

   1. _____ they met, they discovered they had a lot in com-

   mon.

   2. Carmen enrolled in an art class _____ she had a crush

   on the instructor.

   3. Kenny had to drive his mother to the market _____ she

   needed to go shopping.

4. Sheila has not had a weekend free _____ she started back to school.

5. _____ he did not know how to spell the word correctly, Danny felt stupid.

6. _____ they are together, they can't keep their hands off each other.

7. Manny bounced the basketball _____ he waited for his friend.

8. I can never figure out my checkbook balance _____ I use a calculator.

9. Students are eligible for financial aid _____ they maintain a "C" average.

10. We'll go out for pizza _____ we finish early.

Punctuation

As you have probably noticed, clauses beginning with a subordinating conjunction can come before or after an independent clause. When the dependent clause comes before the independent clause, follow it with a comma. If the dependent clause follows the independent clause, no punctuation is necessary.

Wherever she went, her adoring fans mobbed her.

Her adoring fans mobbed her **wherever she went.**

APPLICATION

If a sentence is punctuated correctly, write **C** in the blank. If it is not punctuated correctly, add the necessary comma.

EXAMPLE: _____ Whenever I see her, she is smiling.

1. _____ While they were eating dinner someone pounded on the door.

2. _____ I plan to go to the Caribbean even if it is hurricane season.

3. _____ Whenever Marla studies she has the radio blaring full blast.

4. _____ Because the jeans were on clearance my aunt bought them for me.

5. _____ My sister brought her boyfriend home so that my mother could check him out.

6. _____ Even though it's raining the soccer game will go on as scheduled.

7. _____ Carla went to lunch with her friends whenever they could think of a reason to celebrate.

8. _____ Jesse will be accepted into the Honors Program if he can improve his Spanish grade.

9. _____ Because I needed the money I got a job as a singing waiter.

10. _____ After the movie was over the audience applauded.

Joining Sentences with Subordinating Conjunctions

Subordinating conjunctions are important writing tools because they allow you to **stress a main idea, and, in the same sentence, give additional information about the main idea, like explaining the circumstances, reasons, times, and places of its occurrence.** As a general rule, put your most important idea in the independent clause and the other information in the dependent clause.

Although I enjoy music, I hate my music appreciation course.
(The emphasis is on the dislike of the music appreciation course, but the information in the dependent clause explains more about the source of the writer's dislike.)

Because she wanted to get more experience working with children, Emilia volunteered at a day care center.
(The emphasis is on the volunteering, but the dependent clause explains why she wanted to volunteer in the first place.)

APPLICATION

Join each pair of sentences into a single sentence using an appropriate subordinating conjunction. Be sure to punctuate each resulting sentence correctly.

EXAMPLE: Everyone agrees about the importance of education.
No one wants to pay for it.

Although everyone agrees about the importance of

education, no one wants to pay for it.

1. Melissa has five children below the age of ten.
She has made the dean's list every semester.

_____

_____

2. Jackie arrived at the party.
The police crashed through the door.

_____

_____

3. The cat was walking across the roof.
The earthquake struck.

_____

_____

4. Her father's cousins lived in North Dakota.
Her family went there every summer.

_____

_____

5. Dana won't look at an outfit.
It costs over a hundred dollars.

_____

_____

6. The boy begged his mother to buy him the shoes.
All his friends had the same kind.

_____

_____

7. Sean went to college.
His wife worked as a bus driver.

_____

_____

8. Adam searched through his briefcase for a disk.
He turned on the computer.

_____

_____

9. Britta got her law degree.
She filed for divorce.

_____

_____

10. The professor had high grading standards.
Her classes were always full.

_____

_____

▼ CHAPTER REVIEW

- Use **subordinating conjunctions** to **join ideas by stressing the relationship of one idea to another.**
- **Subordinating conjunctions** tell **why, where, when, how,** or **how much or little.**

    Why: because, so that

    Where: where, wherever

    When: after, as, before, since, until, when, whenever, while

    How: as, as if, unless, although, though

    How much or little: as far as, as long as

- **A clause that begins with a subordinating conjunction** is a **dependent clause.** A dependent clause cannot stand alone as a sentence; it must be joined to an independent clause.
- If a **dependent clause comes before the independent clause,** follow it with a **comma.** If the **dependent clause follows the independent clause, no punctuation** is necessary.

PRACTICE

Test your familiarity with subordinating conjunctions by circling the subordinating conjunctions and underlining the dependent clauses that they introduce. The first sentence has been done for you.

The Question of Bilingual Education

[1]In general, (as long as) public education has existed in the United States, schoolchildren have been taught in English. [2]From the 1970s on, however, educators have debated about the best way to teach the large numbers of children entering American schools unable to speak, read, and write in English. [3]One argument is that these children will learn English quickly if they are placed in an English language classroom because it is the only language they will hear and use. [4]Opponents of this argument believe non-English-speaking children will be educationally lost unless they are taught primarily in their native languages until they are ready to be "mainstreamed" into all-English classes. [5]People in favor of native language teaching, also called bilingual education, say non-English-speaking children should learn subject matter like math and history in their own language. [6]At the same time, they would learn English as a separate subject until they could communicate fluently in the new language. [7]Because both groups believe strongly in the rightness of their positions, this educational debate will continue as long as the United States is made up of people with many different languages and cultures.

CHAPTER 14

Using Semicolons and Transitions

▼ CHAPTER PREVIEW

You have learned two methods for joining ideas: using coordinating conjunctions and using subordinating conjunctions.

I learned a lot from Professor Schwartz, **so** I decided to take another English course from her.

Because I learned a lot from Professor Schwartz, I decided to take another English course from her.

Another way to join two ideas is to use a **semicolon,** either by itself or together with a word or several words.

I learned a lot from Professor Schwartz; I decided to take another English course from her.

I learned a lot from Professor Schwartz; **consequently,** I decided to take another English course from her.

I learned a lot from Professor Schwartz; **as a result,** I decided to take another English course from her.

In this chapter, you will practice joining ideas using a semicolon and become familiar with the various words that can be used with a semicolon to join ideas.

A Professional Writer Uses Semicolons to Join Ideas

About the Reading: Leslie Marmon Silko was born in Albuquerque, New Mexico, in 1948. Of mixed ancestry—Laguna Pueblo, Mexican, and white—Silko grew up on the Laguna Pueblo Reservation. She has written several novels; the latest is called *Almanac of the Dead* (1991). One of her most acclaimed novels is *Ceremony* (1977), which tells about Tayo, a troubled Native American war veteran. The novel details Tayo's quest for spiritual renewal, which takes him back to his Indian past. In the selection that follows, Tayo is searching for some spotted cattle that once belonged to his people.

As You Read: Pay close attention to the author's use of semicolons, which have been printed in bold type.

From *Ceremony*

[1]He stopped at a wide shallow stream and dismounted while the mare drank. [2]She had traveled for hours without water; now she swelled out her sides drinking. [3]She let out a deep sigh when she was finished and shook herself; she was tired. [4]As he led her away from the stream, he felt the muscles in his thighs get shivery, and his knees were tight and sore from hours in the saddle and from kneeling on the rocks to cut the wire. [5]His hands hurt, and his fingers were still swollen with blisters from the pliers. [6]He knew what was happening. [7]In the sky above the clearing, Orion had fallen over the south edge; he was running out of night. [8]His stomach tensed up again. [9]Whatever night this was, he still had a big hole cut in their fence, and he had to find the cattle and get them out before the fence riders found the break.

After You Read: Refer to the reading selection to complete the following items:

1. A semicolon is used to join two clauses that could stand alone as sentences by themselves. Write the two clauses in sentence 2 as separate sentences.

   _____

   _____

2. The word ***now,*** which follows the semicolon in sentence 2, signals what kind of relationship between the two clauses? Circle the letter preceding the correct answer.

   a. An addition: One thing happened in addition to another.

   b. A time relationship: One thing happened before another.

   c. A cause/effect relationship: One thing caused the other.

3. In which sentence is a semicolon used to join a description of the horse's behavior to a comment on what that behavior means?

_____

4. In which sentence is a semicolon used to join a description of the night sky with a comment about what the change in the sky means to Tayo? _____

Semicolons

Use a semicolon to join independent clauses that could stand alone as sentences.

> Student diversity has been a fact for some time on most college campuses; faculty and administration are now beginning to pay attention to this fact.

Main clause: Student diversity has been a fact for some time on most college campuses.

Main clause: Faculty and administration are now beginning to pay attention to this fact.

Use a semicolon by itself to join two ideas that are closely related in meaning.

> Her journalism instructor was impressed by her work; he recommended her for an award.

> The service was terrible; we vowed never to shop there again.

You can easily see the relationship between good work and the desire to reward it or between bad service and a decision to avoid it in the future, so a semicolon is a good choice to join the ideas in these sentences. Notice that the next word after the semicolon is not capitalized.

APPLICATION ONE

In the following sentences, add the necessary punctuation to join independent clauses. If independent clauses are separated by a coordinating conjunction (**for, and, nor, but, or, yet, so**) put a comma in the blank; if there is no coordinating conjunction between them, put a semicolon in the blank.

> EXAMPLE: Jerome started out as a boxboy ___;___ now he manages the supermarket.

1. The house looked abandoned _____ windowpanes and doors were missing.

2. We know we should recycle plastic bags and newspapers _____ but we don't always do it.

3. I can't find my car keys _____ I'll never get there on time.

4. Marilyn did not want to go to the party _____ nor did Courtney.

5. The History Club picnic was scheduled for the first weekend in May _____ the planning had to be completed before spring break.

6. My uncle Tony spent most of his life working as a mechanic _____ but at forty he decided to become an engineer.

7. The young boy didn't have much money _____ so he bought his mother's birthday gift at a thrift shop.

8. Leila was working a forty-hour week _____ yet she found time to volunteer as a literacy tutor.

9. Vinnie loved to argue _____ he decided to become a lawyer.

10. The classroom seemed half-empty _____ but the instructor informed me that I would be unable to add the course.

APPLICATION TWO

Each of the following independent clauses is the first part of a sentence. Add a semicolon and another independent clause. Be sure that the ideas in the two clauses are closely related.

> EXAMPLE: The teacher was absent ; the students went wild.

1. She had been warned repeatedly _____

   _____

2. The woman heard a noise outside _____

   _____

3. My high school counselor helped me a lot _____

   _____

4. Joe never got over his car accident _____

   _____

5. My dad joined the Coast Guard right out of high school ____

   _____

   _____

6. Linda's husband is addicted to spy novels _____

   _____

7. Everyone who hears that song loves it _____

   _____

8. The cable channel went off the air _____

   _____

9. Phil Jong and his wife have three children under the age of five

   _____

10. The admissions office sent me to the registrar's office _____

    _____

Using Semicolons with Transitions

Sometimes, you may wish to stress the relationship between ideas, or you may feel that the relationship between two ideas might not be obvious to the reader. You have several options for joining these ideas. You can use a coordinating conjunction or a subordinating conjunction to suggest how the ideas are related.

I wanted to be a creative writer, **but** I'm working in a bank.

Although I wanted to be a creative writer, I'm working in a bank.

A third option for joining these ideas is to use a semicolon together with a word or words that emphasize the relationship between the ideas.

I wanted to be a creative writer; **instead,** I'm working in a bank.

Words that point out relationships between ideas are called **transitions.** They tell the reader what transitions, or changes, in meaning to expect between one idea and another. Transitions can be single words, like *instead,* or they can be several words together. Here is a list of transitions frequently used with a semicolon to join two independent clauses.

COMMON TRANSITIONS

accordingly	consequently	in other words	on the other hand
after all	even so	indeed	otherwise
also	finally	instead	similarly
anyway	for example	meanwhile	specifically
as a matter of fact	for instance	moreover	still
as a result	furthermore	nevertheless	subsequently
at any rate	hence	next	then
at the same time	however	nonetheless	therefore
besides	in addition	on the contrary	thus
certainly	in fact		

As in the case of a comma and a coordinating conjunction, when a transition is used with a semicolon to join two clauses, each clause remains an independent clause that could stand alone as a sentence.

He seems to be popular, but I don't like him.

Main clause: He seems to be popular.

Main clause: But I don't like him.

He seems to be popular; however, I don't like him.

Main clause: He seems to be popular.

Main clause: However, I don't like him.

APPLICATION

In each sentence, circle the semicolon and the transition. Then underline verbs twice and subjects once. Remember that a transition and a semicolon must join two independent clauses, so you will find at least one subject and one verb in each clause.

EXAMPLE: Hosea wanted to take calculus; however, the class was already full.

1. I decided not to buy lunch; otherwise, I would not have had enough money to pay the bus fare.

2. Jodi wanted to be a model; accordingly, she registered with an agency.

3. The ticket windows were closed; moreover, the phone lines were jammed.

4. Lorenzo was disappointed not to have won the competition; however, he was glad to receive an honorable mention.

5. Felicity sang in the choir; subsequently, she was hired to sing backup on a commercial.

6. The volleyball team practiced only once a week; nevertheless, they won the tournament.

7. Our cat always has fleas; as a result, it has a standing flea dip appointment with the vet.

8. She expected to graduate near the top of her class; at any rate, she expected to be in the top 10 percent.

9. The tutors at the college writing lab were all busy with students; meanwhile, the lines outside grew longer.

10. Jordan is known for his great sense of humor; at the same time, he is famous for his enormous appetite.

Meaning of Transitions

Different transitions stress different relationships between ideas.

1. Use words like **consequently, therefore, thus, as a result,** and **accordingly** to show **cause and effect.**

   She studied her notes every night; **consequently,** she did well on the test.

2. Use words like **however, nevertheless, instead, on the contrary,** and **even so** to show **contrast.**

   He had meant to pay the ticket; **however,** he had forgotten about it.

She did not mind the extra responsibility at all; **on the contrary,** she enjoyed meeting the challenges of her new job.
(**On the contrary** is used after a negative statement containing words like **not** and **no.**)

3. Use words like **furthermore, in addition, moreover,** and **besides** to show **addition.**

Cara received an AA degree in liberal studies; **furthermore,** she completed all of her general education requirements for a BA degree.

4. Use words like **subsequently, at the same time, then,** and **meanwhile** to show **time** relationships.

Luan searched for work day after day; **meanwhile,** his savings disappeared.

5. Use **otherwise** to show an **alternative.**

She had better pay the telephone bill; **otherwise,** the service will be shut off.

APPLICATION

Write an appropriate transition in each blank. Be sure to pay close attention to the relationships between ideas when choosing a transition.

EXAMPLE: Peter failed Spanish twice; _nevertheless_, he signed up to spend a semester studying in Mexico.
(**Nevertheless** signals a contrast.)

1. Melanie went to Hawaii last year; _____, she has decided she wants to spend the rest of her life there.

2. He owes back child support payments; _____, he has charged to his limit on all of his credit cards.

3. The first job I ever had was behind the candy counter in a movie theater; _____, I worked in a department store.

4. The doctor told Gustavo to lose some weight; _____, his health was good.

5. My brother's English professor talks a mile a minute; _____, he's always exhausted after an hour in her class.

6. Donna pursued her career as a fire fighter; _____,

she began investing in real estate.

7. The copy machine in the library is broken; _____, the

microfilm I wanted to use is missing.

8. The students at the scholarship luncheon ate everything in sight;

_____, the administration decided to order more food

next year.

9. The children in the day-care center fought all day long;

_____, Carline decided to go back to school to prepare for

a new career.

10. Melchor discovered a day-old bakery surplus store; _____,

he also discovered that the products tasted like sawdust.

Punctuation

When a transition is used after a semicolon to join two clauses, it is most often followed by a comma; however, you can leave the comma out after short transition words, like **then** and **next.**

> Jolene wanted an "A" in the class; **however,** she did not want to work for it.

> Aaron closed all of the windows and shut the door; **then** he turned up the music full blast.

Because the comma after the transition makes the reader pause for a second, it draws attention to and emphasizes the relationship between ideas that is described by the transition word.

APPLICATION

Use a semicolon, a transition, and a comma (if necessary) to add another independent clause onto each independent clause.

EXAMPLE: Murray wished for a car **; however, he continued to go**

to work by bus.

1. Lex was afraid of cats _____

   _____

2. Trina's boyfriend was mysterious about his past _____

   _____

3. Paula and Emilio decided to get married _____

   _____

4. Rico grew up in an immigrant Sicilian family _____

   _____

5. My family's idea of a fun vacation is going to visit relatives _____

   _____

6. Sylvia was determined to succeed in college _____

   _____

7. Before going to work, he made sure that the house was perfectly

   clean _____

   _____

8. Matt, Ron, and Mike decided to spend the day at the mall _____

   _____

9. Ray had never been able to balance his checkbook _____

   _____

10. Her health plan did not cover vision _____

    _____

Joining Sentences with Semicolons

Used with a semicolon, transitions are particularly powerful writing tools to join two main clauses. Use transitions when you **especially want to emphasize the relationship of one clause to the other.** Compare the use of transitions to the use of conjunctions:

I learned the mechanics of playing the piano, **but** I never learned the joy of it. (coordinating conjunction)

I learned the mechanics of playing the piano; **however,** I never learned the joy of it. (transition)

Although many of the students came from poor educational backgrounds, they were all determined to succeed in the course. (subordinating conjunction)

Many of the students came from poor educational backgrounds; **nonetheless,** they were all determined to succeed in the course. (transition)

Notice how the transition word, by calling attention to itself with two marks of punctuation, focuses your attention on the relationship it is describing.

APPLICATION

Use a semicolon and a transition to join each of the following sentence pairs into one sentence with two independent clauses. Be sure to punctuate the resulting sentence correctly.

EXAMPLE: Mrs. Tritle made an offer on a three-bedroom house. She found a condominium she liked better.

Mrs. Tritle made an offer on a three-bedroom house;

then, she found a condominium she liked better.

1. His aim in life was to marry a wealthy woman. He was unable to meet a single one.

2. The call-in show had a toll-free phone line for listeners' calls. The number was always busy.

3. Gerland needed three units to qualify for a student discount on her car insurance. She enrolled in an astronomy class.

4. The discount store on Marine Avenue was always mobbed and had terrible service.
   The prices were the best in town.

   _____

   _____

5. For an entire semester she had wanted to talk with him.
   She didn't know how to take the first step.

   _____

   _____

6. Frieda describes herself as an animal rights activist.
   She continues to eat meat.

   _____

   _____

7. Bill's job required a two-hour daily commute.
   He loved his work.

   _____

   _____

8. I get hay fever every time I cut the grass.
   I can't afford a gardener.

   _____

   _____

9. She had to catch a train at 7:00 P.M.
   At 5:30 she was still trying to decide what to pack.

   _____

   _____

10. My sister always studies first thing in the morning.
    She drinks two cups of coffee and gets ready for class.

    _____

    _____

▼ CHAPTER REVIEW

- Use a **semicolon** to **join independent clauses that could stand alone as complete sentences.**
- Use a **semicolon by itself** to **join ideas that are closely related in meaning.**
- **Words that point out relationships between ideas** are called **transitions.**
- Use a **semicolon along with a transition** to **join two independent clauses** when you want to **emphasize the relationship between the ideas in the clauses.**
- In general, put a **comma after a semicolon and a transition,** but you can **leave out the comma after short transitions** if you wish.
- In your writing, **use a semicolon alone or with a transition** to **join two sentences into one** when you want to **stress the relationship between the ideas in each sentence.**

PRACTICE

Test your familiarity with semicolons and transitions by inserting a semicolon or a semicolon and an appropriate transition in each of the blanks.

Indian Removal Act

[1]Relations between the United States government and the Native American peoples have, in large part, been dictated by the government's desire for land. [2]Whenever the government needed more land, terms of existing treaties and claims to property were often ignored _____ this fact is illustrated by the Indian Removal Act of 1830. [3]The Indian Removal Act of 1830 gave the president power to force native peoples living east of the Mississippi River to move to areas in the West that would be designated as Indian territory _____ Native Americans were forced to leave their homelands. [4]Not only did they suffer the pain of losing everything that was familiar to them, but they faced disease, starvation, and even death during the relocation process _____ so many of the Cherokees suffered and died during a forced move from Georgia to Okla-

homa in 1838 that their route became known as the Trail of Tears. [5]The U.S. government promised the Native Americans that they would be able to live in their new homes forever ＿＿＿＿＿＿ this promise was forgotten during the westward expansion of the late nineteenth century.

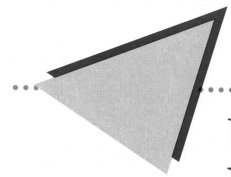

CHAPTER **15**

Using Relative Pronouns

▼ CHAPTER PREVIEW

You have practiced joining ideas using conjunctions and semicolons.

Idea one: He is a wonderful person.

Idea two: Everyone adores him.

> He is a wonderful person, **and** everyone adores him. (coordinating conjunction)
>
> **Because** he is a wonderful person, everyone adores him. (subordinating conjunction)
>
> He is a wonderful person; everyone adores him. (semicolon)

Yet another way to join ideas into a single sentence is to put one idea into a clause beginning with a **relative pronoun** like *who, whom,* or *that.*

> He is a wonderful person, **whom** *everyone adores.*

In this chapter, you will learn to use relative pronouns to join ideas and practice punctuating clauses that begin with these words.

A Professional Writer Uses Relative Pronouns

About the Reading: As vice president of the Center for Applied Linguistics in Washington, D.C., Allene Guss Grognet has been active in second-language learning and immigrant services. The selection that follows is taken from "Elderly Refugees and Language Learning," a 1989 article by Grognet that originally appeared in *Aging* magazine, which is published by the Administration on Aging of the Department

190

of Health and Human Services. Grognet was assisted in writing the article by Mary Schleppegrell and Brenda Bowmen. In the article, Grognet focuses on the difficulties that older refugees have with learning English; the selection that follows discusses the particular difficulties of immigration for older Southeast Asian refugees.

As You Read: All of the relative pronouns are printed in bold type, and the clauses they introduce are italicized. Notice which words serve as relative pronouns, and pay close attention to the way the underlined clauses function in their sentences.

From "Elderly Refugees and Language Learning"

[1]Since 1975, approximately 1 million refugees have come to the U.S. from Vietnam, Cambodia, and Laos. [2]They range from highly educated, multilingual former cabinet ministers to non-literate hilltribe people **who** *practiced slash and burn agriculture.* [3]Fleeing from one's homeland and starting over again in a strange country is traumatic for refugees of any age. [4]For elderly Southeast Asian refugees, it has been particularly difficult. [5]At a time in their lives when they should be looking forward to the respect and reverence **that** *traditional Asian society affords elders*, they find themselves transplanted to a culture **which** *is focused on youth.* [6]They have lost their homes, probably many of their family members, and, most of all, their honored status.

After You Read: Refer to the reading to complete the following items:

1. List the three relative pronouns that appear in the reading.

   _____   _____   _____

2. Write the clause that begins with **who.**

   _____

3. The pronoun **who** refers to which people described in sentence 2? (circle one)

        former cabinet member   hilltribe people

4. Write the clause that describes what kind of respect and reverence the older refugees would have gotten in their homelands.

   _____

   _____

5. In sentence 5, what information is given about American culture in the clause that begins with **which?**

Relative Pronouns

The words **which, who, whom, that,** and **whose** are called **relative pronouns.** Clauses beginning with relative pronouns **identify or give additional information about a noun or pronoun in a sentence.**

> The students **who** *flunked the test* demanded to see the dean.
> (The italicized clause identifies which students.)

> The paramedics worked on the man **whose** *leg had been broken.*
> (The underlined clause identifies which man.)

> My grandmother, **who** *is eighty-five years old,* came to this country from Japan.
> (The underlined clause gives additional information about the grandmother.)

Use a clause that begins with a relative pronoun to expand a sentence by adding specific details describing a person or thing.

> The thunder frightened the children.

> The thunder, *which roared from the sky,* frightened the children.
> ("which roared from the sky" gives specific details that describe the sound of the thunder.)

> The thunder, *which roared from the sky,* frightened the children, *who huddled beneath their bedcovers.*
> ("who huddled beneath their bedcovers" adds details that describe the behavior of the children.)

Notice that **clauses beginning with relative pronouns,** like clauses beginning with subordinating conjunctions, are **dependent clauses** that can never stand alone as sentences. They must be connected to independent clauses.

APPLICATION

Complete each sentence by supplying the missing words after the relative pronouns.

> *EXAMPLE:*   Her new shoes, which **were made in Italy**, were quite expensive.

1. The fender that _____ looks terrible.

2. Mr. Lieu was looking for a secretary who _____

_____ .

3. Annie, who _____ , is an excellent tennis player.

4. Darren, whose _____ , got a new car for graduation.

5. He waited for Amin, who _____ .

6. The student, who _____ and got caught, was sorry that

_____ .

7. MTV, which _____ , is a cable television channel.

8. The high school that _____ was vandalized last night.

9. Professor Kalash, whom _____ , gives difficult exams.

10. Many parents object to music that _____ .

Meaning and Function

The relative pronoun gets its meaning from another noun or pronoun in the sentence.

I got an "A" on the paper **that** *I wrote for my geography class.*
    (**that** refers to paper)

Mr. Kim, **who** *owns the liquor store,* was held up last night.
    (**who** refers to Mr. Kim)

Notice that **clauses introduced by relative pronouns come directly after the words they describe.**
    Sometimes the relative pronoun is the subject of its clause; other times, it is not.

S   V
The cow **that** *won first prize at the fair* was run over by a milk truck.

S   V
She left him a message, **which** *he claimed never to have received.*

The word **who** is always a subject; **whom** and **whose** are never subjects.

S   V
She is the woman **who loves me.**

S   V
Joshua is someone **whom I trust.**

S   V
Here comes Anne, **whose son won the award.**

Choose relative pronouns carefully.

1. Use **who, whom,** and **whose** to refer to **people.**

   Anisha went to visit her uncle, **who** lives in India.
       (**who** = **uncle**)

2. Use **which** to refer to **things** or **animals.**

   That lamp, **which** my roommate bought at a garage sale, has
   never worked right.
       (**which** = **lamp**)

3. Use **that** to refer to **things, animals,** or **people.**

   Chelsea ordered a hamburger **that** came with a salad and fries.
       (**that** = **hamburger**)

   The team **that** wins this game will win the tournament.
       (**that** = **team**)

APPLICATION ONE

In each sentence, circle the relative pronoun, and underline the
clause it introduces. Then draw an arrow from the relative pronoun
to the word that it identifies or describes.

   EXAMPLE: My parents live in a house that is over 100 years old.

1. In the summer, local residents avoid the beach, which is usually

   crowded with tourists.

2. She wore the wedding dress that her mother had worn.

3. Notre Dame University, which is in Indiana, has an excellent

   reputation.

4. Teenagers who are rebellious sometimes make the best parents

   later on.

5. Monterey, which has a famous aquarium, is in Northern California.

6. Hockey is a sport that can often get violent.

7. When Walt Disney looked at an empty field, he saw possibilities

   that no one else saw.

8. Attending classes while holding a job is not something that everyone can do successfully.

9. My Aunt Mary, who once worked as a roller-skating messenger, is an interesting character.

10. Having children is probably one of the biggest responsibilities that a person can ever take on.

APPLICATION TWO

Write an appropriate relative pronoun in each blank.

EXAMPLE: Rafael, _____who_____ lives in the apartment next door, surprised a burglar.

1. Selena, _____ I met in my algebra class, is now in my calculus class.

2. The visitor slept on the sofa _____ folds out into a bed.

3. The play _____ he directed got a great review in the college paper.

4. I cannot resist shoes _____ are on clearance.

5. Lori, _____ brother is a DJ, has an amazing CD collection.

6. Clint found a stray cat _____ turned out to be a valuable show animal.

7. His stepbrother, _____ everyone thinks is nice, is cruel to him.

8. We visited the amusement park _____ has one of the most famous roller coasters in the United States.

9. Ronica, _____ book I borrowed, has a twin sister.

10. The washing machine, _____ they had just paid off, broke down the day after the warranty expired.

Punctuation

Sometimes clauses beginning with relative pronouns need commas, and other times they do not.

1. **Use commas** with a clause introduced by a relative pronoun if the **information in the clause is *not* necessary** to identify a person or thing. If the clause comes in the middle of a sentence, put a comma before and after it. If the clause comes at the end of a sentence, put a comma before it.

   Geraldo, **who drives a Porsche,** pays a high insurance premium.
   ("who drives a Porsche" gives additional information about Geraldo; it does not identify him.)

   I used to live in Compton, **which is a suburb of Los Angeles.**
   ("which is a suburb of Los Angeles" gives additional information about Compton; it is not necessary to identify the city.)

2. **Do not use commas** with a clause introduced by a relative pronoun if the clause gives information **necessary** to identify people or things.

   It is usually unwise to date people **who are married.**
   ("who are married" identifies which people it is unwise to date.)

   To eliminate confusion about punctuating *that* and *which* clauses, **use *that* to introduce necessary information,** and **use *which* to introduce unnecessary information.**

   The dog **that lives down the street** bit a child.
   ("that lives down the street" is necessary to identify which dog.)

   Batman Returns, **which is the sequel to *Batman,*** stars Danny DeVito as the Penguin.
   (The information that *Batman Returns* is a sequel is not necessary to identify the film because the film is named.)

APPLICATION

Underline each relative clause. If a clause contains necessary information, put **N** in the blank. If it contains unnecessary information, put **U** in the blank and add commas.

EXAMPLE: **N**   My instructor won't read essay exams that are written in pencil.

_____ 1. At a police auction, Sasha bought a car that had belonged to a drug dealer.

_____ 2. People who have sleep disorders should seek medical treatment.

_____ 3. He was very proud of his son John who had a role on a television soap opera.

_____ 4. I recently had dinner with Professor Kinimaka whose ancient history course I took a few years back.

_____ 5. She is reading Savage Warrior which is a steamy romance novel.

_____ 6. Crystal who has two older sisters at this school knows everyone on campus.

_____ 7. Leon whose mother wanted him to be a priest, was more interested in a career in the movie industry.

_____ 8. He picked up the folder that was on the table.

_____ 9. Diane whom I had met once before remembered me immediately.

_____ 10. Willard whose best friend was a rat was a disturbed adolescent.

Joining Sentences Using Relative Pronouns

Use a relative pronoun to join sentences when one sentence gives information identifying or describing a person or thing in another sentence.

Sentence 1:   Public Enemy is a controversial rap group.

Sentence 2:   The group's music contains disturbing lyrics.

Combined: Public Enemy, whose music contains disturbing lyrics, is a controversial rap group.

Or: Public Enemy is a controversial rap group, whose music contains disturbing lyrics.

APPLICATION

Use the relative pronoun in parentheses to join each pair of sentences into a single sentence. Be sure to place the relative pronoun directly after the person or thing it describes, and be sure to punctuate the resulting sentence correctly.

EXAMPLE: Three workers were laid off last week.
They had been with the company for over ten years.

(who) **Three workers who had been with the company**

for over ten years were laid off last week.

_____

1. Starter's jackets have the names of athletic teams on them.
   Starter's jackets are popular with gang members.

   (which) _____

   _____

2. Erin finally found a job.
   The job let her make her own hours around her school schedule.

   (that) _____

   _____

3. Protesters picketed the home of the judge.
   The judge let the defendant go free.

   (who) _____

   _____

4. Rhianna decided to take a business class.
   The class met on Tuesday and Thursday nights.

   (that) _____

   _____

5. In the corner of the room sat a desk.
   The desk was covered with papers.

   (which) _____

   _____

6. Rod Stewart was making records when my mother was young.
He is now making videos for my generation.

(who) _____

_____

7. My alarm clock did not go off until 8:30.
I had set it for 6:00.

(which) _____

_____

8. Count Dracula is a popular figure in old monster movies.
His trademark is a bite on the neck.

(whose) _____

_____

9. The political candidate was criticized for attending a nightclub.
The nightclub featured topless dancers.

(that) _____

_____

10. The ceremony honored students.
The students had maintained a grade point average of 3.5 or better.

(who) _____

_____

▼ CHAPTER REVIEW

• The words **which, who, whom, whose,** and **that** are **relative pronouns. Relative pronouns introduce clauses that identify or give additional information about a noun or pronoun in a sentence.**
• **Expand sentences using clauses introduced by a relative pronoun** to add specific details **that describe a person or thing.**
• **A clause that begins with a relative pronoun** is a dependent clause; **it can never stand alone as a sentence.**
• **Sometimes the relative pronoun is the subject of its clause; other times it is not.**
• **Choose relative pronouns carefully.**

1. Use *who, whom,* or *whose* to refer to **people.**
2. Use *which* to refer to **things** or **animals.**
3. Use *that* to refer to **things, animals,** or **people.**

- **Use commas** with a clause introduced by a relative pronoun **if the information in the clause is *not* necessary** to identify a person or thing. **Do not use commas if the information in the clause *is* necessary** to identify a person or thing.
- In your writing, **use a relative pronoun to expand a sentence by adding details about a person or thing or to join sentences when one sentence gives information about a person or thing in another sentence.**

PRACTICE

To test your familiarity with relative pronouns and the clauses they introduce, circle relative pronouns and underline the clauses they introduce in the following paragraph. Be sure to include the entire clause when you underline.

No Irish Need Apply

[1]The phrase "No Irish Need Apply," which was frequently posted on the doors of American businesses between the mid-1800s and the 1920s, reflected the intense discrimination that Irish immigrants of this period faced in their attempts to find jobs, housing, and acceptance in the United States. [2]Before the great Irish famine of 1847, which resulted in the death or emigration of half of the Irish population, some Irish had come to the United States in search of better lives. [3]But the terrible destruction of the famine caused thousands of Irish to flood into the United States from 1847 on. [4]Those with high hopes of new lives in America soon discovered they would not receive a welcome here. [5]The only jobs available to these immigrants were positions as unskilled factory laborers or house servants. [6]Both kinds of work, which paid low wages, were considered by "native" Americans to be the only appropriate jobs for immigrants who were widely believed to be inferior to native-born Americans. [7]Most Irish im-

migrants, whose native language was Gaelic, found themselves targets of discrimination because of their foreign language and accented English; others found themselves disliked for being a Catholic minority in a Protestant country. [8]Some Americans even argued the Irish were racially inferior. [9]Newspapers discussed the dirtiness and stupidity of the Irish and described physical resemblances between apes and the Irish as proof that the Irish were subhuman.

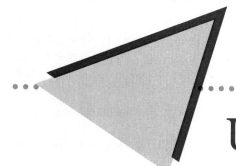

Using Phrases

▼ CHAPTER PREVIEW

As you have learned, **to** + **verb** and **-ing phrases** can function as nouns, but they can also be used for joining ideas.

Used as Nouns:

Driving a car is not too difficult.

To drive competitively is a different matter.
(In both sentences, the **phrases** in boldface type act as subjects.)

Used for Joining Ideas:

Joining ideas using a **to** + **verb phrase:**

Idea one: Albert wanted to receive a "B" in the class.

Idea two: He needed to earn an "A" on the final.

Combined: **To receive a "B" in the class,** Albert needed to earn an "A" on the final.

Joining ideas using an **-ing phrase:**

Idea one: Helen was thinking of taking out a fast-food franchise.

Idea two: She ate at every McDonald's, Jack-in-the-Box, Carl's, Wendy's, and Burger King in the county.

Combined: **Thinking of taking out a fast-food franchise,** Helen ate at every McDonald's, Jack-in-the-Box, Carl's, Wendy's, and Burger King in the county.

By putting the information from one sentence into an **-ing** or **to** + **verb phrase,** the writer in each example was able to join that information to a second sentence. In this chapter, you will practice joining ideas using **to** + **verb** and **-*ing* phrases.** You will also learn how to avoid making the two most common errors that occur when these two methods are used to combine ideas.

A Professional Writer Uses *To* + Verb and -*ing* Phrases

About the Reading: Amy Tan is a Chinese-American whose ethnic heritage is reflected in her fiction. In addition to writing essays and numerous short stories, she has written two novels. Her first book, *The Joy Luck Club* (1989), was enthusiastically received by critics and made into a film. Her second novel, *The Kitchen God's Wife* (1991), was on the best-seller list. The selection that follows is taken from *The Joy Luck Club*, which tells the stories of a group of Chinese-American daughters, all born in the United States, and their Chinese-born mothers, who came to the United States to escape strife in their native country. The story reprinted here is told by Jing-Mei Woo, one of the daughters.

As You Read: Notice that **-*ing*** and **to** + **verb phrases** have been printed in bold type. Pay particular attention to how these phrases function in a sentence and where they appear in a sentence.

From *The Joy Luck Club*

[1]Five months ago, after a crab dinner **celebrating Chinese New Year,** my mother gave me my "life's importance," a jade pendant on a gold chain. [2]The pendant was not a piece of jewelry I would have chosen for myself. [3]It was almost the size of my little finger, a mottled green and white color, intricately carved. [4]To me, the whole effect looked wrong: too large, too green, too garishly ornate. [5]I stuffed the necklace in my lacquer box and forgot about it.

[6]But these days, I think about my life's importance. [7]I wonder what it means, because my mother died three months ago, six days before my thirty-sixth birthday. [8]And she's the only person I could have asked, **to tell me about life's importance, to help me understand my grief.**

After You Read: Refer to the reading selection to answer the following questions:

1. What **-*ing* phrase** appears in the first sentence?

2. The *-ing* **phrase** describes which word in the sentence?

_____

3. Circle the answer that best describes where in the sentence the
   -ing **phrase** comes.

   beginning   middle   end

4. What two phrases begin with *to* + **verb?**

_____

_____

5. Circle the letter preceding the answer that best describes the function of the *to* + **verb** phrases in sentence 8.

   a. Tell what the writer would like to have happen.

   b. Tell when the information in the rest of the sentence occurred.

   c. Tell how the action in the rest of the sentence occurred.

6. Where in the sentence do these phrases appear? _____

Using *To* + Verb and *-ing* **Phrases**

To join ideas, use a *to* + **verb phrase** to tell what a person or animal
wants to do (purpose or goal). The *to* + **verb phrase** joins what the
person wants with what the person has to have or do to get it
(method).

> She wanted to prevent the killing of animals for their fur. (goal)
>
> She organized a petition to ban the selling of fur coats. (method)

Combined: **To prevent the killing of animals for their fur,** she
organized a petition to ban the selling of fur coats.

> The college wants to attract minority professors. (goal)
>
> The college advertises instructional openings in minority-
> targeted publications. (method)

Combined: **To attract minority professors,** the college adver-
tises instructional openings in minority-targeted publications.

To + **verb phrases** can occur at the beginning of a sentence, in the
middle of a sentence, or at the end of a sentence.

> **To prevent bugs from eating your plants,** spray the plants
> with soapy water.

Martin is, **to use his own words,** the product of a dysfunctional family.

You will need a wok **to make authentic Chinese stir fry.**

Use *-ing* **phrases** to join details that tell *why, when,* and *how* to another idea.

Idea one: Mr. Pedrone arrived in this country.

Idea two: He found a job as a waiter.

Combined: **Arriving in this country,** Mr. Pedrone found a job as a waiter.
(The *-ing* **phrase** tells *when* Mr. Pedrone found his job.)

Idea one: The actress was licking her lips seductively.

Idea two: She looked straight into the camera.

Combined: **Licking her lips seductively,** the actress looked straight into the camera.
(The *-ing* **phrase** tells *how* the actress behaved as she looked into the camera.)

Like a *to* + **verb phrase,** an *-ing* **phrase** can occur at the beginning of a sentence, in the middle of a sentence, or at the end of a sentence.

Listening for his mother's key in the lock, the thirteen-year-old boy tuned the television to the Playboy channel.

His mother, **hearing heavy panting,** peered in the window.

The boy found himself on restriction, **spending every afternoon for a week in his room.**

APPLICATION

Underline any *to* + **verb** or *-ing* **phrases.**

EXAMPLE: Working in the scorching sun, the apricot pickers quickly grew hot and fatigued.

1. Looking for the house address, Miranda drove over the curb and onto someone's lawn.

2. Lighting a candle, Missy made her way to the breaker box.

3. The dog snarled at the intruder, forcing the man into a corner.

4. To prepare his new baseball glove, Ty spent hours oiling it and shaping it.

5. Curtis, to get his mother to let him stay out late, complimented her on her new haircut.

6. Marianne soon learned the new song, practicing it for two hours each night .

7. Screaming as loud as he could, the toddler threw himself on the floor of the market.

8. To sound professional in the interview, Russell went over sample questions beforehand.

9. Trying to find day care for her children, Leona called the county for a list of approved facilities.

10. Daniel, arriving an hour late for his date, searched desperately for a believable excuse.

Punctuation

Use commas with **to** + **verb** and **-ing phrases** that add nonessential information.

1. Put a comma after an introductory phrase.

   Putting on her jacket, Michelle waited for her friend to arrive.

2. Put commas around a phrase that comes in the middle of a sentence unless the information in the phrase is necessary to identify the word it describes.

   Liz, **hurrying to get to her psychology class on time,** ran a red light.
   (The phrase in boldface type is *not* necessary to identify Liz.)

   The files **containing my military records** were destroyed in a fire.
   (The phrase in boldface type is necessary to tell which files.)

3. Put a comma before a phrase that comes at the end of a sentence if it merely adds information to the sentence. If it identifies or describes the word just before it, omit the comma.

   In his lectures, Professor Hill refers to all doctors as "she," **to avoid stereotyping physicians as men.**

   She watched the monkeys **swinging from the trees.**

APPLICATION

In each sentence, underline *to* + **verb** and *-ing* **phrases** and add commas wherever necessary.

> EXAMPLE: To bolster her self-confidence, Mrs. Chang took a martial arts course.

1. Looking for love Gerry joined the Singles Connection.
2. Anita expecting a promotion was disappointed when all her boss wanted was a date.
3. To honor both their mothers the couple named their daughter Carilu.
4. Whistling cheerfully Seth waited for his next victim.
5. Marnie found a kitten meowing in a ditch on the side of the road.
6. To gain firsthand experience with animals Shanna took a job at a pet store.
7. Paulina searching for her birth certificate found a pile of unpaid bills.
8. Hoping to start her own business my neighbor attended a small business seminar.
9. To solve their rodent problem the tenants called an exterminator.
10. Justin had no right to take the car without permission.

Avoiding Dangling and Misplaced Phrases

Unless it is acting as a noun, a *to* + **verb phrase** or an *-ing* **phrase** gives information about another word that appears in the same sentence. In the following sentence, the phrase in boldface type gives information about Kindra:

> **Looking in the showroom window,** Kindra saw the car of her dreams.
> (Who was looking? Kindra was looking.)

Be sure to place a phrase in a sentence so that it clearly refers to a particular word. You will never go wrong if you place the phrase directly before or after the word it tells about.

> **Listening to her stereo,** Jenny woke her parents.
> (Who was listening? Jenny was listening.)

Dr. Zamora, **searching frantically for his lost lecture notes,** had an anxiety attack.

(Who was searching frantically? Dr. Zamora was.)

When a phrase appears to describe the wrong word, the sentence can be confusing or silly.

Chewing contentedly on a rubber bone, I watched the puppy.

(Who was chewing? I? That's what the sentence seems to say.)

To correct a phrase that appears to describe the wrong word, move it so that it is next to the word it tells about.

I watched the puppy **chewing contentedly on a rubber bone.**

In this example, the phrase was merely **misplaced,** so it could be corrected by simply moving it to the right place in the sentence. Sometimes, however, a sentence may not contain a word that the phrase could logically describe.

Flying at a tremendous speed, the sound barrier was broken.

(Who or what was flying? There is no word in the sentence to answer this question.)

Because there is no word in the sentence that tells who or what was flying at a tremendous speed, the phrase is left **dangling** with nothing to hook onto. To correct a dangling phrase, rewrite the sentence so that it contains a word for the phrase to describe.

Flying at a tremendous speed, the pilot broke the sound barrier.

(Who or what was flying? The pilot was flying.)

Or:

Flying at a tremendous speed, the aircraft broke the sound barrier.

(Who or what was flying? The aircraft was flying.)

APPLICATION
....

Most of the following sentences contain misplaced or dangling phrases. Rewrite these sentences to correct misplaced and dangling phrases. If a sentence is correct, put **C** on the line.

EXAMPLE: Crawling on the rug, I noticed the baby seemed tired.

Crawling on the rug, the baby seemed tired.

1. My sister spotted her stolen car having lunch in a restaurant.

_____

_____

2. I noticed a stain on my blouse eating a burrito.

_____

_____

3. To improve his grades a miracle was prayed for.

_____

_____

4. Leaving the movie theater, we decided to go out for coffee.

_____

_____

5. A celebrity underwear auction was held in a Hollywood theater featuring such items as Madonna's bustier and Tom Cruise's briefs.

_____

_____

6. Reciting poetry in a loud voice, the dog listened attentively to Professor Pratt.

_____

_____

7. Awakening in the ambulance, the attendant noticed the patient.

_____

_____

8. To get the children's attention, the camp counselor walked on his hands.

_____

_____

9. Wearing only a string bikini, Martin watched the roller skater cruise past.

_____

_____

10. To impress her former classmates at the reunion, a complete makeover was considered by Nadine.

_____

_____

Joining Sentences Using -*ing* and *To* + *Verb* Phrases

To + **verb** and **-*ing* phrases** are important writing tools because they allow you to join one sentence to another without adding an additional clause.

Sentence one: Evelyn was learning to water-ski.

Sentence two: She broke her collarbone.

Two clauses: When Evelyn was learning to water-ski, she broke her collarbone.

-*ing* Phrase + **clause:**   Learning to water-ski, Evelyn broke her collarbone.

And, because you can move these phrases around in a sentence, they can give your sentences variety.

Having won the lottery, Dhong decided to buy a new house.

Dhong, **having won the lottery,** decided to buy a new house.

As with dependent clauses, you will probably want to put your most important idea in an independent clause and put additional information about intention or circumstances in a phrase.

Sentence one: Harris lost his job making farm equipment.

Sentence two: Harris found work as a bodyguard for a rap singer.

Independent clause + dependent clause:

Harris, **who lost his job making farm equipment,** found work as a bodyguard for a rap singer.

After he lost his job making farm equipment, Harris found work as a bodyguard for a rap singer.

Independent clause + phrase:

Losing his job making farm equipment, Harris found work as a bodyguard for a rap singer.

In all three sentences, the stress is on finding work, which appears in the independent clause.

APPLICATION

Use an *-ing* **phrase** or a *to* + **verb phrase** to join each pair of sentences into a single sentence.

EXAMPLE: Freddie found his lost skate.
            It was lying in the driveway.

            Freddie found his lost skate lying in the driveway.

1. Her brother rushed her to the hospital.
   He drove as fast as he could.

   _____

   _____

2. Ronica opened the kitchen door suddenly.
   Ronica knocked a tray of dishes out of the busboy's hands.

   _____

   _____

3. Cassandra wanted to attend her boyfriend's twenty-first birthday party.
   Cassandra obtained a fake ID.

   _____

   _____

4. The lead singer got out of his limousine.
   The lead singer was pulled into the crowd of screaming fans.

   _____

   _____

5. Heather wanted to avoid her parents.
    Heather hid behind a parked car.

    _____

    _____

6. Rachel hurried home from work.
    Rachel forgot to pick up the children from day care.

    _____

    _____

7. Noel and Alyson grabbed a snack from the snack bar.
    Noel and Alyson hurried off to class.

    _____

    _____

8. He needed to find a singing messenger.
    He looked in the yellow pages under "Delivery."

    _____

    _____

9. He wore a wolfman mask.
    He terrified the children at the Halloween party.

    _____

    _____

10. I was walking along the edge of the water.
    I stepped on a dead fish.

    _____

    _____

▼ CHAPTER REVIEW

- Use a *to* + **verb phrase** to **join what a person or animal wants to do** (purpose or goal) **with the method for achieving it.**
- Use *-ing* **phrases** to **join details that tell why, when, and how** to **another idea.**
- *To* + **verb** and *-ing* **phrases** can **appear at the beginning of a sentence, in the middle of a sentence, or at the end of a sentence.**
- Punctuating *to* + **verb** and *-ing* **phrases:**

  1. Put a **comma after an introductory phrase.**
  2. Put **commas around a phrase that occurs in the middle of a sentence unless the information in the phrase is necessary to identify the word it describes.**
  3. Put a **comma before a phrase that comes at the end of a sentence unless it identifies or describes the word just before it.**

- To **avoid a misplaced** or **dangling phrase, be sure a phrase describes a word that is actually in the sentence, and put the phrase next to the word it tells about.**
- In your writing, **use** *-ing* **and** *to* + **verb phrases to join one sentence to another without adding an additional clause** and **to give your sentences variety.**

PRACTICE

Test your familiarity with using *-ing* and *to* + **verb phrases** by underlining these phrases in the following paragraph:

Please Don't Eat or Cage That Woman!

[1]Have you ever thought about the kinds of words we use to describe one another?[2] Looking closely at English-language words used to describe women, you might be surprised at the number of these words that are also used to refer to food items or to animals. [3]Comparing women to food, we refer to them as *tarts, sweetie pies, sharp cookies,* and *cute tomatoes.* [4]We say that a woman has "a peaches and cream complexion," and little girls, the nursery rhyme explains, are made of "sugar and spice." [5]Parents, naming their daughters, have come up with first names like *Cherry* or *Candy* to pin on their delectable offspring. [6]Managing to escape comparison to a food item, a woman risks being compared to an animal. [7]A woman who nags is a *shrew* or a *bitch.* [8]Young women are *chicks;* old ones are *biddies.* [9]An attractive woman might be judged "a fox," and an unattractive woman described as "a dog" or "a cow." [10]Showing spunk, a woman is

"a tigress"; acting submissive, she is "a kitten." [11]Terms like *catty* and *bitchy* are used to label certain negative traits. [12]Sometimes animal terms are combined with another word to come up with a label. [13]Putting on a pair of skis, a young woman immediately becomes a "ski bunny." [14]Exhibiting permissive behavior, she becomes a "sex kitten." [15]While all of these terms sound pretty silly when you stop to examine them, you might ask yourself if perhaps they reveal something about the way our society has traditionally viewed women.

CHAPTER 17

Joining Ideas in Your Writing

▼ CHAPTER PREVIEW

In each chapter of this unit, you have learned a different method for joining ideas. In this chapter, you will have a chance to compare these different methods and consider the effect on your writing of using one method instead of another. Then you will be given a choice of writing assignments, followed by a sample student essay written on one of the topics. Finally, you will be asked to use the techniques for joining ideas to revise your own essay.

Using Different Techniques to Join Ideas

Whenever you as a writer use one method of joining ideas instead of another, you are making a choice that affects the meaning as well as the style of your writing. Look at the different methods for combining the two sentences that follow, and think about the effect each method has on meaning.

Sentence one: Teresa won the lottery.

Sentence two: She began to spend money foolishly.

1. Teresa won the lottery, and she began to spend money foolishly.
2. As soon as Teresa won the lottery, she began to spend money foolishly.
3. Teresa won the lottery; then, she began to spend money foolishly.
4. Teresa, who had won the lottery, began to spend money foolishly.
5. Having won the lottery, Teresa began to spend money foolishly.

In sentences 1 and 3, the two ideas—the winning and the spending—seem to be of equal importance because each is in its own independent clause, but the word **then** in sentence 3 explains that the foolish spending behavior occurred after the actual winning. Sentences 2, 4, and 5 stress the spending over the winning by putting only the spending in an independent clause. The words "as soon as" in sentence 2 focus attention on just how soon after winning Teresa began her foolish spending. In sentence 4, the winning seems to be almost incidental to the spending. Because the winning would logically seem to be an important factor in the spending, sentence 4 is probably the weakest choice.

In your writing, once you have gotten all of your thoughts laid out on paper, go back and try different patterns for arranging and joining your ideas until you are satisfied that you have made the best choices.

APPLICATION

Experiment with the different methods for joining ideas that have been outlined in this unit. Use two different methods to combine each pair of sentences into one sentence. Try to use every method at least once before you complete the exercise.

EXAMPLE: Mrs. Potts was afraid of muggers.
Mrs. Potts clutched her purse tightly.

a. **Mrs. Potts, who was afraid of muggers, clutched her purse tightly.**

b. **Mrs. Potts was afraid of muggers, so she clutched her purse tightly.**

1. My sister is majoring in business.
My sister really wants to be a country and western singer.

a. _____

b. _____

2. The children were driving their mother crazy.
The children had been fighting with one another all day.

a. _____

b. _____

_____

_____

3. The old roller coaster climbed the steep incline.
   The old roller coaster was creaking and straining.

a. _____

_____

_____

b. _____

_____

_____

4. My sister is going to marry Jose Villegas.
   The couple will live in Mexico City.

a. _____

_____

_____

b. _____

_____

_____

5. The singing telegram was intended for Mrs. Kioto.
   Mrs. Kioto had already left the building.

a. _____

_____

_____

b. _____

_____

_____

Writing Assignments

Choose one of the following topics to develop into an essay:

1. Tell about a family incident that illustrates the character of one of your family members. Perhaps someone started trouble within the family by spreading gossip or revealing a secret. Or, maybe someone's generous act showed just how selfless that person is.
2. Describe a family incident that influenced you in some significant way. Perhaps the birth of a much younger sibling affected your views on parenting, or perhaps a divorce brought you closer to one parent or forced you to grow up quickly.
3. Tell about a time that a close friend or a relative did something that either made you proud or let you down. Perhaps a parent finally completed a high school or college degree, or maybe a brother or sister failed to make good on a promise to you. Try to focus on one specific action or achievement rather than on your pride or disappointment about a person's overall behavior.

   To get started, you might want to make a quick list of all your family members or of occurrences in your family that stick out in your mind. Once you have chosen a particular incident to write about, try freewriting about the incident to bring the details alive in your mind. You can clarify the significance of the incident or action by trying to name it and describe its impact in a single sentence, such as one of the following:

> When my mother worked all Christmas vacation to pay my way to cheerleading camp, I finally realized what a wonderful mom she was.

> When I first found out that I was adopted, I began to question who I really was.

> It was a proud moment for me and for my whole family when my father received his high school diploma at the age of forty-five.

A Student Responds to One of the Writing Assignments

About the Reading: The essay that follows was written by Deborah Garza, who says she "loves writing." Garza, who is nineteen years old, has not yet declared a major, but she is interested in the field of business management. While she is attending college, Garza also works as a cashier in a drugstore.

As You Read: Notice how the writer uses a specific incident to reveal the character of her father. Pay attention to her use of details to make this incident real for the reader and to her comments about the influence that her father's behavior has had on her own life goals.

The Shark

It was the summer of 1988. I was sixteen years old, and I was about to see someone whom I had not seen or spoken to for five years—my father. I had been invited by his wife to a party being given at his house. I wore a bright red sweater and a black miniskirt, unlike the clothes I wore at the age of eleven when he last saw me. I wanted him to see that I wasn't a little girl anymore. I was excited to see him because it had been so long since I had, but at the same time, I was angry at him for allowing so much time to go by without calling or coming to see me.

1

When I arrived at the house, everyone greeted me very politely. It was a very beautiful house. It was two stories high, it was big, and it was very nicely furnished. When I saw my father, he gave me a hug, and he said hello. He began to tell me how he had tried to get in touch with me, but he had lost my number. I knew he was lying because he had my grandmother's phone number and he knew exactly where I lived. If he had really tried to get in touch with me, he would have. At that point, I was angry because he actually thought I was stupid enough to believe his story. My father was there for about ten minutes when he stood up and said he would be back because he had something to do. I said okay, and I waited.

2

Four hours went by, and I knew he wasn't coming back. Everyone waited for him to return before dinner was served, but they also realized that he wasn't coming back. His whole family was angry at him for doing what he had done. I was angry too, and although everyone was being very nice to me, I didn't want to be there. I wanted to go home. If he did decide to come back, I didn't want to be there. I told his wife that I really wasn't in the mood for a party. She told me she understood, and she took me home. When I got home, I told my mom what had happened, and she began to tell me how she had known he would do something like that. My mom hated my father, so naturally she was angry. That night I cried myself to sleep. I couldn't understand what type of a father would do what he had done.

3

It's been almost four years now since that summer day at my father's house. I'm nineteen years old, I work, and I go to school. I guess you can say I turned out okay, thanks to my mom. I don't like my father, I don't care about him, and I don't want to see him. I can say, though, that he does have something to do with what I'm doing today and who I will be tomorrow. In a sense he has influenced me in a big way. I want to graduate from college, have a good career, and have nice things, and I want to show him that I did those things without needing his help or having him around. I want to show him that my mom did a pretty good job raising me without him. He hasn't been around for most of my life, and he hasn't been a father to me; therefore, I don't consider him

4

one. How can a person whom I dislike so much influence me in a good way? Well, as funny as it may sound, he has.

The last I heard, his wife had divorced him and kicked him out of her house. He now lives in an apartment all alone, and he doesn't have a job. In my eyes my father is like a shark who travels alone along a lonely sea. People tend to fear sharks and stay away from them. I don't fear my father because I have no real reason to, but I do plan to stay away from him. If given the chance, a shark will pull you right in and kill you. My father will travel through life alone, just like a shark, because, no matter what, this man will never be a father to me, and I will never be his daughter.

5

....

After You Read: Refer to the student essay to complete the items that follow:

1. This essay does not contain one particular sentence that states the topic and main idea. All of the following sentences contain ideas from the essay. Circle the letter preceding the sentence that you think best states the author's *main* point.

   a. My father hurt me deeply when I was sixteen years old.

   b. In a curious way, having a no-good father turned out to be a positive influence on me.

   c. I was both excited and angry at the prospect of seeing my father again.

2. What specific details in the first paragraph help you picture the writer? What information lets you know her state of mind?

   _____

   _____

   _____

3. What insight do you get into the father from the writer's description of their conversation in paragraph 2?

   _____

4. In the following sentence, the verb in bold type is not in the correct tense.

   I wore a bright red sweater and a black miniskirt, unlike the clothes I **wore** at the age of eleven when he last saw me.

   Instead of the past tense form, the verb **wore** should be in the form used to tell about a past action that occurred before another past action: **had** + past participle.

I wore a bright red sweater and a black miniskirt, unlike the clothes I **had worn** at the age of eleven when he last saw me.

Cross out the incorrect verb form in bold type in the following sentence, and write in the correct form above it:

My father **was** there for about ten minutes when he stood up and said he would be back because he had something to do.

5. In the first sentence of paragraph 3, the writer has used a comma and a coordinating conjunction to join the two ideas. Join these same two ideas using first a semicolon and then a subordinating conjunction.

    semicolon: _____

    _____

    subordinating conjunction: _____

    _____

6. The writer also used a comma and a coordinating conjunction to join the two ideas in another sentence in paragraph 3: "She told me she understood, and she took me home." Join these same two ideas using two different methods.

    a. _____

    _____

    b. _____

    _____

Revising Your Writing by Joining Ideas

Joining ideas in your own writing can serve two purposes: it can eliminate choppy sentences (many short sentences in a row), and it helps you develop style as a writer. Look over your essay and find at least two sentences that could be joined together into one sentence. Use any of the methods discussed in this unit to join these sentences.

The easiest—and so the most common—method for joining two ideas into one sentence is a comma and a coordinating conjunction, usually the word ***and.*** Look over the sentences in your essay to identify those that use a comma and a coordinating conjunction to join ideas. Revise at least one of these sentences by using one of the other methods to join ideas.

▼ CHAPTER REVIEW

- To avoid choppy sentences and develop your writing style, **join ideas** using the following methods:

  1. Comma and a coordinating conjunction (FANBOYS)
  2. Subordinating conjunction
  3. Relative pronoun
  4. *To* + **verb** phrase or *-ing* phrase

Highlights

Coordinating Conjunctions

- The **coordinating conjunctions** are *for, and, nor, but, or, yet,* and *so* (FANBOYS). Use **coordinating conjunctions** to **join words, phrases, and clauses.**
- To **avoid** writing a **run-on sentence** or a **comma splice,** be sure to **join independent clauses with both a comma and a coordinating conjunction.**

Subordinating Conjunctions

- Use **subordinating conjunctions,** like *because, after,* and *although,* to **join ideas by stressing the relationship of one idea to another. Subordinating conjunctions tell *why, where, when, how,* or *how much or little.***
- A **clause that begins with a subordinating conjunction** is a **dependent clause.** A dependent clause cannot stand alone as a sentence; it must be joined to an independent clause.
- If a **dependent clause comes before the independent clause,** follow it with a **comma.** If the **dependent clause follows the independent clause, no punctuation** is necessary.

Semicolons

- Use a **semicolon** to **join independent clauses that could stand alone as complete sentences.**
- Use a **semicolon by itself** to **join ideas that are closely related in meaning.** Use a **semicolon along with a transition** to **join two independent clauses** when you want to **emphasize the relationship between the ideas in the clauses.**
- In general, put a **comma after a transition that follows a semicolon,** but you **can leave out the comma after short transitions** if you wish.

Relative Pronouns

- The words *which, who, whom, whose,* and *that* are **relative pronouns.**
- **Use relative pronouns to introduce clauses that identify or give additional information about a noun or pronoun in a sentence.**
- A **clause that begins with a relative pronoun** is a dependent clause; it **can never stand alone as a sentence.**
- Use **commas** with a clause introduced by a relative pronoun **if the information in the clause is *not necessary*** to identify a person or thing. **Do not use commas if the information in the clause *is necessary*** to identify a person or thing.

To + *Verb Phrases and* -ing *Phrases*

Use a *to* + **verb phrase** to **join what a person or animal wants to do** (purpose or goal) **with the method for achieving it.**

- Use *-ing* **phrases** to **join details that tell** *why, when,* **and** *how* **to another idea.**
- *To* + **verb** and *-ing* **phrases** can **appear at the beginning of a sentence, in the middle of a sentence, or at the end of a sentence.**
- Punctuating *to* + **verb** and *-ing* **phrases:**

1. Put a **comma after an introductory phrase.**
2. Put **commas around a phrase that occurs in the middle of a sentence unless the information in the phrase is necessary to identify the word it describes.**
3. **Put a comma before a phrase that comes at the end of a sentence unless it identifies or describes the word just before it.**

- To **avoid a misplaced** or **dangling phrase, be sure a phrase describes a word that is actually in the sentence, and put the phrase next to the word it tells about.**

Joining Ideas in Your Writing

- In your writing, avoid choppy sentences and give your sentences variety by joining ideas:

1. Use **coordinating conjunctions to join two or more ideas into a single sentence.**
2. Use **subordinating conjunctions** to join ideas when you want to **stress the relationship of one idea to another.**
3. Use a **semicolon** by itself to join ideas that already have a **clear relationship.** Use a **semicolon with a transition** when you want to put a strong **emphasis on the relationship between the ideas.**
4. Use **relative pronouns** to join sentences when one sentence gives **information about a person or thing** in another sentence.
5. Use *to* + **verb** and *-ing* **phrases** to **join one sentence to another without adding an additional clause.** When you use *to* + **verb** and *-ing* **phrases** to join ideas, put **ideas that are less important** in the phrases, and leave the main idea in the independent clause.

PRACTICE

Use the following sentences to test your mastery of the material in Unit Four. If you have difficulty, go back and look over the explanations in Chapters 12–17.

A. Use a coordinating conjunction to join each pair of sentences into one sentence. If the new sentence contains two independent clauses, be sure to put a comma before the coordinating conjunction.

EXAMPLE: The game ended early.
Everyone decided to go out for pizza.

The game ended early, so everyone decided to go out

for pizza.

Or:

The game ended early, and everyone decided to go out

for pizza.

1. Deborah wanted to go to the movies.
Her parents wouldn't let her use the car.

_____

_____

_____

2. Martina left the party late.
Tony left the party late.

_____

_____

_____

3. He ate nonfat yogurt for lunch.
He had a pizza for an afternoon snack.

_____

_____

_____

4. Clyde wants to win the 10-K race this weekend.
He has been training for months.

_____

_____

_____

5. Pauline controlled her temper.
   She could not afford to lose her job.

   _____

   _____

   _____

B. Use a subordinating conjunction to join each pair of sentences into a single sentence. Be sure to add commas if necessary.

   EXAMPLE: My alarm did not go off.
               I was late for the exam.

               Because my alarm did not go off, I was late for

               the exam.

1. Sue was waiting for her interview.
   She began to feel sick.

   _____

   _____

   _____

2. Hector washed his car and went to the bank.
   He picked up Karen for their date.

   _____

   _____

   _____

3. I am planning to leave for Vermont for a family visit.
   The semester ends.

   _____

   _____

   _____

4. The CD player was not working right.
   I decided to return it to the store.

   _____

   _____

   _____

5. Classes do not end until May 28th.
   I am supposed to start my new job on the 24th.

   _____

   _____

   _____

C. Use either a semicolon alone or a semicolon *and* a transition to join the following sentence pairs into one sentence. Add commas if necessary.

   EXAMPLE: The weather report called for snow.
   Jack had packed only shorts and T-shirts.

   The weather report called for snow; unfortunately, _____

   Jack had packed only shorts and T-shirts. _____

   _____

1. The new instructor had an impressive educational background.
   He had never actually taught a class before.

   _____

   _____

   _____

2. Barry decided not to go out for dinner after all.
   He was not at the restaurant when Michael Jordan showed up.

   _____

   _____

   _____

3. The morning was cold and rainy.
My car refused to start.

_____

_____

_____

4. Coretta is an incredibly picky eater.
No one invites her to dinner.

_____

_____

_____

5. The dog ignored the rawhide bone and doggy treats.
He went straight for Doug's new running shoes.

_____

_____

_____

D. Use a relative pronoun to join each pair of sentences into one sentence. Add commas whenever necessary.

    EXAMPLE: Jack never heard the siren.
                 Jack was listening to his Walkman.

                 Jack, who was listening to his Walkman, never heard

                 the siren.

1. Emily's uncle was a POW in Vietnam.
He never discusses his experiences in Southeast Asia.

_____

_____

_____

2. My English professor talked about Thoreau.
   Thoreau acted crazy and refused to pay his taxes.

   _____

   _____

   _____

3. Pedro admired the bookcases.
   He had built the bookcases from scratch.

   _____

   _____

   _____

4. The young woman is waiting outside the dean's office.
   The young woman wants to appeal her grade.

   _____

   _____

   _____

5. Jamal Wilson is being scouted by the NFL.
   His sister is a close friend of mine.

   _____

   _____

   _____

E. Use a **to** + **verb** phrase or an **-ing** phrase to combine each
   sentence pair into a single sentence. Add commas as needed.

   EXAMPLE: She wanted a degree in zoology.
   She would have to transfer to a different college.

   To get a degree in zoology, she would have to

   transfer to a different college.

1. Pierre was going 85 miles per hour.
    Pierre didn't see the policeman waiting on the side street.

    _____

    _____

    _____

2. Ophelia turned the corner.
    Ophelia bumped right into her chemistry professor.

    _____

    _____

    _____

3   He wanted to help the homeless in his neighborhood.
    He organized a food and clothing drive.

    _____

    _____

    _____

4. The man began to roar with laughter.
    The man was sitting next to me.

    _____

    _____

    _____

5. Lonny lost his construction job due to the slow economy.
    Lonny decided to get training as a plumber.

    _____

    _____

    _____

F. Use any two methods you have studied in this chapter to join the following sentence pairs into single sentences. Add commas if necessary.

EXAMPLE: Harry left his family and friends in Reno.
                       Harry took a job in New York.

       a. **Leaving his family and friends in Reno, Harry took a**

       job in New York.

       b. **Harry left his family and friends in Reno and took a**

       job in New York.

1. The child received a prize for good citizenship.
     Her parents looked on proudly.

       a. _____

       _____

       _____

       b. _____

       _____

       _____

2. Aretha wanted tickets for the playoffs.
     Aretha waited in line for six hours.

       a. _____

       _____

       _____

       b. _____

       _____

       _____

3. Raj inherited $20,000 from his aunt.
   He immediately bought a new car.

   a. _____

   _____

   _____

   b. _____

   _____

   _____

4. Domingo is studying law at Harvard.
   He still finds time to volunteer in the Big Brother program.

   a. _____

   _____

   _____

   b. _____

   _____

   _____

5. Ebony started babysitting when she was twelve years old.
   Today she has a degree in child development and owns a preschool.

   a. _____

   _____

   _____

   b. _____

   _____

   _____

Using Modifiers

CHAPTER 18

Using Adjectives

▼ CHAPTER PREVIEW

In Unit 4, you studied methods for joining sentences. In this unit, you will learn about **modifiers,** words that add information to a basic sentence. The sentences that follow have both a subject and a verb, but the sentences are rather dull.

The man put on his shoes.

The tree grew in the yard.

Adding just a couple of words, however, can make the sentence much more vivid for the reader.

The **athletic** man put on his **running** shoes.

The **gnarled** tree grew in the **neglected** yard.

The words in boldface type in each sentence are called **adjectives.** Each adjective **describes a noun** in the sentence. In this chapter you will learn about the **function, forms, and placement of adjectives.**

A Professional Writer Uses Adjectives

About the Reading: Born in Puerto Rico in 1952, Judith Ortiz Cofer moved with her family to New Jersey in 1955. She is a poet, novelist, and essayist. The selection that follows is taken from a longer essay called "Silent Dancing," which originally appeared in *The Georgia Review* and is included in a 1990 collection of essays and poems by Cofer also entitled *Silent Dancing.* Reprinted in *The Best American Essays 1991*, the essay focuses on Cofer's memories of her youth prompted by viewing a home movie.

As You Read: The adjectives in the selection have been printed in bold type. Notice what types of words function as adjectives and which words these adjectives describe.

....

From "Silent Dancing"

[1]**One** New Year's Eve we were dressed up like **child** models in the **Sears** catalogue: **my** brother in a **miniature man's** suit and **bow** tie, and I in **black patent-leather** shoes and a **frilly** dress with **several** layers of crinoline underneath. [2]**My** mother wore a **bright red** dress **that** night, I remember, and **spike** heels; **her long black** hair hung to **her** waist. [3]Father, who usually wore **his navy** uniform during **his short** visits home, had put on a **dark civilian** suit for the occasion: we had been invited to **his uncle's** house for a **big** celebration. [4]Everyone was **excited** because **my mother's** brother Hernan—a bachelor who could indulge himself with luxuries—had brought home a **movie** camera, which he would be trying out **that** night.

....

After You Read: Refer to the reading selection to complete the following items:

1. Look carefully at the words in sentence 1 that are described by adjectives. Write these words in the appropriate blanks:

    One _____   bow _____

    child _____   black patent-leather _____

    Sears _____   frilly _____

    my _____   several _____

    miniature man's _____

2. Circle the answer that names the type of words you wrote in the blanks in question 1.

    prepositions   conjunctions   nouns   verbs

3. Which adjectives are colors?

    _____

4. In sentence 1, what adjective tells *how many* layers of crinoline?

    _____

5. In sentence 2, what adjectives tell *whose* mother and *whose* waist?

_____

6. In sentence 3, what adjective tells *what kind* of visits?

_____

7. In sentence 4, what adjective tells *which* night?

_____

Using Adjectives

An adjective describes a noun or pronoun.

> The **tattered** coat hung on the **dusty** rack.
> (The adjective ***tattered*** describes the noun ***coat.*** The adjective ***dusty*** describes the noun ***rack.***)

> It was **only** he.
> (The adjective ***only*** describes the pronoun ***he.***)

An adjective tells *which, what kind, how many or how much,* or *whose.*

> **that** bike (which bike)

> **mountain** bike (what kind of bike)

> **one** bike (how many bikes)

> **Juan's** bike (whose bike) or **his** bike (whose bike)

Notice that many different types of words can function as adjectives, as long as the words describe a noun or pronoun.

> **Campus** parking is impossible! (noun describing another noun)

> I lost **my** pen. (pronoun describing a noun)

> Someone stole **Americo's** car. (***'s*** word describing a noun)

APPLICATION ONE

Circle each adjective and draw an arrow from the adjective to the noun it describes.

EXAMPLE: The (stray) dog sniffed the (discarded) sandwich.

1. He drove the battered car into his driveway.

2. The spoiled cat eats only smoked fish.

3. Tran's brother is a preschool teacher.

4. Doris grew up in a small town in Kansas.

5. The suspicious clerk followed the two girls.

6. She insisted on buying the hideous earrings.

7. Those neighbors are always making noise.

8. He rented a studio apartment.

9. Derek slowly filled out the complicated form.

10. Two students in the English class dropped out after the first day.

APPLICATION TWO

In each blank, write a word that can function as an adjective.

EXAMPLE: A ___screaming___ girl burst into the ___crowded___ room.

1. _____ hours later, they found the _____ car.

2. The _____ bill arrived today.

3. Mary Beth got a(n) _____ job after she graduated.

4. _____ wife had been a(n) _____ dancer in her youth.

5. My _____ class is _____.

6. Her _____ birthday party was a surprise.

7. Alex enrolled his _____ sons at a(n) _____ preschool.

8. Nel is afraid of _____ animals.

9. Craig works as a(n) _____ engineer.

10. _____ people usually eat lunch at the _____ restaurant.

Comparatives and Superlatives

When adjectives are used to compare two or more people or things, they have special forms.

He has a **newer** car than I have.

Mohammed is the **tallest** person in his family.

Use the **comparative** form to **compare two persons or things.** The comparative form ends in *-er* or follows the word *more.*

He has **longer** hair than his sister.
(Add *-er* to a one-syllable adjective like *long.*)

Jeremy is **luckier** than I was.
(With a two-syllable adjective ending in *y,* such as *lucky,* drop the *y* and add *-ier.*)

This course gets **more difficult** every day.
(Put *more* before an adjective of two or more syllables that does not end in *y,* such as *difficult.*)

Do not use both *more* and *-er* together.

Incorrect: She was more sadder than I was.

Correct: She was sadder than I was.
(Notice, as in the case of *sad* and *sadder,* you will sometimes need to double the final letter of an adjective before you add *-er.*)

Use the **superlative** form to **compare three or more persons or things.** The superlative form ends in *-est* or follows the word *most.*

Fala is the **youngest** of five sisters.
(Add *-est* to a one-syllable adjective like *young.*)

Carlos is the **funniest** person I've ever met.
(With a two-syllable adjective ending in *y,* such as *funny,* drop the *y* and add *-iest.*)

That is the **most ridiculous** thing I ever heard.
(Put *most* before an adjective of two or more syllables that does not end in *y,* such as *ridiculous.*)

Do not use *most* and *-est* together.

Incorrect: He was voted the most sexiest man on television.

Correct: He was voted the sexiest man on television.

Some common adjectives are irregular; you will have to memorize their comparative and superlative forms if you don't already know them.

	COMPARATIVE	SUPERLATIVE
good	better	best
bad	worse	worst
little	littler, less*	littlest, least*
many	more	most
some	more	most
much	more	most

*Use **littler** and **littlest** to describe size; use **less** and **least** to describe an amount.

APPLICATION ONE

Write the comparative and superlative forms of each adjective.

	COMPARATIVE	SUPERLATIVE
EXAMPLE: nice	nicer	nicest
1. heavy	_____	_____
2. dumb	_____	_____
3. mad	_____	_____
4. good	_____	_____
5. silly	_____	_____
6. intelligent	_____	_____
7. athletic	_____	_____
8. great	_____	_____
9. happy	_____	_____
10. proud	_____	_____

APPLICATION TWO

In the blank, write either the comparative or the superlative form of the adjective in parentheses. Use the comparative to compare two things; use the superlative to compare three or more.

EXAMPLE: My grandmother is the __**most elegant**__ woman I
have ever met. (elegant)

1. It was my _____ nightmare. (bad)

2. My uncle is _____ than I am. (young)

3. Jorinda's apology was _____ than Alisa's. (sincere)

4. He is a lot _____ now than he was five years ago. (heavy)

5. *Oprah* is the _____ afternoon talk show. (popular)

6. Trudie is the _____ of the five sisters. (talented)

7. He studies _____ than I do, but he gets better grades.

   (little)

8. Sonia is convinced that her child is the _____ child

   on the planet. (smart)

9. Each of my psychology teachers is _____ than the

   last one. (crazy)

10. Since his hair transplant, women have found Art _____

    than ever. (attractive)

Demonstrative Adjectives

This, these, that, and ***those*** are **demonstrative adjectives.** Use
demonstrative adjectives to **point out (or demonstrate) which noun**
you mean.

> He wants to buy **that** motorcycle in the window.
>   (***That*** points out which motorcycle.)

> I am taking **these** curtains back to the store.
>   (***These*** points out which curtains.)

Demonstrative adjectives are the only adjectives that change form to
show singular or plural.

SINGULAR	*PLURAL*
this	these
that	those

Use **this** and **that** before singular nouns; use **these** and **those** before plural nouns.

> I hate **this** class! (**class** is singular)
>
> Romero brought me **these** flowers. (**flowers** is plural)
>
> Vanessa made **that** wine herself. (**wine** is singular)
>
> My aunt just loves **those** ashtrays made from abalone shells. (**ashtrays** is plural)

APPLICATION

Circle the correct demonstrative adjective in parentheses.

> *EXAMPLE:*   How did you ever get (that, (those)) tickets?

1. Estefan found (that, those) same shorts on sale for $20.00.
2. (This, These) slides are not safe for young children.
3. Do (this, these) shoes come in size eleven?
4. The writing lab is located in the basement of (this, these) building.
5. (This, These) information is crucial.
6. Patricia's mother attended (that, those) classes when Patricia was ill.
7. She forgot to pay (that, those) bills.
8. My first husband, Elvis, gave me (this, these) blender for our tenth anniversary.
9. Have you seen (that, those) violent new movie?
10. (This, These) assignment is harder than it looked.

Placement of Adjectives

Adjectives usually come right before the words they describe.

> Grampa Hector is not a **young** man any more.
>   (**Young** describes **man.**)

> The **three** dolphins leaped from the water.
>   (**Three** describes **dolphins.**)

Adjectives that follow linking verbs (*is, feels, seems,* and so on) can describe the subject of the linking verbs, or they **can describe a noun or pronoun that renames the subject.**

> The new three million dollar science building is **hideous.**
>   (**Hideous** describes the subject **building.**)

The new three million dollar science building is a **hideous** eye-sore.
> (**Hideous** describes the noun *eyesore.*)

APPLICATION

Draw an arrow from each italicized adjective to the noun or pronoun it describes.

    EXAMPLE: That dog is *uglier* than either of its parents.

1. Jeri has the *curliest* permanent I've ever seen.

2. It takes *four* hours to drive to his sister's house.

3. My *favorite* holiday is Cinco de Mayo.

4. Justin wrote a *wonderful* essay about his childhood.

5. I met *Bailey's* grandfather at graduation.

6. *That* textbook is used in all of the introductory courses.

7. Krissie felt *confident* that she could finish the assignment on time.

8. She tried unsuccessfully to fix the *screen* door.

9. He was often teased about his *loud* snoring in class.

10. Special Services supplied an *experienced* interpreter to sign the performance for nonhearing audience members.

▼ CHAPTER REVIEW

- An *adjective* **describes a noun or pronoun.**
- An **adjective** tells *which, what kind, how many or how much,* or *whose.* **Many different types of words can function as adjectives,** as long as the words describe a noun or pronoun.
- Use the **comparative** form (*-er, more*) of an adjective to **compare two persons or things.**
- Use the **superlative** form (*-est, most*) of an adjective to **compare three or more people or things.**
- Use **demonstrative** adjectives (*this, these, that, those*) to **point out which noun** you mean.
- **Adjectives usually come right before the words they describe. However, an adjective that follows a linking verb can describe the subject of the verb.**

PRACTICE

Test your familiarity with the function of adjectives by drawing an arrow from each of the italicized adjectives to the noun or pronoun it describes.

Aztlán

[1]Aztlán is the name given to the *mythic* homeland of the *Aztec* peoples. [2]The actual *Aztec* civilization of *central* Mexico, which existed when *Spanish* explorers arrived in the 1500s, was quite advanced in *many* areas. [3]The Aztecs were known for *their* use of astronomy and their *military* skill. [4]The Aztecs had established numerous *urban* centers and had made alliances with other *native* tribes. [5]They had also developed a *sophisticated* system of barter and exchange. [6]Although the Spaniards, led by Cortés, conquered the *Aztec* empire and claimed *its* territories and minerals for Spain, the *Aztec* civilization remains a *powerful* symbol for *many* Mexican-Americans. [7]The "search for Aztlán" has come to represent the search for *one's* identity in the civilizations of the *Mexican* Indians who ruled Mexico before the Europeans imposed their *own* values and beliefs on the region.

CHAPTER **19**

Using Adverbs

▼ CHAPTER PREVIEW

In Chapter 18, you learned about adjectives, words that describe a noun or pronoun.

My father can't stand **loud** music.

In the preceding sentence, the word **loud** is an adjective describing music.

The baby shrieked **loudly.**

In this sentence, the word **loudly** looks similar to the adjective **loud,** but it is not an adjective. Instead, it is an **adverb.** Adverbs are **words that describe a verb, an adjective,** or **another adverb.** In the sentence, **loudly** tells how the baby **shrieked,** so it describes a verb.

In this chapter, you will study adverbs and learn how they work in a sentence. You will also learn the different forms of adverbs.

A Professional Writer Uses Adverbs

About the Reading: Diana Hume George is a professor of English and women's studies. Her essays, poetry, and reviews have appeared in numerous publications. Her second volume of poetry, *The Resurrection of the Body,* was published in 1989. She has also written two book-length works examining the poetry of others. The selection that follows is taken from "Wounded Chevy at Wounded Knee," an essay that appeared originally in *The Missouri Review* and was reprinted in *The Best American Essays 1991.* The essay centers on George's recollections about her first husband, a carnival worker from the Seneca tribe. These memories are triggered when she and her second husband visit Wounded Knee, "site of the last cavalry massacre of the Lakota in 1890 and of the more recent confrontation between the FBI and the American Indian Movement."

245

As You Read: In the reading, adverbs have been printed in bold type. Notice what kinds of words function as adverbs and what types of words these adverbs describe.

From "Wounded Chevy at Wounded Knee"

[1]A few years ago, my son Bernie went through a period when he chose to remove himself from my world and go live in his father's, from which I'd taken him when he was three. [2]I did**n't** try to stop him, even though I knew he was hanging out with people who lived **dangerously.** [3]I used to lie in bed unable to go to sleep because I was wondering what tree he'd end up wrapped **around** with his dad. [4]He was a minor, but I was **essentially** helpless to prevent this. [5]If I'd forced the issue, it would **only** have made his desire to know a forbidden world **more** intense. [6]He lived **there** for months, and I **slowly** learned to get to sleep at night. [7]Mothers ca**n't** save their children. [8]And he had a right.

After You Read: Refer to the reading selection to complete the following items:

1. Which four adverbs end in **ly?** _____

   _____

2. The **n't** in the contractions **didn't** and **can't** stands for what adverb? _____

3. In sentence 6, what adverb tells *where* he lived? _____

4. In sentence 2, what adverb tells *how* the people lived? _____

5. In sentence 4, what adverb describes the adjective **helpless?**

   _____

6. In sentence 6, what adverb describes the verb **learned?**

   _____

Using Adverbs

Use an **adverb** to **describe a verb, an adjective,** or **another adverb.**

Kyle uses foul language **constantly.**
(**Constantly** describes the verb **uses.**)

My geography instructor is **quite** interesting.
(***Quite*** describes the adjective ***interesting.***)

She spent the lottery money **very** quickly.
(***Very*** describes the adverb ***quickly.***)

Adverbs tell *when, where, how,* and *under what condition.*

My uncle arrived **yesterday.** (When did he arrive?)

The mall is one block **north** of her house. (Where is the mall?)

Jerome dunked the basketball **easily.** (How did he dunk the ball?)

She is **certainly** entitled to a share of the money. (Under what condition is she?)

The words ***not*** and ***never*** are always adverbs. They give the opposite meaning to the verb or adverb they describe.

The boy was **not** sleepy. (He is the opposite of sleepy.)

Many adverbs are **formed by adding** *-ly* **to adjectives.**

ADJECTIVE	ADVERB
attractive	attractively
honest	honestly
easy	easily
perfect	perfectly

Be careful not to confuse adjectives with adverbs because they often look so similar. The following adjectives and adverbs are often confused.

CONFUSING ADJECTIVE / ADVERB PAIRS

Adjective	Adverb
awful	awfully
bad	badly
poor	poorly
quick	quickly
quiet	quietly
real	really
sure	surely

The adverb form of the adjective ***good*** is ***well.*** Be careful not to confuse these two. The only time that ***well*** is an adjective is when it refers to someone's health.

Francesca is a **good** worker. (adjective describing ***worker***)

Francesca works **well** with others. (adverb describing ***works***)

Francesca is feeling **well.** (adjective describing Francesca's health)

APPLICATION ONE

Circle the appropriate adjective or adverb form in parentheses.

EXAMPLE: (Sudden, (Suddenly) the earthquake shook the house.

1. I am (perfect, perfectly) willing to follow your suggestions.
2. Peter answered the phone before he was (full, fully) awake.
3. He was (real, really) late for his first day at work.
4. Salsa goes (good, well) with any food.
5. Roxanne fell and hurt herself (bad, badly).
6. Hector will (sure, surely) get a raise next month.
7. Vivian and Nigel had an (awful, awfully) argument.
8. The exam was (extreme, extremely) difficult.
9. He played (poor, poorly) in the last game.
10. The professor took a (quick, quickly) look at his notes.

APPLICATION TWO

Use each adverb in a sentence of your own.

EXAMPLE: (shortly) **I will be there shortly.** _____

1. (generously) _____
2. (well) _____
3. (everywhere) _____
4. (quickly) _____
5. (yesterday) _____
6. (really) _____
7. (easily) _____
8. (too) _____
9. (badly) _____
10. (unexpectedly) _____

Comparatives and Superlatives

Like adjectives, many adverbs have special forms to compare two or more people or things.

Herman drove **faster** than the speed limit.

Melinda ran **slowest** of all of the competitors.

Use the **comparative** form to **compare two persons or things.** The comparative form ends in *-er* or follows the word *more.*

He arrived **later** than his girlfriend.
>   (Add *-er* to a one-syllable adverb. If the adverb already ends in *e,* like *late,* just add *-r.*)

Elaine sings even **more beautifully** than her sister.
>   (Use *more* with adverbs of two or more syllables, including adverbs that end in *-ly.*)

Use the **superlative** form to **compare three or more persons or things.** The superlative form ends in *-est* or follows the word *most.*

Gary jumped **highest** of all.
>   (Add *-est* to a one-syllable adverb like *high.*)

She gave of her time **most generously.**
>   (Use *most* with adverbs of two or more syllables, including adverbs that end in *-ly.*)

Two irregular adverbs that often give students difficulty are *well* and *badly.* If you don't already know their comparative and superlative forms, you will need to memorize them.

	COMPARATIVE	SUPERLATIVE
well:	better	best
badly:	worse	worst

APPLICATION

Write the comparative and superlative forms of each adverb.

	COMPARATIVE	SUPERLATIVE
EXAMPLE: gently	**more gently**	**most gently**
1. calmly		
2. carefully		
3. soon		
4. well		
5. suddenly		
6. quietly		

7. badly   _____   _____

8. hard   _____   _____

9. carelessly   _____   _____

10. fast   _____   _____

Placement of Adverbs

You can put adverbs in several places in a sentence. They usually appear in one of four positions:

1. At the beginning of the sentence.

> **Carefully,** the policeman pushed open the door.
> (Put a comma after an adverb that appears at the beginning of a sentence.)

2. In front of a verb or between a helping verb and a main verb.

> Mr. Contreras **finally** decided to change jobs.

3. Right after the verb.

> The baby babbled **happily** in its playpen.

4. At the end of the sentence.

> The driver slammed on his brakes **suddenly.**

Be careful when placing an adverb after the verb that you do not create an awkward sentence.

Awkward: The nurse left quietly the room.

Better: The nurse quietly left the room.

APPLICATION
....

Write an appropriate adverb in each space.

> *EXAMPLE:*   <u>Ferociously</u>, the cat sprang at the bird.

1. The young boy waited _____ for his turn at bat.

2. The irate motorist glared _____ at the car that cut him off.

3. Late for school, Jess _____ threw on his clothes.

4. Kim removed the label _____ .

5. _____, Gabriel received the news of his college acceptance.

6. Gene Begay ran _____ than anyone in the neighborhood.

7. Sheena reacted _____ when she heard the news.

8. The dog _____ responded to its master's command to at-

    tack.

9. _____, they embraced one another.

10. _____, the small girl ripped the paper from the birthday

    gift.

▼ CHAPTER REVIEW

- Use an **adverb** to **describe a verb, an adjective, or another adverb.**
- Adverbs tell *when, where, how,* and *under what condition.*
- The words *not* and *never* are always **adverbs.**
- **Many adverbs are formed by adding *-ly to adjectives.***
- Many adverbs have **special forms** to **compare** people or things. Use the **comparative form** (*-er, more*) to **compare two persons or things.** Use the **superlative form** (*-est, most*) to **compare three or more persons or things.**
- Adverbs usually appear in one of **four positions:**

    1. At the beginning of a sentence.
    2. In front of a verb or between a helping verb and a main verb.
    3. Right after the verb.
    4. At the end of a sentence.

PRACTICE

To test your knowledge of adverbs, circle all of the adverbs in the paragraph that follows.

The Little Rock Crisis

[1]"The Little Rock Crisis" is the name widely given to a series of events that took place in Little Rock, Arkansas, during the 1957 school year. [2]On September 4, Arkansas National Guardsmen with drawn bayonets stopped a fifteen-year-old African-American girl at the entrance to Little Rock's Central High School and motioned her

back into a crowd that loudly threatened her. [3]The legal issue behind this frightening confrontation was the Little Rock School Board's acknowledgement that it had to desegregate the city's public schools. [4]The moral issue behind the desegregation decision was embodied in nine African-American teenagers, aged fourteen to sixteen. [5]In spite of the opposition of much of the city's population, these young people had bravely volunteered to be the first to integrate the school system; as a result, they became deeply and personally involved in the struggle for civil rights. [6]In thinking back on the events of that school year, most of the "Little Rock Nine," as the teenagers were called, vividly remember their experiences. [7]Now middle-aged, the Little Rock Nine can still clearly recall their terrifyingly close calls with violence, ranging from threats against them to the reality of violence when the high school was overrun by a mob. [8]On that occasion, the teenagers were dramatically rescued by police who drove them safely home. [9]One of the Nine remembers politely thanking her driver for the ride; looking back, she feels that she should have said, "Thank you for my life."

CHAPTER 20

Using Prepositional Phrases

▼ CHAPTER PREVIEW

So far in this unit, you have looked at **single words** that add details to sentences by describing nouns, pronouns, or verbs. Sometimes, a **group of words** can add details to a sentence by describing nouns or verbs.

> She went.

> She went **to the library.**

In the first sentence, you cannot tell where the person went. These details are supplied in the second sentence by a **prepositional phrase that tells *where.***

> He noticed the stares.

> He noticed the stares **of the saleswomen.**

In the first sentence, you cannot tell who was staring. The second sentence puts this information in a **prepositional phrase** that **describes the noun *stares.***

In this chapter, you will study prepositional phrases, and learn which words go with certain prepositions and which prepositions might give you trouble in your writing.

A Professional Writer Uses Prepositional Phrases

About the Reading: Irving Howe was born in New York in 1920. In addition to editing volumes of Yiddish poetry, Howe has written and edited a number of books on the topic of American literature. The following selection from *World of Our Fathers* (1976) describes the treatment of newcomers to America arriving at Ellis Island. Ellis Island, located in New York Harbor, served as the official point of entry for European immigrants into the United States from 1892 to 1943. During this period, thousands of immigrants, many of whom spoke no English, were processed daily at Ellis Island by overworked U.S. officials.

As You Read: The prepositional phrases in the reading have been printed in bold type. Notice the words that begin and end each phrase, and pay close attention to the way the phrases function in each sentence.

From *World of Our Fathers*

[1]**On Ellis Island** they pile **into the massive hall** that occupies the entire width **of the building.** [2]They break **into dozens of lines,** divided **by metal railings,** where they file **past the first doctor.** [3]Men whose breathing is heavy, women trying to hide a limp or deformity **behind a large bundle**—these are marked **with chalk, for later inspection.** [4]Children **over the age of two** must walk **by themselves,** since it turns out that not all can. [5](A veteran inspector recalls: "Whenever a case aroused suspicion, the alien was set aside **in a cage apart from the rest** . . . and his coat lapel or shirt marked **with colored chalk,** the color indicating why he had been isolated.") [6]One **out of five or six** needs further medical checking—H chalked **for heart,** K **for hernia,** Sc **for scalp,** X **for mental defects.**

After You Read: Refer to the reading selection to complete the following items:

1. List the first word of each phrase in sentences 1 through 4.

   _____

   _____

2. Circle the two answers that best describe the last word in each of the prepositional phrases in sentences 1 through 4.

   noun   adjective   pronoun   adverb

3. In sentence 4, which two phrases appear in a row? _____

   _____

4. In sentence 5, the phrase "apart from the rest" begins with a two-word preposition, **apart from.** Which phrase in sentence 6 begins with a combination of two prepositions? _____

   _____

5. In sentence 3, which prepositional phrase tells *where* the women try to hide imperfections? _____

6. In sentence 4, which phrase tells *how* the children must walk? _____ What phrases tell *which* children must walk? _____

7. In sentence 1, which phrase describes the noun **width?**

   _____

8. In sentence 6, which phrase describes the pronoun **one?**

   _____

9. In sentence 5, which phrase describes the verb **marked?**

   _____

Prepositional Phrases

A **prepositional phrase** is a **group of words that begins with a preposition, ends with a noun or pronoun, and includes any words in between.** The noun or pronoun that comes at the end of a prepositional phrase is called the **object** of the preposition.

> Sally arrived early **at the college library.**
> (**At** is the preposition and the noun *library* is the object.)

> Walter split his time **between his classes and his job.**
> (**Between** is the preposition, and the nouns *classes* and *job* are the objects. The preposition **between** often takes more than one object.)

COMMON ONE-WORD PREPOSITIONS

about	beside	of
above	between	off
across	by	on
after	during	outside
against	except	over
along	for	past
among	from	since
around	in	through
at	inside	throughout
before	into	to
behind	like	toward
below	near	under

underneath	upon	within
up	with	without

COMMON PREPOSITIONS OF MORE THAN ONE WORD

along with	in addition to	out of
because of	in spite of	similar to
except for	next to	

Use a **prepositional phrase to describe a noun, a pronoun, or a verb.**

His father is the man **in the coat and tie.**
("in the coat and tie" describes the noun *man*)

My roommate was dating someone **with red hair.**
("with red hair" describes the pronoun *someone.*)

Rene swam **across the pool.**
("across the pool" describes the verb *swam.*)

Use **prepositional phrases,** like adjectives and adverbs, to **answer questions like** *where, when, whose, why, how, which,* and *what kind.*

The woman talked **throughout the entire movie.** (when)

The instructor assigned a whole book **of short stories.** (what kind)

My aunt always dresses **in style.** (how)

Because of his illness, Santiago was unable to attend class. (why)
(Use a comma after an introductory phrase.)

Note: Be sure that you do not mistake **to** + **verb** for a prepositional phrase. Remember that **to** + **verb** (**to go, to see, to eat,** and so on) cannot be a prepositional phrase because the object of the preposition cannot be a verb; it must be a noun or pronoun.

You may wish to use **more than one prepositional phrase in a single sentence.**

Late **for work,** Brigette applied her makeup **on the subway.**

My brother **in the army** was sent **to Saudi Arabia.**

You may wish to use **two or more prepositional phrases in a row.**

I learned a lot **about human biology in Professor Simm's class.**

The football team went back **to the locker room during half-time for a pep talk from the coach.**

Copyright © 1994 Macmillan College Publishing Company

APPLICATION ONE

Underline any prepositional phrases. Remember, a sentence may have more than one prepositional phrase or no prepositional phrases at all.

EXAMPLE: Carlos gave his placement test <u>to the woman</u> <u>at the desk</u>.

1. The lifeguard's whistle fell into the pool.
2. Yolanda enrolled in the nursing program.
3. Wayne found himself between a snarling dog and a six-foot fence.
4. In summer, the children visit their father in Louisiana.
5. The student's tears dropped onto his paper when he saw the grade of "D."
6. Our flight from Detroit to Dallas was delayed.
7. The African history class was the most interesting course I ever took.
8. Just after Henry financed his car, the interest rate plunged to an all-time low.
9. One of the most difficult times for Kewani was his first year in the United States.
10. The intruder tied the couple to a chair.

APPLICATION TWO

Add a prepositional phrase to each sentence.

EXAMPLE: The **in the front row** man spoke first.

1. The truck driver unloaded the cargo.

2. Zachary punched Nathan.

3. She wanted to travel.

4. Smiling nervously, the young man stepped forward.

5. Jeanie introduced her new boyfriend.

6. The final exam was scheduled.

7. Rochelle decided to see a doctor.

8. Clem and Loren drove off.

9. Zolinda volunteered to work.

10. I will meet you.

Expressions

Certain words combine with prepositions to form fixed expressions. When you use one of these words, be sure to combine it with the preposition your reader will expect.

COMMON PREPOSITIONAL EXPRESSIONS

acquainted with	depend on	shocked at
addicted to	fond of	similar to
apply for	identical to	specialize in
approve of	interested in	succeed in
consist of	interfere with	take advantage of
contrast with	object to	worry about
convenient for	pleased with	
deal with	reason with	

Sometimes the same word can team up with different prepositions to form expressions with different meanings. Notice the different meanings formed by combining various prepositions with the words **agree, angry, differ,** and **grateful.**

EXPRESSION	EXPRESSION USED IN A SENTENCE
agree on (a plan)	They **agreed on** a divorce settlement.
agree to (someone's proposal)	She **agreed to** the conditions of the contract.
angry about or at (a person or thing)	Her husband was **angry about** her spending.
	Sam was **angry at** the delay.
angry with (a person)	The professor was **angry with** the counselor.
differ from (a thing)	An adverb **differs from** an adjective.
differ with (a person)	I have to **differ with** you on that point.
grateful for (something)	The family was **grateful for** the church's help.
grateful to (someone)	Corinne is **grateful to** her professor for his good advice.

APPLICATION

Circle the correct expression in parentheses.

EXAMPLE: She was (addicted to, addicted on) talk radio shows.

1. The expensive meal (consisted on, consisted of) a microscopic piece of fish and three tiny carrots.
2. Everyone in the class was (fond for, fond of) Mrs. Watanabe.
3. John (took advantage of, took advantage for) the two-for-one coupon.
4. Jeremy, Karyn, and Sasha (agreed to, agreed on) a schedule to work on their group research project.
5. Hilary's parents do not (approve of, approve on) her punker boyfriend.
6. I (differ from, differ with) my parents on political issues.
7. Garrett tried not to (worry on, worry about) his upcoming chemistry midterm.
8. Credit card companies often encourage students to (apply to, apply for) their own credit cards.
9. My history professor's structured teaching style certainly (contrasts on, contrasts with) my English professor's informal style.
10. Peter's quiz grades are (identical to, identical with) Alissa's quiz grades.

Troublesome Prepositions

If you are like many other student writers, you may have difficulty with a few prepositions.

1. ***in* and *on*.** To indicate time, use ***in*** before months or years used without any other dates and before seasons. Use ***on*** before days of the week, before holidays, and before months followed by a date.

    She started classes **in** August.

    Dee was born **in** 1975.

    In winter, people tend to get depressed.

    Final exams start **on** May 20.

    They always watch fireworks **on** the Fourth of July.

    The registrar's office will be closed **on** Monday.

    To indicate a place, use ***in*** to mean "inside of," and use ***on*** to mean "on top of " or "at a particular place."

    The professor finally found a pen **in** his desk.

    He visited his grandparents **in** Guatemala.

    I'm sure I left the book **on** the table.

The people she baby-sits for live **on** Pine Avenue.

2. *like.* Use **like** to mean "similar to." Don't confuse **like** with **as if,** which is a subordinating conjunction that takes a subject and a verb.

Her brother looks **like** Eddie Murphy.

Like my mother, I prefer reading to watching television.

S   HV   MV
He acted **as if** he had never seen a VCR before.

3. *before, since, after,* **and** *as.* **Before, since, after,** and **as** can be either prepositions or subordinating conjunctions. To decide whether they are used as prepositions, look to see whether they are followed by a subject and verb. If they are followed by a subject and verb, they are acting as subordinating conjunctions; if not, they are acting as prepositions.

I promised to meet her **before** class. (preposition)

S   V
I promised to meet her **before** I went to class. (subordinating conjunction)

APPLICATION

In each blank, write an appropriate word from the following list.

PREPOSITIONS	SUBORDINATING CONJUNCTIONS
as	
in	as
on	as if
like	before
before	since
since	after
after	

EXAMPLE: The instructor told us to put our blue books

_____**on**_____ our desks.

1. My father was born _____ Santo Domingo.

2. We always go to my uncle's _____ Christmas Eve.

3. Our literature professor acts _____ she has read every

book ever written.

4. My little brother eats just _____ a pig.

5. Professor Gonzalez was ill _____ Thursday.

6. _____ my friend warned me, parking was a nightmare the first day of classes.

7. I try to avoid going to school _____ the summer.

8. Jolene spent the summer _____ Connecticut working with children of AIDS patients.

9. Professor Horowitz lives _____ Crenshaw Boulevard.

10. If you want a room, you must make a reservation _____ April 4.

▼ CHAPTER REVIEW

- A **prepositional phrase** is a **group of words that begins with a preposition, ends with a noun or pronoun, and includes any words in between.**
- Use a **prepositional phrase to describe a noun, a pronoun, or a verb.**
- Use **prepositional phrases to answer questions like** *where, when, whose, why, how, which,* and *what kind.*
- Certain **words combine with prepositional phrases to form fixed expressions.**
- Be careful when using **troublesome prepositions** such as *in* and *on, like, before, after,* and *since.*

PRACTICE

Test your familiarity with prepositional phrases by underlining each of the prepositional phrases in the following paragraph.

Hero Street, U.S.A.

[1]The story of Hero Street, U.S.A., is the story of the lives and heroism of Mexican-American residents on a single street in the town of Silvis in northwestern Illinois. [2]Thousands of Mexicans came to the United States fleeing the revolution that tore apart their country from 1910 to 1917. [3]Some of these people found work with the Rock Island Railroad in the small town of Silvis. [4]Here the

Mexicans were allowed to live in boxcars, and their children were able to attend public schools. [5]By 1928, the Mexicans had saved enough money to buy a strip of unwanted land at the west end of town. [6]Twenty-two families built their homes on the muddy stretch known as Second Street. [7]When World War II began, the people of Second Street sent their sons, sometimes as many as six or seven boys from the same family. [8]When the Korean War broke out, Second Street continued to send its young men. [9]In all, 57 men from Second Street fought in World War II and Korea, the largest number of servicemen from the same ethnic background to come from any one area of comparable size during these conflicts. [10]Eight of these young men were killed in the line of duty. [11]This enormous sacrifice by the families on one short street sparked a movement to change the name of Second Street. [12]On Memorial Day in 1971, Second Street finally became Hero Street, U.S.A.

Using Modifiers in Your Own Writing

▼ CHAPTER PREVIEW

In the preceding chapters of this unit, you have learned that modifiers like adjectives, adverbs, and prepositional phrases can be used to add details to sentences. In this chapter, you will learn how you can use adjectives, adverbs, and prepositional phrases to add information to your writing and make it more lively. Then you will be given a choice of writing assignments, followed by a sample student essay on one of the topics. Finally, you will practice revising your own essay based on what you have learned in this unit.

Expanding the Sentence with Details

When a journalist covers a story for a newspaper, he or she must answer questions like *who, when, where,* and *how many* in order to give readers the complete story. When you write an essay, your reader needs this information too. On a sentence level, you can often supply this information with adjectives, adverbs, and prepositional phrases.

Melvin Johnson threatened to jump.

This sentence contains a basic fact, and it has a specific noun and verb, but it still leaves a lot of questions unanswered. Notice how adding various modifiers affects the basic sentence.

Melvin Johnson threatened to jump **off the bridge.** (prepositional phrase telling *where*)

Melvin Johnson threatened to jump off the **Golden Gate** Bridge. (adjective telling *which* bridge)

Thirty-year-old, unemployed Melvin Johnson threatened to jump off the Golden Gate Bridge. (adjectives telling *what kind* of man Mr. Johnson is)

Copyright © 1994 Macmillan College Publishing Company

On Sunday afternoon, thirty-year-old, unemployed Melvin Johnson threatened to jump off the Golden Gate Bridge. (prepositional phrase telling *when*)

On Sunday afternoon, thirty-year-old, unemployed Melvin Johnson threatened **repeatedly** to jump off the Golden Gate Bridge. (adverb telling *how* he threatened)

Not only do the modifiers in this final sentence add details, but they also make the sentence more interesting.

In your writing, once you have gotten the basic facts on paper, go back and see if you can make your writing more precise by adding modifiers that give information like *what kind, how, where,* or *when.*

APPLICATION

Rewrite each sentence adding at least two modifiers.

> *EXAMPLE:*   Max walked.
>
> **Max walked slowly toward the door.**

1. Johanna whispered.

   _____

2. The woman spent her check.

   _____

3. Lucille and Armando shouted.

   _____

4. Peter called his girlfriend to discuss their plans.

   _____

5. The Porsche sped.

   _____

Writing Assignments

Choose one of the following topics to develop into an essay:

1. Describe an event that marked a milestone or achievement in your life. Graduation, marriage, childbirth, anniversary, notification of a promotion—all of these mark a change or accomplishment in life. As you describe the event, try to include details that re-create

the event for your reader, and be sure to let the reader know why the event holds such significance for you.

2. Tell about a time that peer pressure caused you to act in a way that you would not otherwise have acted. This action may have been positive, like taking college prep courses instead of the easier ones, or it may have been negative, like taking drugs. Besides describing the way you acted in response to peer pressure, let the reader know how this action has affected you in the long run.

To choose a topic, you might try one or both of the following:

1. Brainstorm the types of things that people consider to be milestones or achievements. To get you started, think of all the occasions for which you can buy Hallmark cards.
2. Make a list of the kinds of things that people are pressured into by others. To get started, you might make headings like school things, social things, personal things, physical things, and work things.

Once you have chosen what you are going to write about, try focusing on one of the prewriting strategies from Unit 1 on your particular topic. You might want to brainstorm the details leading up to and surrounding an achievement, for example, or you might want to freewrite about the peer pressure you responded to. To clarify the direction your essay will take, try completing one of the following sentences (or make up a similar one of your own):

_____ was a real milestone in my life.

_____ was one of my proudest achievements.

Peer pressure caused me to do something _____.

A Student Responds to One of the Writing Assignments

About the Reading: The essay that follows was written by 20-year-old Edgar Rivas. Rivas, who enjoys writing, plans to major in microbiology and minor in English. While he is attending classes, Rivas also works as a programmer's assistant.

As You Read: Pay close attention to the way this student writer uses modifiers to add details to his essay. Notice also how he opens and closes his essay.

....

My Achievement

The big event was about to begin, and anxiety and enthusiasm ran in the air. All my fellow students looked gorgeous.

1

Most of the guys were wearing black suits with matching ties and shirts. Their shiny shoes reflected the lighting of the big football field. The girls looked so beautiful. Their high heels and their dazzling dresses made them all look like princesses. I remember how everyone began waltzing down the path as the enchanting old melody of graduation was being performed by the elegant band. As I waltzed down that path I could only admire the wonders that had been done with the football field, as if it had been enchanted or something of the sort. There were hundreds of white, black, and silver balloons all over the field; the red bleachers had been all replaced by white bleachers where the spectators were to be seated. At the center of the rich green field, hundreds of white chairs had been placed like the rows of a church. I was excited by the audience. All that cheering, yelling, and shouting of names made everything much more exciting. The applause made me feel proud, not only of myself, but also of everyone else. There I was among all my other classmates who had perhaps struggled for the past four years to finally get high school over with. The ceremony began as the class president gave a speech, which lasted only a few minutes. Everyone was quiet; the graduates were stiff, anxious to hear their names being called to proudly receive that diploma they'd waited for. I was nervous, but patiently waiting my turn.

For me, finishing high school wasn't that easy. My first two **2** years of high school were perhaps the roughest. Getting used to the system and the new teachers, choosing the right people to hang around with and so on—all of that was just too complex. I made a few friends throughout the years, friends who were good, even excellent students. But there were also those who weren't so perfect—the trouble makers, the no self-esteem ones, who are always trying to drag others into their no-good life, the ones who decide to dip out of school whenever they feel like it.

I hate to admit that I had been dragged by those students **3** whose future only ends in misery. I had started off good in high school, making A's and B's, but once I joined, or was being pressured to join, that gang of isolated lowriders, my grades dropped tremendously low. I began cutting class sometimes for a whole week, perhaps two weeks. I would leave campus just to go smoke grass with my friends. I would usually meet them in back of the school, and from there we would go to Victor's house, which was only a few blocks away from school. Sometimes I wouldn't even go to school. I would just go straight to his house in the mornings to spend the whole day there with them. We would just smoke and listen to some old records. At the time, I didn't know what I was getting myself into. I had only a few months to graduate from high school, but instead, I got kicked out for too many absences. I didn't really care. I would still hang out with those lazy friends of mine.

One night I saw a special report on TV, showing how the **4** dropout rates had increased, and how some dropouts had ended up on the streets, some of them becoming drug dealers. It was sad, but for some strange reason, I felt connected with that percentage of dropouts. A lot of thoughts came to mind. Confused and isolated, I decided to look back at my grades, and to see all the awards I had once earned, and I realized how little by little I was throwing off my life.

After a conference with the principal and my parents, I returned to school. I began to attend regularly; I even did some extra time in detention to clear my bad record. I studied harder to finish school in good standing. I wanted to bring my grades up and make up the time I had wasted. During that period, I made new friends whose time was spent productively in school activities. I made every effort to avoid my old peers. From this side of the picture, I could see where their lives were going to end up. I began to think of my future and how I wanted to be a successful engineer and to be recognized as someone important, not as a loafer. I wanted to go to college and make my dreams a reality. But I knew that would depend on my hard work and efforts. With extra work and effort, I believe everyone can accomplish everything. **5**

The night was clear and full of excitement, the audience stood up on their feet, all the names had been called, and the principal was ready to introduce the class of 1990. As the class was introduced, all of the students switched their tassels from left to right and tossed their caps up in the sky. As I switched my tassel from left to right, I knew I had taken the first step toward making my dreams a reality. My diploma was the key to the next door in my life. I knew there would be challenges and obstacles ahead, but if I was able to graduate from high school, I could also achieve a career. In the future, I could only see myself being successful. My parents would be proud of me, and I would also be proud of myself. In the future, I will look back and laugh at the crazy things I once did with those crazy friends of mine. **6**

In my hands I carried the key to the future, my high school diploma. **7**

After You Read: Refer to the student essay to complete the following items:

1. Circle the letter of the sentence that best sums up the main idea of the essay:

   a. My high school graduation was a night I'll never forget.

   b. Graduating from high school had a special importance for me because I almost became a high school dropout.

   c. My high school diploma provided the key to my future.

2. The essay begins with the description of a scene—a high school graduation. How effective do you find this introduction? Is it a

good lead-in to the student's explanation of how he came to be participating in graduation? Explain.

_____

_____

_____

3. In what paragraph toward the end of the essay does the writer return to the description of the graduation ceremony? _____ How well do you think this strategy works to tie the parts of the essay together? _____

_____

_____

4. This writer uses a lot of modifiers to add details to his essay. Look closely at the first paragraph and complete the items that follow:

a. List five adjectives that appear in the first paragraph.

_____

b. List three adverbs that appear in the first paragraph.

_____

c. Copy down an appropriate prepositional phrase from the first paragraph to illustrate each function:

Tell *where* _____

Tell *which one* _____

Tell *what kind* _____

Tell *how long* _____

5. In the following sentence from paragraph 3, the adjective in bold type is being used incorrectly as an adverb.

I had started off **good** in high school, making A's and B's, but once I joined, or was being pressured to join, that gang of isolated lowriders, my grades dropped tremendously low.

What word should the writer use instead of **good**? _____

Using Modifiers to Add Details to Your Writing

Using modifiers to add details to your writing serves two purposes: It gives the reader additional information, and it makes your writing more interesting. Try the following revision strategy to add details to your essay:

1. Look over your essay and find two nouns that are not described by an adjective. Add adjectives to describe these nouns.
2. Locate two words in your essay—verbs, adjectives, or adverbs—that could be described by an adverb other than **only, never, not,** or **always.** Add adverbs to describe these words.
3. Add a prepositional phrase to at least two of the sentences in your essay.

▼ CHAPTER REVIEW

• Use modifiers like **adjectives, adverbs,** and **prepositional phrases** to **add informative details** to your writing and make it more **interesting.**

Highlights

Adjectives

- An **adjective describes a noun or pronoun** by telling *which, what kind, how many or how much,* or *whose.* Many **different types of words can function as adjectives** as long as the words describe nouns or pronouns.
- Use the **comparative** form (*-er, more*) of an adjective to **compare two persons or things.** Use the **superlative** form (*-est, most*) of an adjective to **compare three or more people or things.**
- Use **demonstrative** adjectives (***this, these, that, those***) to **point out which noun** you mean.
- **Adjectives usually come right before the words they describe. However, an adjective that follows a linking verb can describe the subject of the verb.**

Adverbs

- Use an **adverb** to **describe a verb, an adjective, or another adverb.** Adverbs tell *when, where, how,* and *under what condition.*
- **Many adverbs are formed by adding *-ly* to adjectives.** The words ***not*** and ***never*** are always **adverbs.**
- Many adverbs have **special forms** to **compare** people or things. Use the **comparative form** (*-er, more*) to **compare two persons or things.** Use the **superlative form** (*-est, most*) to **compare three or more persons or things.**
- Adverbs usually appear in one of **four positions:**

  1. At the beginning of a sentence
  2. In front of a verb or between a helping verb and a main verb
  3. Right after the verb
  4. At the end of a sentence.

Prepositional Phrases

- A **prepositional phrase** is a **group of words that begins with a preposition, ends with a noun or pronoun, and includes any words in between.**
- Use a **prepositional phrase to describe a noun, a pronoun, or a verb.**
- Use **prepositional phrases to answer questions like** *where, when, whose, why, how, which,* and *what kind.*
- Certain **words combine with prepositional phrases to form fixed expressions,** such as "apply for" or "fond of."
- Be careful when using **troublesome prepositions** such as ***in, on, like, before, after,*** and ***since.***

270

Copyright © 1994 Macmillan College Publishing Company

In Your Writing

- Use **adjectives, adverbs, and prepositional phrases** to **add details for information and interest.**

PRACTICE

Use the sentences that follow to test your mastery of the material in Unit 5. If you have difficulty, go back and review the information in Chapters 18–21.

A. Put an adjective in each blank in the following sentences:

    EXAMPLE: The _____**embarrassed**_____ girl began to giggle.

1. Both professors assigned _____ books.

2. The _____ child bit his _____ sister.

3. My grandmother is a(n) _____ woman.

4. The _____ student spoke _____ English.

5. The two teenaged boys ordered _____ large pizzas just for themselves.

6. The _____ instructor was upset by the student's _____ behavior.

7. Andrea enrolled in a(n) _____ course.

8. Sergio felt _____ about giving his in-class presentation.

9. _____ sister lives in a(n) _____ part of town.

10. The _____ dog lay on a(n) _____ rug.

B. Put an adverb in each blank in the following sentences:

    EXAMPLE: _____**Cautiously**_____, Vinny put his hand in the snake's cage.

1. Marcel _____ complained about the lack of sunshine in Oregon.

2. The firefighters _____ extinguished the flames.

3. The young woman waited _____ as a clerk looked over her application for food stamps.

4. The tired child wailed _____.

5. _____, Hilda awaited the results of her math placement test.

6. The police officers _____ responded to the call for help.

7. Have you _____ decided what you want to order off the menu?

8. The car in front of ours stopped _____.

9. The new father held the baby _____.

10. Mr. Miyamoto _____ offered to drive.

C. Circle the correct adverb or adjective form in parentheses.

    EXAMPLE: Her homemade strudel tastes really (well, (good)).

1. (Impatient, Impatiently), the crowd waited for the speaker to begin.
2. She is the (more selfish, most selfish) woman I know.
3. I read the directions (careful, carefully) before I began.
4. He is (more easier, easier) to get along with than his wife.
5. Amy had a (real, really) difficult time saving money.
6. I (sure, surely) hope so.
7. The old roof leaked (bad, badly) whenever it rained.
8. Maria's presentation was (more thoughtful, more thoughtfully) prepared than mine.
9. Albert is (awful, awfully) scary in his monster costume.
10. Of all my friends, Teri lives (most extravagant, most extravagantly).

D. Add a prepositional phrase to each sentence.

                                      out of her chair
    EXAMPLE: The woman fell˄

1. I remember my first day.

2. Wally was not prepared.

3. The parents proudly introduced their children.

4. The boa constrictor escaped.

5. The movie was a big disappointment.

6. The files contained incriminating information.

7. The book tells about notorious women.

8. Worried, he scanned the horizon.

9. A sign said, "No shoes, no shirt, no service!"

10. The Perez family finally bought their dream home.

UNIT **6**

Maintaining Consistency and Parallelism

CHAPTER **22**

Consistency in Time

CHAPTER PREVIEW

As a general rule, if you begin writing in the past tense, stay in the past tense; if you begin writing in the present tense, stay in the present tense. The paragraph that follows shifts back and forth between the past and the present:

> As I **walked** into the room, I immediately **knew** I **was** in trouble. Every student **has** a blue book, and everyone **has** a pen. The eyes of each person **are riveted** on the blackboard, where the teacher **was writing** an essay question. I **realized** that I **do**n't **have** any materials and I **do**n't **have** a clue about how to answer the question. Then, just as I **am** about to panic, it **dawned** on me that I **was** in the wrong classroom.

The paragraph should be all in the present:

> As I **walk** into the room, I immediately **know** I **am** in trouble. Every student **has** a blue book, and everyone **has** a pen. The eyes of each person are riveted on the blackboard, where the teacher **is writing** an essay question. I **realize** that I **do**n't **have** any materials and I **do**n't **have** a clue about how to answer the question. Then, just as I **am** about to panic, it **dawns** on me that I **am** in the wrong classroom.

Or it should be all in the past:

> As I **walked** into the room, I immediately **knew** I **was** in trouble. Every student **had** a blue book, and everyone **had** a pen. The eyes of each person **were riveted** on the blackboard, where the teacher **was writing** an essay question. I **realized** that not only **did** I not **have** any materials but I **did**n't **have** a clue about how to answer the question. Then, just as I **was** about to panic, it **dawned** on me that I **was** in the wrong classroom.

Copyright © 1994 Macmillan College Publishing Company

The term *consistency* means "being the same throughout." To keep your writing consistent in time, you need to avoid shifting from one tense to another for no good reason. In this chapter, you will practice maintaining **consistency in time.**

A Professional Writer Maintains Consistency in Time

About the Reading: Poet Garrett Hongo is Japanese-American. He was born in Hawaii but came with his family to Los Angeles, where he grew up. His 1988 collection of poetry, entitled *The River of Heaven*, was a finalist for the 1989 Pulitzer Prize in poetry. When he is not in Hawaii, Hongo is associate professor of English and director of creative writing at the University of Oregon. The selection that follows is taken from an essay called "Kubota," which appeared originally in *Ploughshares*. In this essay, Hongo tells about his grandfather, Kubota, who was born in Hawaii but was sent by his Japanese-born father to Hiroshima, Japan, for a formal education. His ties with Japan would cause Kubota to come under suspicion by the FBI after the bombing of Pearl Harbor. At the time that Hongo writes, his grandfather is no longer alive.

As You Read: Verbs in the reading have been printed in bold type. Pay close attention to Hongo's use of tense.

From "Kubota"

[1]I **am** Kubota's eldest grandchild, and I **remember** him as a lonely, habitually silent old man who **lived** with us in our home near Los Angeles for most of my childhood and adolescence. [2]It **was** the fifties, and my parents **had emigrated** from Hawaii to the mainland in the hope of a better life away from the old sugar plantation. [3]After some success, they **had sent** back for my grandparents and **taken** them in. [4]And it was my grandparents who **did** the work of the household while my mother and father **worked** their salaried city jobs. [5]My grandmother **cooked** and **sewed, washed** our clothes, and **knitted** in the front room under the light of a huge lamp with a bright three-way bulb. [6]Kubota **raised** a flower garden, **read** up on soils and grasses in gardening books, and **planted** a zoysia lawn in front and a dichondra one in back. [7]He **planted** a small patch near the rear block wall with green onions, eggplant, white Japanese radishes, and cucumber. [8]While he **hoed** and **spaded** the loamless, clayey earth of Los Angeles, he **sang** particularly plangent songs in Japanese about plum blossoms and bamboo groves.

After You Read: Refer to the reading to complete the following items:

1. List the verbs in sentences 4 through 8.

2. Are the verbs you listed in question 1 in the past or present tense?

   _____

3. Circle the letter of the answer that best completes the following statement: The verb **had emigrated** in sentence 2 uses **had** + past participle because
   a. the action described took place before now.
   b. the action described took place before the time the author is remembering.
   c. the action described takes place in the present.

4. List the verbs in sentence 1.

5. Which verbs in sentence 1 are in the present tense? _____

   Which are in the past tense? _____

6. Given the information that Kubota is no longer alive when Hongo writes, can you think of a logical reason that Hongo might use both present and past tense in the same sentence?

   _____

   _____

   _____

Consistency in Time

To maintain **consistency in time,** avoid shifting from one tense to another without a good reason.

Shift in time: We **arrived** at the halfway point on the trail.

Suddenly, snowflakes **begin** to fall.

Consistent: We **arrived** at the halfway point on the trail.

Suddenly, snowflakes **began** to fall.

Consistent: We **arrive** at the halfway point on the trail.

Suddenly, snowflakes **begin** to fall.

The sentences in the first example are not consistent with one another: The first sentence is in the past tense, and the second one is in the present tense even though the actions being described should be happening at the same time. In the second example, both actions are in the past tense; in the third example, they are both in the present tense.

APPLICATION

Underline the first verb in each sentence, and then circle the verb in parentheses that is consistent with the underlined verb.

> EXAMPLE: Whenever my grandfather <u>speaks</u>, my father (listens,)
> listened).

1. As soon as Delilah walks in from work, she (plops, plopped) down on the sofa.
2. We were having breakfast when the tornado (hits, hit).
3. The students laughed hysterically when the light fixture (falls, fell) on Professor Evans' head during his lecture on gravity.
4. Cheryl and Guy waited in line until the ticket booth (opens, opened).
5. Whenever he turns on the radio, his roommates (complain, complained).
6. My husband put my new top in the dryer and (shrinks, shrank) it.
7. While Annique was eating her salad, blue cheese dressing (drips, dripped) down her chin.
8. The self-conscious child blushed when her pushy mother (forces, forced) her to sing for company.
9. At midnight, she finally closes her book and (goes, went) to bed.
10. After he searched for weeks, Armando (finds, found) the perfect job as a women's trainer at the gym.

Time Relationship

Sometimes you will need to combine different tenses to reflect accurately the time relationship between actions.

Last year, I **wanted** to quit college, but now I **am considering** graduate school.

(I **wanted** in the past, but I **am considering** right now.)

When you encounter a combination in past and present tenses, ask yourself if a shift in tense makes sense or not. If the shift is not consistent with meaning, it is incorrect.

Incorrect: Whatever time I **arrived** on campus, I **have** trouble finding a parking space.

(There is no reason to shift from past to present.)

Correct: As a small boy, Huey **wanted** to be a lion tamer; today he **is** an elementary school teacher.

(He **wanted** in the past, but he **is** right now.)

APPLICATION

In the blank, write the correct tense of the verb in parentheses. Consider the meaning of the sentences when you choose the verb.

EXAMPLE: As soon as Elias wakes up, he _____**does**_____ one

hundred sit-ups. (does, did)

1. They were walking down the street when the blackout

   _____. (occurs, occurred)

2. After they moved away from home, Jackie and Rory

   _____ an apartment together. (rent, rented)

3. Uri bought a dog and immediately _____ the animal in an

   obedience class. (enroll, enrolled)

4. Sara went out on a boat for the first time and _____ terri-

   bly seasick. (becomes, became)

5. They were on their way to a baseball game when their brakes

   _____. (fail, failed)

6. Whenever she gets mad, Joan stomps out and _____ the

   door. (slams, slammed)

7. Prudence works hard and _____ even harder. (plays,

   played)

8. When she first got a secretarial job, she thought she would love it

forever; now, she _____ to be a real estate agent. (wants, wanted)

9. When Raul stood up to get his diploma, his family _____. (cheers, cheered)

10. At the age of fourteen, Jessica ran away from home and _____ to make her own way in the world. (begins, began)

▼ CHAPTER REVIEW

- To maintain **consistency in time,** avoid shifting from one tense to another without a good reason.
- If you **combine different tenses to reflect the time relationship between actions,** ask yourself if there is a good reason to shift from one tense to another.

PRACTICE

To test your ability to maintain consistency in time, circle the verb tense in parentheses that best maintains consistency.

Soaps

[1]Soap operas—which got their name because they were sponsored by manufacturers of soap products—(**originate, originated**) in the 1930s, when radio (**provide, provided**) entertainment for Americans who (**are, were**) anxious for relief from the poverty and stress (**cause, caused**) by the Great Depression. [2]Today, millions of Americans (**watch, watched**) one or more soaps on a regular basis. [3]In fact, according to researchers, soap operas now (**are, were**) so popular that sometimes soaps fans actually (**confuse, confused**) the world of the soap opera with the reality of daily life. [4]Contrary to popular opinion, soaps fans (**are, were**) not exclusively female; in fact, today large

numbers of men (**watch, watched**) soaps. [5]Nor, increasingly, (**are, were**) the majority of soaps fans people at home with small children. [6]One of the most interesting statistics about the modern soap opera fan (**reveals, revealed**) that college students (**make, made**) up a large portion of the audience. [7]People who are at work during the day routinely (**tape, taped**) their favorite soaps and (**view, viewed**) them in the evenings. [8]In an increasingly complex and hurried America, why (**do, did**) so many people find soap operas so compelling? [9]Research (**suggests, suggested**) that Americans (**find, found**) comfort in watching the troubles of others, believing that their own lives, however bad, (**are, were**) not as bad as those of the soap opera characters. [10]Research also (**shows, showed**) that the main theme of the soap operas—the power of family—(**holds, held**) endless fascination for viewers.

CHAPTER 23

Maintaining Consistency in Person

▼ CHAPTER PREVIEW

Just as you need to maintain consistency in time when you write, you also need to maintain consistency in **person.** If you are writing to or about people in general, you should not suddenly switch to addressing the reader as *you.* The sentence that follows is not consistent in person:

> **People** should not drink and drive; otherwise, **you** are a potential killer.

If you consider what this sentence actually says, it does not make sense. If other people drink and drive, that doesn't make *you* a potential killer; it makes *them* potential killers. The sentence makes more sense after it has been revised for consistency:

> **People** should not drink and drive; otherwise, **they** are potential killers.

Or:

> **You** should not drink and drive; otherwise, **you** are a potential killer.

In this chapter, you will learn more about the concept of person and practice maintaining consistency in person.

A Professional Writer Maintains Consistency in Person

About the Reading: Whitney Otto has taught creative writing and composition at various colleges in Southern California. Her first novel, *How to Make an American Quilt,* was published to critical acclaim in 1991. The novel is actually a collection of seven interrelated short stories interspersed with seven chapters that give historical information and technical instructions about quilt making. Each short story is the story of one of the women in the Grasse Quilting Circle. Because of the unique structure of the novel, Otto uses *I* in some sections, *you* in others, and *she* or *people* in still others. The selection that follows is composed of pieces taken from different chapters.

As You Read: Pay close attention to the boldface words in each excerpt, and try to discern the author's reason for choosing the words she does for each excerpt.

Excerpts from *How to Make an American Quilt*

1. **I** refused, at an early age, to be a specter in **my** own world. **I** decided that **I** would not be whisked away, so **I** sought to anchor **myself** to society, to make them see *me,* Anna Neale, child of a black mother (deceased) and a white father (whereabouts unknown and unacknowledged); gave birth to one child, **my** daughter, Marianna Neale; became undisputed leader and founder of the Grasse Quilting Circle (recognized nationally for superior and original work).

2. As **you** prepare to join **your** blocks, affix them to the diningroom wall or pin them to a set of drapes or arrange them upon the bed **you** share with **your** husband. **You** want to imagine how they will look once bound together.

3. Many of **their** neighbors cannot recall a time when **Glady Joe** and **Hy** were not "old." It seemed that **the two sisters** had always been languishing somewhere in **their** senior years, as if **they** had somehow executed the leap from girlhood to middle age to senior citizen, lacking any sort of transitional areas in between.

After You Read: Refer to the preceding excerpts to complete the following items:

1. Which excerpt addresses the reader directly? _____ List

   the words that are printed in bold type in that excerpt:

   _____

2. Which excerpt tells a person's story from the person's own point of

   view? _____ List the words that are printed in bold type in

   that excerpt: _____

3. Which excerpt relates information about someone other than the person speaking? _____ List the words that are printed in bold type in that excerpt: _____

Consistency in Person

English has three **persons:**

First person (the person speaking)—*I, we, us, our, ours*

Second person (the person being spoken to)—*you, your, yours*

Third person (the person or thing being spoken about)—*he, she, it, they, his, her, hers, its, their, one, anyone, a person, people*

When you write, you need to decide if you wish to speak directly to your reader (*you*), if you wish to speak personally (*I, we*), or if you wish to speak generally (*he, she, one, a person*). Your decision will depend on what you are writing and to whom you are writing.

Be sure to use the second person (*you*) only when you are speaking directly to the reader.

To change a tire, **you** will need to get the jack out of the trunk.
(In this case, the writer is giving instructions directly to the reader.)

Use the first person (*I, we*) when you write about a personal experience.

I could feel my leg twisting as the 270-pound linebacker threw himself on **me.**
(In this sentence, the writer is describing his own experience.)

Otherwise, use the third person.

People who buy homes today must consider a number of mortgage options.

Maintain consistency in person by sticking to one person.

Not consistent:	**College students** must budget their time, or **you** will spend a lot of late nights studying.
Consistent:	**College students** must budget their time, or **they** will spend a lot of late nights studying.
Consistent:	**You** must budget your time, or **you** will spend a lot of late nights studying.

APPLICATION

Circle the word or words in parentheses that are consistent with the rest of the sentence.

> *EXAMPLE:* If a person likes night life and shopping, (you, he or she) might find living in the country a bore.

1. Working students must decide (their, your) schedules carefully.
2. I enjoy aerobics because (you, I) feel so good after a workout.
3. Our high school science teacher wouldn't let (you, us) touch the chemistry equipment (yourself, ourselves).
4. Jermaine likes to go out with Marlena because (you, he) can be himself with her.
5. You will need a number 2 pencil to fill in (their, your) answer sheet.
6. Beginning swimmers should stay out of heavy surf until (you, they) have more experience.
7. When Teresa and her sister jog in the morning, (you, they) can see the sun come up.
8. If anyone wants to add this class, (you, he or she) must show the instructor proof of registration.
9. I'm finding I have to do a lot a memorizing if (I, you) want to get a passing grade in French.
10. If people want to be professional writers, (you, they) should consider taking a creative writing course.

▼ CHAPTER REVIEW

- **To maintain consistency in your writing, do not shift needlessly from one person to another.**
- **Determine which person to use based on what you are writing and to whom you are writing.**

PRACTICE

In each paragraph, test your ability to maintain consistency in person by writing an appropriate pronoun in each blank.

A. [1]If you want to get the best buy for your money nowadays,

_____ must be willing to forget about name brands. [2]When

you go to the supermarket, _____ need to read the ingredients on labels rather than just reading the name on the label. ³_____ will find that many store brands have the same contents as name brands; in fact, you might be surprised to learn that they are made by the same companies. ⁴When you shop for clothing, _____ will get more for your fashion dollars if _____ avoid designer labels. ⁵If you could watch clothing being manufactured, _____ would often see the same sewing machine operator making a designer jean and a J. C. Penney jean—from essentially the same pattern and material.

B. ¹When people talk about diseases, _____ often use words usually used to discuss war and crime. ²When a person gets cancer, for instance, _____ is described as a cancer *victim.* ³A disease like cholera is thought of as a serial killer that goes on a spree, *striking down* everyone who comes into contact with contaminated food sources. ⁴The AIDS virus, like an invading army, *invades* the body's cells. ⁵People who don't know that they are carriers of contagious disease are likened to *time bombs* because _____ could begin spreading a *deadly* disease without warning. ⁶Physicians, accordingly, become warriors or police officers; _____ arm themselves with medicine and technology to *fight* disease, even declaring *war* on a particular disease.

CHAPTER 24

Maintaining Parallel Structure

▼ CHAPTER PREVIEW

Read the two sentences that follow:

To get exercise, Eduardo likes to surf and jogging.

To get exercise, Eduardo likes to surf and to jog.

The first sentence may sound a bit awkward to you. An experienced reader who reads "to surf and" expects to read another **to** + **verb** item. In the second sentence, the reader's expectations are fulfilled by "to jog."

When **items joined by** *and* **or** *or* and **items in a list or series** are expressed in similar grammatical elements, such as the *to* + *verb* elements in the second sentence, they are said to be **parallel.**

In this chapter, you will practice using **parallel structure** for grammatical correctness and learn how using parallel structure can stress relationships between ideas.

A Professional Writer Uses Parallel Structure

About the Reading: The selection that follows is taken from a unique book called *The Meaning of Life* put together by David Friend and the editors of *Life* magazine. Three hundred people, from scientists to photographers, were asked to answer one question: What is the meaning of life? Their replies were limited to 250 words, or, in the case of photographers, to one photo. The paragraphs reprinted here are taken from the response given by Rosa Parks, a woman often credited with initiating the civil rights movement. Rosa Parks' 1955 arrest for refusing to sit in the back of the bus sparked a successful bus boycott in Montgomery, Alabama. Eventually the U.S. Supreme Court found Montgomery's discriminatory bus laws unconstitutional, and the power of collective behavior made itself felt. Parks has recently completed her autobiography.

As You Read: Many of the parallel elements have been printed in bold. Pay close attention to Parks' use of parallel structure not only to maintain grammatical correctness, but also to stress the relationship of one idea to another.

······

From *The Meaning of Life*

[1]Human beings are set apart from the animals. [2]We have **a spiritual self, a physical self** and **a conscience.** [3]Therefore, we can make choices and are responsible for the choices we make. [4]We may choose **order and peace,** or **confusion and chaos.** [5]**If we choose the former, we may cultivate and share our talents with others.** [6]**If we choose the latter, we will isolate and segregate others.** [7]We can also expand our vision to include the universe and the diversity of its people, or we can remain **narrow** and **shallow** and isolate those who are unfamiliar.

[8]To this day I believe we are here on earth to live, grow up, and do what we can to make this world a better place for all people to enjoy freedom. [9]Differences of **race, nationality** or **religion** should not be used to deny any human being citizenship **rights** or **privileges.** [10]Life is to be lived to its fullest so that death is just another chapter. [11]Memories of **our lives, our works** and **our deeds** will continue in others.

······

After You Read: Refer to the reading selection to complete the following items:

1. In sentence 2, what word is repeated at the beginning of each parallel element? _____

2. Copy the parallel elements from sentence 4 in the blanks below. Then label the nouns (N) and circle the coordinating conjunction in each element.

   _____   _____

3. In sentence 9, what three nouns are listed in a series?

   _____ _____ _____

   What two nouns are joined by *or*?

   _____ _____

4. In sentence 11, what one word precedes each noun in the parallel

   elements? _____

5. Occasionally, entire sentences can be parallel to one another.

   Which two sentences in this reading are parallel? _____

   What structural similarities can you find between these two sen-

   tences? _____

   _____

   How are the sentences related in meaning? _____

   _____

Parallel Structure

Use similar grammatical structures for items in **lists or series,** as
well as items joined by **and** or **or.**

> She told the child **to take out the trash** or **to forget his al-
> lowance.** (**to** + **verb** phrases)

> Nan stomped **through the living room** and **out the front door.**
> (prepositional phrases)

> Kevin married a woman **who enjoys sports** and **who has a ter-
> rific personality.** (**who**- clauses)

> Elvina's new watchdog is **mean, ugly,** and **loud.** (adjectives)

APPLICATION ONE

Practice identifying parallel elements by circling the element in each
group that is not like the others.

EXAMPLE: beautiful

attractive

witty

(has a great sense of humor)

1. under the stairs   2. red

   beneath the sink   like the ocean

   the liquor cabinet   black

   over the stove   green

3. taking a test
   making notes
   parking the car
   listen to the lecture

4. typewriters
   computers
   xerox machines
   taking dictation

5. slowly
   sadly
   thoughtfully
   work

6. who is talking
   which she recognized
   he intends to go
   that he deserves

7. taken his time
   to buy a new car
   hoped for the best
   seen the future

8. look
   eat
   listen
   being

9. she being homesick
   she visited her mother
   she bought a ticket
   she packed her bags

10. to drink coffee
    to exchange gossip
    to the lunchroom
    to meet people

APPLICATION TWO

Underline the parallel items in each of the sentences that follow:

EXAMPLE: Federico was an outstanding golfer and a champion swimmer.

1. Lisa and Margie shared a love of rare books and old movies.
2. Dr. Billings gave a speech on the state of the college and the need for reform.
3. The students giggled helplessly after the speaker tripped over the microphone cord and fell off the stage.
4. The art history majors and the engineering majors found that they had few goals in common.
5. Lorenzo and Marguerite despised dogs and children.
6. Linda had a troubled son who dropped out of school at 16 and who was arrested at 18.
7. Confused by the pressures of modern life, Mr. Vaca drove his aged mother to soccer practice and took his five-year-old son to the convalescent home.
8. Sonia trimmed the bushes, mowed the lawn, and swept the driveway.

9. Jim decided to join a gym and to take up jogging.

10. Maurice loved going to the races and betting on the horses.

Parallel Structure with Word Pairs

Whenever you use word pairs like *either . . . or, neither . . . nor, not only . . . but also,* or *both . . . and* to join ideas, make sure that the sentence elements that follow the second word of the pair are parallel to those that follow the first.

Not parallel:	He wanted either **to order the chicken** or **the fish.**
Parallel:	He wanted either **to order the chicken** or **to order the fish.**
Parallel:	He wanted to order either **the chicken** or **the fish.**

APPLICATION

After the second word of each pair, write an element that is parallel to what comes after the first word of the pair.

> *EXAMPLE:*   Jessie had neither read the material nor
>
> **brought home her book**_____.

1. Helen liked both to ski and _____.

2. The man at the door was neither a friend nor _____.

3. Doug is either going to the state university or _____

_____.

4. Lelani wanted both a family and _____.

5. That woman is in either my geography class or _____.

6. Neither Eddie nor _____ went on to college.

7. After graduation, Tricia wants either to go to law school or

_____.

8. Marlow not only despises dogs but also _____.

9. Both Carlton and _____ are in Professor Weiner's English

class.

10. Rika was voted not only student body president but also

_____ .

Parallel Structure for Effect

Use parallel structure to achieve balance in your writing and to stress relationships between ideas.

> Roger drove out of the bustling, crowded city. Then he entered the prairie, which was vast and empty.

These sentences are grammatically correct. However, the idea in the sentences might be expressed in a more balanced or effective manner by putting them in parallel structure and placing them in a single sentence.

> Roger drove out of the bustling, crowded city and into the vast, empty prairie.

Occasionally, make whole sentences parallel to one another to stress their relationship.

> Before he returned to college, Rafael's goals were unfocused, his lifestyle was self-destructive, and his future looked depressing. After he returned to college, Rafael's goals became clear, his lifestyle changed dramatically, and his future became bright.

APPLICATION

In items 1–8, fill in the blanks with parallel elements. In items 9 and 10, add a parallel sentence.

> EXAMPLE: Cristina <u>joined the army</u> and <u>had three children</u> before enrolling in college.

1. After _____ and _____, Arthur

   finally made it to school.

2. Ariel is known both for her _____ and for her

   _____ .

3. After a year of trying to _____, _____,

   and _____, Marissa is about to collapse.

4. The panicked cat ran _____ and _____ .

5. Professor Tyo is often described as _____ and

_____ .

6. Marlon has worked as _____, _____,

and _____ .

7. Lonnie never _____, nor did he ever _____ .

8. Horace drove _____ while his wife drove _____ .

9. Dave got a degree in philosophy in 1990.

_____

10. It is easy to buy the book and bring it to class.

_____

▼ CHAPTER REVIEW

- Use **similar grammatical structures** for **items in lists or series,** as well as **items joined by _and_ or _or._**
- **Whenever you use word pairs** like _either . . . or, neither . . . nor, not only . . . but also,_ or _both . . . and_ **to join ideas, make sure that the sentence elements that follow the second word of the pair are parallel to those that follow the first.**
- **Use parallel structure to achieve balance in your writing and to stress relationships between ideas.**

PRACTICE

Test your knowledge and understanding of parallel structure by underlining all examples of parallel structure in the following reading.

The Farmworkers' Theater

[1]One of the least remembered of the 1960s struggles for civil rights in the United States took place in the grape fields of Delano, California. [2]Angered and frustrated by their living and working conditions, Filipino and Mexican farmworkers decided to go on strike. [3]Under the leadership of Cesar Chavez, they organized themselves into a union—the United Farmworkers of America. [4]Reaction to the

Delano strike led to political actions, including a grape boycott. [5]It also inspired many young people to consider the lives and problems of migrant farmworkers. [6]One young man who was deeply interested in the farmworkers' struggle and who decided to do something about it was Luis Valdez, an English major at San Jose State College. [7]Valdez was the child of migrant farmworkers and was himself a field worker by the age of six. [8]In spite of the fact that his early schooling was constantly interrupted as his family followed the crops, Valdez won a scholarship to college, where he majored in English. [9]In 1965, the year after his graduation from college, Valdez became involved with the Delano farmworkers' struggle by founding a group to assist the grape boycott and the farmworkers' strike. [10]This group, which Valdez called El Teatro Campesino (The Farmworkers' Theater), would, he decided, put on short plays which Valdez called *actos*. [11]These one-act plays used humor to educate and to entertain the workers, and did so using both the English language and the Spanish language. [12]From the beginning, El Teatro Campesino was a political and a popular success. [13]It not only proved to be a vital part of the farmworkers' struggle but also proved to be a major influence in American drama.

Strengthening Your Writing Through Consistency and Parallel Structure

▼ CHAPTER PREVIEW

In the previous chapters of this unit, you have studied the concepts of consistency and parallel structure. In this chapter, you will be looking at how using parallel structure can strengthen your writing. Then you will be given a choice of writing assignments, followed by a sample student essay written on one of the topics. Finally, you will be asked to revise your own essay for consistency in person and time and for parallel structure.

Using Parallel Structure for Effect

As you learned in the previous chapter, using parallel form for items joined by *and* and for items in a series is a matter of being grammatically correct. However, using parallel wording to stress the relationship between ideas is a matter of stylistic choice. Both of the following sentences are grammatically correct, yet only the second one contains parallel elements:

> Patti is someone who knows her own mind; furthermore, she is not afraid to say what she thinks.

> Patti is someone who knows her mind and who says what she thinks.

The second sentence focuses the reader on the two traits by repeating the word **who** and describing the traits in similar terms. In your writ-

Copyright © 1994 Macmillan College Publishing Company

ing, use parallel elements not only to emphasize similarities (as in the preceding example), but also to stress contrasts.

> Trini is the smartest person I know when it comes to school knowledge· however, he knows little about practical things.

> Trini is the smartest person I know when it comes to school knowledge; he is the stupidest person I know when it comes to practical knowledge.

The second example repeats the word pattern of the first half of the sentence in the second half of the sentence to make the reader think about the relationship between the ideas in the two halves.

Whenever you write, always maintain parallel structure in series and items joined by *and.* Experiment with parallel elements in your writing when you want to place a special emphasis on the relationship between ideas.

APPLICATION

A lot of writers and speakers have used parallel structure to make powerful points or witty statements. Look at the parallel patterns in what they have written, and see if you can put your own words in the same patterns.

EXAMPLE: To err is human, to forgive divine.
—Alexander Pope

To ____**punish**____ is ____**easy**____,

to ____**discipline challenging**____.

1. Give me liberty or give me death.
   —Patrick Henry

   Give me _____ or give me _____.

2. I came to bury Caesar, not to praise him.
   —William Shakespeare

   I came to _____, not to _____.

3. We must stop talking about the American dream and start listening to the dreams of Americans.
   —Reubin Askew

   We must stop _____, and start _____.

Writing Assignments

Choose one of the following topics to develop into an essay:

1. Share one particular incident that illustrates why you feel a commitment to something you do. This something might be a job, a hobby, or an activity that you engage in regularly. Perhaps you had a particularly rewarding experience as a volunteer worker, or maybe you got a tremendous feeling of excitement playing guitar with your band one night. Try to include details that will make the reader share what you felt. You might want to use the present tense as the student writer does in "To Save a Life."

2. Tell about a job-related experience that taught you something about yourself or about life in general. Perhaps a horrendous day working in a day-care center made you decide you weren't ready to have children yet; maybe helping a particular student while working as a peer tutor made you decide to become a teacher. Try to include details that will re-create this experience for the reader.

To help you decide on a particular experience or incident to write about, first try making a list of every job—paid or volunteer—that you have ever held. Then make a list of any hobbies and interests you have. After you have finished, look over your lists to see what ideas you get.

Once you have decided on a topic, use a prewriting strategy from Unit 1 to help you generate ideas and come up with details. Then try to focus your essay by writing a single sentence that sums up the main idea. This sentence might look something like one of the following:

Doing volunteer work with abused children makes me feel good about myself.

My job as a salesclerk taught me that everyone deserves to be treated with respect.

A Student Responds to One of the Writing Assignments

About the Reading: The essay that follows was written by Nancy Poirier. She is both a college student and, as you will learn from her essay, an emergency medical technician. Poirier, 31 years old, is majoring in nursing, with a career goal of becoming an emergency room nurse.

As You Read: Notice the specific information the writer gives about the incident she describes, the equipment she works with, and the people she comes in contact with. Pay attention also to how the writer's use of the present tense makes you feel almost like you are there with her.

To Save a Life

Moments after the ambulance engine is turned off, the call comes over the air. Mike is the driver, and so I sit in the passenger seat, enjoying the ride and thinking about a friend's question earlier today: "Why are you an EMT (Emergency Medical Technician)?" We speed through intersections blaring the sirens, cursing the stupidity of drivers who insist on ignoring a large, fast-moving vehicle with red and yellow flashing lights. As usual, we do not know what this call is, but as we make the final turn, the sight of sheriffs' vehicles in front of our destination narrows the choices.

1

This call will be a person assaulted or possibly a heart-attack victim. Before I can unbuckle my seat belt, the sheriff is at my side of the ambulance. When I ask, "What do we have?" he just replies, "He's HIV positive. It doesn't look good." At this point, a male is approaching us, announcing that our patient has a very weak pulse. With the jump bag—an extensive first aid kit—slung over my shoulder, I climb the stairs of the house, the silence becoming more apparent the closer we get to the front door. The sheriff and the male who had met us outside the ambulance stay behind. It is only 2:00 P.M. and a sunny December day, yet the house is dimly lit, as if even the sun was afraid to enter this house of a man dying with AIDS.

2

After we stand in the doorway for several moments, our eyes adjust to the darkness. A group of people are huddled together at the back of the dining room. No words come from their mouths; no tears fall from their eyes. As we make our way toward the group, we see our patient lying on the floor face down. It almost seems as if he had been trying to make it out of the house so as not to die where his family lives. But he had fallen face down in midstride. As I roll the patient to a supine position to assess if, in fact, he is still breathing, I can feel the pain of the group huddled in the corner, as if the air has carried it and laid it on my shoulders. I want to vent my anger at these people. They could have helped him while they waited for us to arrive. I want to scream, "Why did you keep him lying like this when you should have rolled him over and started to breathe for him? Don't you know that you breathe once every five seconds into his mouth while you pinch his nose shut?" My anger at the ignorance of these people goes quickly as I start to breathe my life into him while Mike assembles the bag valve mask (BVM).

3

We have barely started CPR when the Fire Department arrives. The captain immediately starts throwing around orders

4

for us to put on face masks for our protection in case this co-matose man should involuntarily produce projectile vomit. With masks on our faces, we then carry the patient out of the house and into the back of the ambulance. I am doing chest compressions while another medic is ventilating Fred (our patient) with the BVM. The second medic is monitoring my compressions on the EKG machine. As the ambulance pulls away from the house, the second medic says, "Don't overexert yourself; he's got AIDS." So my anger at the family is now transferred to this medic, who thinks he's God and can decide who we should try to save and who not. I continue to exert all the energy I possess to help Fred's heart start up once again. What seems like hours is only a few short minutes before we roll up to Martin Luther King Hospital.

Mike pulls the gurney out, and I climb onto the side of the gurney and continue to do compressions. Mike and the other medics push Fred and me into the emergency room. The sight of a person in full arrest always catches the attention of everyone in the waiting room, so when we exit the ER, people that do not even know this man approach me. They are looking at my eyes for the answer they fear, yet are afraid to ask. I search the faces, hoping to remember the family so I can give them a copy of the run sheet, which is just a bill, the part I hate the most, for I know they want to know what is going on behind those doors, and I am not supposed to say anything. This time I cross the line as his wife stands looking at me, too afraid to speak. I place her hand in mine, and as gently as I can, tell her, "He has a pulse now. The doctors are with him, and soon someone will come to talk to you."   **5**

I go to the waiting ambulance, clean it and then push the button of the microphone to announce to the dispatcher that we are "10–8" (on the air and available). We have saved a life today. I know why I'm an EMT.   **6**

After You Read: Refer to the student essay to complete the following items:

1. This essay does not contain one sentence that sums up the writer's main point. Based on the information in the essay, complete the following unfinished summary sentence:

   _____ makes working as an EMT a fulfilling job.

2. List three specific details about the people—their behavior, their words, the way they look—that help you picture what is being described.

   _____

   _____

3. Think about the writer's inclusion of terms like EMT, BVM, and "full arrest." Are all terms adequately explained? What, if anything, do they add to the essay?

_____

_____

_____

4. Why do you think the writer chose to write in the present tense instead of the past tense, since this incident must have taken place in the past?

_____

_____

_____

5. The following sentence from paragraph 3 contains a shift in time from present to past tense. Cross out the past tense verb and write above it the correct present tense form.

It is only 2:00 P.M. and a sunny December day, yet the house is

dimly lit, as if even the sun was afraid to enter this house of a

man dying with AIDS.

6. What person—first, second, or third—does the writer use in this essay? _____

7. Copy the sentence in paragraph 3 that is noticeable for its use of parallel structure.

_____

_____

Revising Your Essay for Consistency and Parallel Structure

Read over the completed draft of your essay to make sure you do not shift from one person to another. Make sure you have used the word *you* only if you mean "the reader." Then, go through and check the verbs in your essay. Make sure that you have not changed from one tense to another without a good reason. Anywhere that you have items in a series or items joined by *and* or *or*, make sure that they are in parallel form.

After you have checked your essay to make sure it is grammatically correct, find a place in the essay—one or possibly two sentences—where you might use parallel structure to stress the relationship between two ideas. Rewrite this material so that it is in parallel form.

▼ CHAPTER REVIEW

- **Use parallel structure in your writing to stress relationships between ideas and to achieve balance.**

Highlights

- To maintain **consistency in time, avoid shifting from one tense to another** without a good reason.
- To maintain **consistency in your writing, do not shift needlessly from one person to another.**
- To maintain **parallel structure,** use **similar grammatical elements for items in lists or series, as well as items joined by** *and* or *or.*
- Whenever you use **word pairs** like *either . . . or* or *both . . . and,* **make sure that the sentence elements that follow** the second word of the pair **are parallel** to those that follow the first.
- In your writing, use parallel structure to **achieve balance** and to **stress relationships.**

PRACTICE

Use the sentences that follow to test your mastery of the material in Unit 6. If you have difficulty, go back and review the information in Chapters 22–25.

A. Circle the correct tense of the verb in parentheses. Keep in mind the meaning of the sentences when you choose the verb tense.

 EXAMPLE: Yesterday, the rain (falls, (fell)) for hours.

1. When I asked Professor Amati to write me a letter of recommendation, I (get, got) the feeling that he (didn't, doesn't) remember me.

2. We were on our way to school when the tire (blows, blew) out.

3. Whenever Karla gets excited, she (does, did) this stupid little dance.

4. Pablo got a new car, and immediately he (runs, ran) into a pole.

5. When she graduated from high school, Alissa wanted to be a nurse; now she (wanted, wants) to be a surgeon.

6. As the crowd applauds wildly, she (returns, returned) to sing one more number.

7. My brother always listens to his stereo while he (did, does) his homework.

8. Lysa and Bret were necking on the couch when his mother (walks, walked) in.

9. Germaine chopped vegetables for a salad while his wife (fires, fired) up the barbecue.

10. Charles likes to go bungee jumping whenever he (had, has) the chance.

B. Circle the word or words in parentheses that are consistent with the rest of sentence.

> *EXAMPLE:*   If a person wants to make a good first impression, (you, he or she) should not arrive three hours late.

1. Rayette likes to get to class early because (you, she) can usually find a seat in the front.

2. If people want to work in the medical field, (you, they) should spend some time volunteering in a hospital.

3. Our Spanish teacher never lets (you, us) speak English during class.

4. I'm finding (you, I) don't have any spare time if (you, I) work and go to school.

5. My father always told us children that (you, we) shouldn't take a handout.

6. After applying unsuccessfully for exciting, high-paying jobs, Jolene finally decided that (you, she) would take whatever job (you, she) could get.

7. I like having a relationship with someone (I, you) can trust.

8. We would be on the bus for six hours, and (we, you) were already bored after the first twenty minutes.

9. All those who intend to go on the trip should make (your, their) reservations as soon as possible.

10. If you watch a lot of violence on television, (one, you) may become numb to its horror.

C. Underline the parallel items in each of the following sentences:

> *EXAMPLE:*   Paul enjoyed reading science fiction and watching old movies.

1. Karin and Tom had a long-distance relationship.

2. Reisha found that she had a lot of extra time and a lot of extra energy after she quit her second job.

3. Whether he was making phone calls or distributing flyers, Andre was always hustling for landscaping work.

4. Ollie wants both to get a degree and to earn a certificate.

5. She wanted to buy a used car with an automatic shift, a cassette player, and a sunroof.

6. Pietro dreamed of coming to America and getting a good job.

7. Looking back on his days as a Little Leaguer, Fernando remembered the thrill of victory but forgot the pain of defeat.

8. The dean of fine arts and the vice president of instruction had a much-publicized feud.

9. The embarrassed restaurant manager offered either to have the woman's suit cleaned or to have her outfit replaced.

10. My sister's children climbed on my garage roof, swung from my hanging planters, and jumped into my fishpond.

D. Fill in the blanks with parallel elements.

EXAMPLE: Nancy had a bird that could both sing the national

anthem and __whistle "Yankee Doodle__."

1. Neither Milton nor _____ could find his class schedule.

2. Latoya plans to move either to Las Vegas or _____.

3. Reuben wanted a career that would give him security and that

_____.

4. She was not only the most beautiful of the sisters but also

_____.

5. Pilar was allergic to her cat, her dog, and _____.

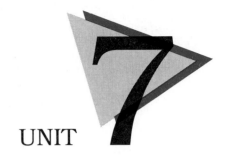

UNIT

Editing for Mechanics

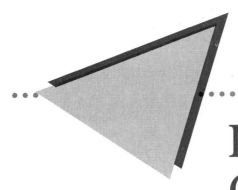

End Marks and Other Markers

▼ CHAPTER PREVIEW

Punctuation marks are often compared to road signs because they tell the reader how to read the words on a page and what to expect from words coming up. The following paragraph has no end marks or other punctuation:

> End marks and other marks of punctuation are valuable aids for the reader as well as important writers tools they signal the end of one idea and the beginning of another they indicate how a particular group of words should be read end marks indicate whether a thought is a statement of fact or a question or even an emotional outburst other marks let the writer show possession or insert additional information or introduce a list

Now read the same paragraph with end marks and other punctuation inserted:

> End marks and other marks of punctuation are valuable aids for the reader as well as important writers' tools. They signal the end of one idea and the beginning of another; they indicate how a particular group of words should be read. End marks indicate whether a thought is a statement of fact or a question—or even an emotional outburst. Other marks let the writer show possession or insert additional information or introduce a list.

Notice how much easier the second paragraph is to read. The wording is exactly the same, but the punctuation marks signal how the words work together to have meaning.

In this chapter, you will learn the function of **end marks, colons and semicolons, apostrophes, dashes and parentheses,** and practice using these punctuation marks.

A Professional Writer Uses End Marks and Other Markers

About the Reading: Kenneth McClane teaches English at Cornell University. He has written seven books of poetry as well as a collection of personal essays entitled *Walls* (1989). The selection that follows is taken from "Walls: A Journey to Auburn," which is included in *The Best American Essays 1988*. The Auburn in the title refers to Auburn Prison, where McClane accompanied eleven teachers from Elmira Community College's inmate higher education program. Before McClane began to read his poetry to a class of 40 inmates, they asked him about his own background. He told them that he was raised in Harlem by "two good parents 'who rode my ass.'" As he explains in the selection, this information "was an oversimplification, if not a direct lie."

As You Read: End marks and other marks of punctuation have been printed in bold. Notice how the various marks function to signal the reader and to help the writer convey his exact meaning.

From "Walls: A Journey to Auburn"

[1]I had been raised in Harlem, but in the most unusual of circumstances. [2]My father was a physician, my mother was a brilliant artist and writer, and I had attended one of the finest—and personally, most ruinous—independent schools in the city. [3]I lived in Harlem, which is to say that I saw much, but I certainly hadn't lived the lives these inmates had: indeed, I had spent my entire life keeping myself at a safe remove from anything which might bring me to Harlem's reality. [4]Yes, I had done a little of this and a bit of that, but I was always at the sidelines. [5]I knew where the deep water was—everyone knew that. [6]But I remained a shore bird.

After You Read: Refer to the reading selection to complete the following items:

1. What punctuation mark is used at the end of every sentence in the reading?

2. What punctuation mark is used in place of a period or semicolon in sentence 3 to attach a second idea that explains the first idea. (If you don't know the name of the mark, just copy the mark in the blank.)

3. In which sentence are dashes (—) used to surround the author's somewhat off-the-topic comment about his school?

   _____

4. In which sentence is a dash (—) used to emphasize a comment added to the end of the sentence?

   _____

5. Two words in sentence 3 contain apostrophes ('). Write these two words in the blanks.

   _____   _____

End Marks

Use a **period,** a **question mark,** or an **exclamation point** to end a sentence.

Vincent made it to class just in time.

Are you ready for the test**?**

I got an "A"**!**

Use a **period** to end any sentence that does not ask a _direct_ question or express a strong command or emotion. Most of your sentences will end with a period.

He asked if I wanted to go to the concert.
   (This sentence reports a question; it does not ask it directly.)

Fill out the registration materials and return them to the front desk.
   (This is an instruction rather than a strong command.)

Use a **question mark** to end a sentence that asks a direct question.

Has Bethany dropped the class?

Use an **exclamation point** to end a sentence that expresses strong feelings.

Keep your eyes off of my paper!

I won!

APPLICATION

At the end of each sentence, insert an appropriate end mark.

EXAMPLE: You will need a Scantron answer sheet for the test.

1. What is Vanna going to do after she graduates
2. Nothing has gone right since I moved into my apartment
3. Andre asked me where the bookstore was
4. Stay away from my sister, you creep
5. Chuck and Romero decided to skip their computer class
6. Latin is not offered at every college
7. It's alive
8. In my high school English class, we had to read a boring book about a whale
9. Everyone had a great time at the Mexican celebration of Cinco de Mayo
10. Does anyone have an extra class schedule

Semicolon and Colon

Use a **semicolon** to join two closely related sentences into one sentence.

Two sentences: We learned the biological facts of life. We never considered the psychological complications.

One sentence: We learned the biological facts of life; we never considered the psychological complications.

Two sentences: Mr. Chang was a shrewd businessman. He was a compassionate employer.

One sentence: Mr. Chang was a shrewd businessman; moreover, he was a compassionate employer.
(Many times, a semicolon will be followed by a transition like *moreover, however,* or *in addition.*)

Use a semicolon to separate a series of items that already contain commas.

Three books often assigned in Native American literature courses are *Ceremony*, written by Leslie Marmon Silko; *Love Medicine*, written by Louise Erdrich; and *The Way to Rainy Mountain*, written by N. Scott Momaday.
(The semicolons help the reader tell where information about one book ends and information about another begins.)

Use a **colon** to direct attention to a quotation or a list.

I'll never forget the advice of my high school counselor: "When you enter a college classroom, sit down, shut up, and, for God's sake, try to stay awake."

Every camper had a list of items to bring: a sleeping bag, a flashlight, a can of insect repellent, and a heavy jacket.

Do **not** use a colon after the words *are, such as,* or *of.*

Incorrect:	The test consisted of: thirty multiple choice questions, ten short answer questions, and an essay question.
Correct:	The test consisted of three parts: thirty multiple choice questions, ten short answer questions, and an essay question.

Use a colon to join two sentences when the second sentence explains or summarizes the first.

Two sentences:	Keisha arrived on time, she brought her materials, she was always prepared, and she participated in class discussion. She was the perfect student.
One sentence:	Keisha arrived on time, she brought her materials, she was always prepared, and she participated in class discussion: she was the perfect student.

Use a colon also after the salutation in some letter formats, between hours and minutes, and between a title and subtitle.

Dear Sir or Madam:

Hernando had to catch the bus at 6:30 A.M.

Professor Cohn assigned a book called *Crosscurrents: Themes for Developing Writers.*

APPLICATION

Insert a colon or semicolon wherever needed in the sentences that follow. Some sentences need no additional punctuation.

EXAMPLE: The test will be on everything in Unit 6: consistency in time, consistency in person, and parallel structure.

1. The Surgeon General issued the following warning "Quitting smoking greatly reduces serious risks to your health."

2. The instructor wanted to make one thing clear she was the boss in the classroom.

3. When the limousine rolled to a stop, George Michael stepped out.

4. Everett wanted to maintain a GPA of 3.5 or better however, he also wanted to maintain his reputation as a master of partying.

5. The program was scheduled to begin at 8 00, but it started 20 minutes late.

6. Yolanda bought a book called *How to Impress Your Boss A Guide to Getting Ahead at Work without Making Coffee.*

7. Alexis is conceited, shallow, and selfish these are her good qualities.

8. The protestors grew rowdy the police became worried.

9. The panel was composed of Professor Dietrich, who teaches American history Professor Quitano, who teaches Spanish and Latin-American Studies and Doctor Hata, who is Vice President of Academic Affairs.

10. Three courses offered this semester through Instructional Television are Humanities I, English 1A, and Business 40.

Apostrophe

Use **apostrophes** to form contractions.

Leticia isn't eligible for financial aid.
    (***Isn't*** is the contracted form of ***is not.*** The apostrophe indicates that the letter ***o*** has been left out.)

COMMON CONTRACTIONS

it's—it is	isn't—is not
don't—do not	hasn't—has not
doesn't—does not	won't—will not
couldn't—could not	could've—could have
wouldn't—would not	would've—would have

Use an **apostrophe** to show **possession** or **ownership.**

I borrowed Tran's notes from last Friday.
    (***'s*** indicates that the notes belong to Tran.)

In some cases you will need to add only the apostrophe to show possession; in others, you will need to add ***'s.***

1. If a word ends in ***s,*** add an apostrophe to show possession.

Phyllis' sister spent a year in India working with Mother Teresa.

2. If a word does not end in ***s,*** add ***'s*** to show possession.

The passenger**'s** side of the car was totaled.

You may find it easier to decide whether to use just an apostrophe or to use **'s** if you ask yourself, "To whom (or what) does it belong?" If the answer ends in **s,** add an apostrophe; if the answer does not end in **s,** add **'s.**

> The boys uniforms were filthy.

To whom do the uniforms belong? The answer, **boys,** ends in **s,** so add only an apostrophe (').

> The boys' uniforms were filthy.

Look at the next sentence.

> The womans dress cost over $2000.

To whom does the dress belong? The answer, **woman,** does not end in **s,** so add **'s.**

> The woman's dress cost over $2000.

The possessive personal pronouns **his, hers, its, ours, yours,** and **theirs** already show ownership, so they do not require an apostrophe.

> **Guy's** father once played professional soccer.
>
> **His** father once played professional soccer.

APPLICATION

In each sentence, if the boldfaced word shows possession, or if it is a contraction, rewrite the word adding an apostrophe. In some cases, the sentence needs no additional punctuation.

> *EXAMPLE:*   The janitor found **Robertas** briefcase behind the chair.
> **Roberta's**

1. **James** mother works on campus.

2. Fran mistakenly walked into the **mens** room.

3. The bird was busily preparing **its** nest.

4. Sawyer **couldnt** play football because of his poor grades.

5. The **boys** skateboards were confiscated by Campus Police.

6. **Isnt** Friday a holiday?

7. The **carpenters** tools were stolen out of his truck.

8. We were really impressed by that comment of **hers**.

9. Alice never understood what her father meant by "a **dogs** life."

10. The **students** groaned when they got their first essays back.

Dashes and Parentheses

Use **dashes** to set off brief comments inserted into a sentence, particularly if you want to emphasize the comments.

> The psychologist gave the couple permission—as if they needed it—to feel anger toward one another.
> ("as if they needed it" is a brief comment inserted into the sentence.)

Use dashes to set off a word or words that rename a noun.

> The student presenters—Wendy Nelson, Marita Jones, and Royal Bennett—received a standing ovation from the class.
> ("Wendy Nelson, Marita Jones, and Royal Bennett" rename **presenters.**)

Use a dash to set off a comment added to the end of a sentence or a series used to introduce a sentence.

> Community colleges, state and private colleges, and state and private universities—all are considered institutes of higher education.
> ("Community colleges, state and private colleges, and state and private universities" comprise an introductory series.)

Use **parentheses** around extra information and brief comments inserted into a sentence.

> Four of the students in the group (the other two had to work) arranged to meet for a study session.

> The price (over $40) was too high for a haircut.

Use parentheses to indicate an abbreviation.

> Our instructor applied to the National Institute for the Humanities (NIH) for money to go to the Library of Congress.

APPLICATION

Insert an appropriate bit of information, comment, series, or abbreviation in each blank.

> EXAMPLE: **Bloodshot eyes, short attention span, coffee-nerves**—all of these are signs of too much late night studying.

1. His brother Duane was drafted by the National Basketball Association (_____).

2. The qualities I look for in a mate—_____—are almost impossible to find.

3. Her first semester Ebony (_____) enrolled in advanced calculus.

4. Her fee (_____) seemed pretty steep for the little amount of work she did.

5. The difficulties of being a student—_____—can discourage even the most eager freshman.

6. The number of graduating students at this institution (_____) has been declining in recent years.

7. _____—raising children is expensive.

8. In only six months, he gained back all of the weight he had lost (_____).

9. My brother—_____— dropped out of college after three semesters.

10. She blamed everything that went wrong in her life—_____—on her parents.

▼ CHAPTER REVIEW

- Use a **period,** a **question mark,** or an **exclamation point** to end a sentence.

  1. Use a **period** to end most sentences.
  2. Use a **question mark** to end a sentence that asks a direct question.
  3. Use an **exclamation point** to end a sentence that expresses strong feelings.

- Use a **semicolon** to join two closely related sentences into one sentence or to separate a series of items that already contain commas.

- Use a **colon** to direct attention to a quotation or a list, or to join two sentences when the second sentence explains or summarizes the first. Use a colon also after the salutation in some letter formats, between hours and minutes, and between a title and subtitle.
- Use **apostrophes** to form contractions and to show possession or ownership.
- Use **dashes** to set off brief comments inserted into a sentence or a word or words that rename a noun. Use a dash to set off a comment added to the end of a sentence or a series used to introduce a sentence.
- Use **parentheses** around extra information and brief comments inserted into a sentence, and use parentheses to indicate abbreviations.

PRACTICE

To test your familiarity with end marks and other marks of punctuation, insert an appropriate marker in each blank in the paragraph that follows.

The Trickster

¹The figure of the "trickster" is found in folktales told around the world ___ ²A god, an animal, an ordinary human being ___ the trickster takes many forms. ³Sometimes, the trickster changes from one form to another ___ a trickster can even change from one sex to the other. ⁴Regardless of shape, the trickster can be distinguished by certain characteristics ___ ⁵First and foremost, this figure is a player of tricks ___ usually mean-spirited tricks ___ that can backfire and lead to humorous situations. ⁶The trickster is often a combination of opposites ___ at the same time creative and destructive, cunning and stupid. ⁷In its most primitive forms, the trickster is driven by its strong appetites ___ for everything from food to sexual gratification. ⁸The trickster is sometimes credited with being responsible for natural phenomenon, such as the movement of the sun, or for originating the characteristics of an animal,

such as the leopard ____ s spots or the bear ____ s stubby tail. [9]In general, tricksters use cunning and ruses rather than bravery or goodness to get what they want. [10]Even today the trickster survives in our popular culture, appearing from time to time as characters like the Roadrunner, Bugs Bunny, or Beetlejuice.

Using Commas

▼ CHAPTER PREVIEW

Commas have three major functions in writing: joining, separating, and enclosing material. In previous chapters you have learned about comma use in bits and pieces. For example, you studied commas when you learned about punctuating independent and dependent clauses, and again when you learned about *-ing* phrases.

This chapter outlines all of the **comma rules;** some of them will be a review of information you have already learned, while others have not been covered anywhere else in the text.

A Professional Writer Uses Commas

About the Reading: Yoshiko Uchida was born in California. During World War II, she and her family were relocated, first to Tanforan Race Track and then to Topaz, a bleak camp in the Utah desert. Uchida received a master's degree from Smith College in Massachusetts. Her publications include *Picture Bride, Journey to Topaz,* and *Desert Exile.* The selection that follows is taken from a story called "Tears of Autumn," which itself forms part of the 1987 novel *Picture Bride.* The main character, Hana, comes to America from her native Japan to be the wife of Taro Takeda, a man she has seen only in an old photograph.

As You Read: Commas have been printed in bold type. Try to figure out why the writer uses commas where she does.

From "Tears of Autumn"

[1]When she set foot on American soil at last**,** it was not in the city of San Francisco as she had expected**,** but on Angel Island**,** where all

third-class passengers were taken. [2]She spent two miserable days and nights waiting, as the immigrants were questioned by officials, examined for trachoma and tuberculosis and tested for hookworm by a woman who collected their stools on tin pie plates. [3]Hana was relieved she could produce her own, not having to borrow a little from someone else, as some of the women had to do. [4]It was a bewildering, degrading beginning, and Hana was sick with anxiety, wondering if she would ever be released.

[5]On the third day, a Japanese messenger from San Francisco appeared with a letter for her from Taro. [6]He had written it the day of her arrival, but it had not reached her for two days.

After You Read: Refer to the reading selection to complete the following items:

1. Circle the letter designating the reason that a comma is needed after the word *last* in the first sentence.

   a. To avoid confusing the reader.

   b. The sentence begins with an introductory dependent clause.

   c. A comma is used with the word *it* to join two clauses together.

2. Look at the information added to the end of the first sentence with a comma: "where all third-class passengers were taken." Is this information necessary to tell which Angel Island, or is it merely giving additional details about Angel Island?

   _____

3. In sentence 4, what two adjectives are separated by a comma?

   _____   _____

4. What word group is added onto the end of sentence 4 with a comma?

   _____

5. In sentence 5, what introductory word group is separated from the rest of the sentence by a comma?

   _____

6. In sentence 6, a comma is used with what coordinating conjunction to join two independent clauses?

   _____

Joining with Commas

Use a comma with a coordinating conjunction (*for, and, nor, but, or, yet, so*) to join two independent clauses that could stand alone as complete sentences.

> He is originally from Guatemala, **but** he has lived in the United States for twenty years.

> Peter is three units short of graduating, **so** he will have to go to summer school.

APPLICATION

In each sentence, circle the coordinating conjunction that joins two independent clauses, and add a comma.

> *EXAMPLE:*   The day was beautiful, so Enzio decided to postpone studying for his history final.

1. Alison learned to play the piano for she wanted to please her grandfather.
2. Wen-Chii wanted to graduate from college yet the English requirement was an obstacle.
3. Buddy had never had a job nor did he intend to get one.
4. Dawn's boyfriend was late for their date so she went out with her girlfriends to teach him a lesson.
5. Edgar wanted to be a rock musician but he had never touched a musical instrument in his life.
6. Cassandra manages to get good grades yet no one has ever seen her study.
7. The network news is always depressing so I have decided to watch the comedy channel instead.
8. The couple argued loudly so the neighbor called the police.
9. She likes her fashion design course for it gives her a chance to be creative.
10. The traffic on the highway was at a standstill so he took another route to work.

Separating with Commas

1. Use a comma to separate an introductory word group from the rest of the sentence.

Introductory dependent clause:

> **After she got off the airplane,** she kissed the ground.

Introductory phrases:

> **Leaving the library,** Melanie set off the alarm.
>
> **In no time at all,** Uri found himself feeling at home in his new country.
>
> > Exception: You may wish to omit the comma after a short prepositional phrase.
>
> **On Friday** we are leaving for Canada.

2. **Use commas to separate items in a series.**

> He always orders exotic foods like **snails, oysters,** and **caviar.**
>
> > Exception: When you join items with **and** or **or,** don't use commas.
>
> Calvin lettered in track **and** baseball **and** soccer.
>
> My grandmother is nothing like the stereotypical **kindly, unassertive, soft-spoken** lady who bakes cookies for her grandchildren.
>
> > Exception: Don't use commas to separate adjectives that could not be joined by **and.**
>
> Jerome bit into the devil's food layer cake.
> ("devil's and food and layer cake" doesn't make sense.)

3. **Use commas to separate items in an address whenever there is more than one item. Do not, however, use a comma between a state and zip code.**

> Her new mailing address is 1204 McConnell Avenue, Los Angeles, California 90045.
>
> He moved to Medford, Oregon, last year.

4. **Treat a date as a series, putting a comma after each item, including the last.**

> We have a date for lunch on Tuesday, August 5, at noon.
>
> She was born on March 12, 1970, in Toledo.
> (Treat the month and day as *one* item.)
>
> The comet should come again in July 2001.
> (Omit the comma if you use only the month and the year.)

5. Use a comma to separate a one-word expression or a tag question from the rest of the sentence.

> **Well,** you certainly took your time getting here.
>
> Lawrence is going to drive on Wednesday, **isn't he?**
>
> **No,** I won't be able to make it.

APPLICATION

Insert commas wherever necessary in the sentences that follow:

> *EXAMPLE:*   After the end of the semester, Pedro intends to transfer.

1. Henry was born on April 15 1969 in Greensboro North Carolina.
2. You will be at the party tonight won't you?
3. She served ice cream coffee and cake.
4. After making a name for himself in business Earl decided to become a street performer.
5. While Marcia was attending classes at the university she was also picking up units at the community college in the summers.
6. Wow that's an impressive grade report.
7. Running in from the rain Albert slipped on the entry floor.
8. Because of the junk piled in the front yard the real estate agent was unable to sell the house.
9. Phyllis just moved to an apartment at 4560 Simpson Avenue Runnemede New Jersey 08078.
10. They were married on Wednesday September 18 1932.

Enclosing with Commas

1. Use commas to enclose words or phrases that are inserted into a sentence if the sentence's meaning would be clear without the words or phrases.

Sentence interrupters:

> The first proposal is, **in my opinion,** the best one.
>
> He wanted, **in the end,** to be more than friends.

Midsentence transitions:

> She decided, **however,** to change her major to psychology.

(If a transition comes at the beginning of a sentence or if it follows a semicolon, you need only the comma after it.)

2. **Enclose nonessential information in commas.**

Walmart, **my mother's favorite place to shop,** is opening a store in my town.
> ("my mother's favorite place to shop" isn't necessary to identify Walmart.)

Mr. Pierce insisted on buying a new BMW, **for which he paid more than a year's salary.**
> (The price is not necessary to identify the kind of car.)

Professor Quayle's house, **which is located two blocks from campus,** looks as if it is about to fall down.
> (The location isn't necessary to identify which house.)

3. **Enclose the name or title of a person you are speaking to directly.**

I'm asking you, **Kenny,** for the last time!

Can you tell me, **Professor,** if you did anything important on the day I was absent?

And now, **my friend,** I want to know all of the juicy details.

APPLICATION

Add commas wherever necessary, and underline the material enclosed in commas.

> *EXAMPLE:*   Mrs. Rodriguez ,my first grade teacher ,just retired.

1. Holy Smokes the tobacco shop at the mall sells cigarettes to underage teens.
2. I think by the way that Dr. Chang will be the next Dean of Fine Arts.
3. I am happy to inform you Ms. Olsen that you have won a new television in the drawing.
4. Her boss who was the last person in the world she wanted to see on her vacation turned up at the same hotel in Mexico City.
5. The violence on American streets is in my opinion the direct result of the breakdown of the American educational system.
6. Roberta who thinks of no one but herself went out of town for two weeks and left her cat alone in the apartment.

7. Wherever you go Gillian I'll always think of you fondly.

8. Donna a single mother of three must work two jobs to pay her bills.

9. Melton decided moreover that he wanted to refurnish his entire apartment.

10. Frank who is incredibly cheap gave his fiancee an engagement ring on which she had to make the payments herself.

▼ CHAPTER REVIEW

- **Use a comma with a coordinating conjunction (*for, and, nor, but, or, yet, so*) to join two independent clauses that could stand alone as complete sentences.**
- **Use a comma to separate an introductory word group from the rest of the sentence.**
- **Use commas to separate items in a series.**
- **Use commas to separate items in an address whenever there is more than one item. Do not, however, use a comma between a state and zip code.**
- **Treat a date as a series, putting a comma after each item, including the last.**
- **Use a comma to separate a one-word expression or a tag question from the rest of the sentence.**
- **Use commas to enclose words or phrases that are inserted into a sentence if the sentence meaning would be clear without the words or phrases.**
- **Enclose nonessential information in commas.**
- **Use commas to enclose the name or title of a person you are speaking to directly.**

PRACTICE

To test your knowledge of commas, read the following paragraph carefully, inserting commas where necessary.

Chief Joseph

[1]In the spring of 1840 probably in Wallowa Valley Oregon Chief Joseph was born. [2]Today Chief Joseph a member of the Nez Perce tribe is remembered as one of the great Native American leaders. [3]The Nez Perces had negotiated treaties with the white settlers who came to Oregon in search of land; however in 1860 gold was discovered on

the Nez Perce land and the settlers were no longer satisfied with the terms of the treaties. [4]The settlers overran part of the Nez Perce reservation and they cheated bullied and murdered the Nez Perce people. [5]The government persuaded some Nez Perce to move to a new and smaller reservation but Joseph's father along with some other tribal leaders refused to sign the new treaty that the settlers offered. [6]In 1871 Joseph's father died and Joseph became the leader of the tribe. [7]Like his father Joseph also refused to give up his people's rights to their land. [8]Using all of his skills as a diplomat Joseph argued that the land was the Mother of the Indians and that it could not be given away or sold. [9]Finally after a series of wars with the settlers and the army Joseph and his people were defeated. [10]In his surrender speech Joseph made the famous statement that he and his people would "fight no more forever." [11]His speech which was also published made Joseph a hero to the American public. [12]But being a hero did not help Joseph's cause. [13]In 1904 Chief Joseph died on a reservation in the state of Washington never having returned to the land he still considered home.

Using Proper Capitalization

▼ CHAPTER PREVIEW

You learned in Unit 1 that the first word of every sentence is capitalized, and that whenever you write your name or someone else's, you begin with a capital letter. Besides these two uses of capital letters, you will need to know only a few basic rules of capitalization. In this chapter, you will learn which types of words to capitalize and which do not begin with capital letters.

A Professional Writer Uses Capitalization

About the Reading: Gish Jen is the daughter of Chinese immigrants. Her real first name is Lillian, but when she was in high school, she renamed herself after the silent film star Lillian Gish. Although Jen wanted to be a writer, her parents expected her to get a practical job, so she stopped writing fiction and briefly attended business school. A graduate of Harvard, Jen believes in the freedom of American life. The selection that follows comes from *Typical American,* Jen's first novel, published in 1991. This book tells the story of Ralph Chang, a Chinese immigrant to the United States, and his struggles to become an American.

As You Read: All capitalized words have been printed in bold type. Pay close attention to the types of words that begin with capital letters.

From *Typical American*

¹**It's** an **American** story: **Before** he was a thinker, or a doer, or an engineer, much less an imagineer like his self-made-millionaire friend **Grover Ding, Ralph Chang** was just a small boy in **China,** struggling to grow up his father's son. ²**We** meet him at age six. ³**He** doesn't know where or what **America** is, but he does know, already, that he's got round ears that stick out like the sideview mirrors of the only car in

town—his father's. [4]**Often** he wakes up to find himself tied by his ears to a bedpost, or else he finds loops of string around them, to which are attached dead bugs. [5]***"Earrings!"*** his cousins laugh. [6]**His** mother tells him something like, **It's** only a phase. [7](**This** is in **Shanghainese.**) [8]**After** a while the other boys will grow up, she says, he should ignore them.

After You Read: Refer to the reading to complete the following items:

1. What two names of people are capitalized in sentence 1?

   _____   _____

2. Sentence 1 and sentence 3 each contain the name of a country that begins with a capital letter. What are these countries?

   _____   _____

3. Sentence 1 contains the capitalized name of a nationality. What is this nationality?

   _____

4. Sentence 7 contains the capitalized name of what language?

   _____

5. In sentence 3, the pronoun ***he*** appears more than once, yet only the first ***he*** is capitalized. Why?

   _____

Rules of Capitalization

1. Capitalize **proper nouns;** proper nouns name *specific* people, places, or things. Do not capitalize common nouns; common nouns name types of people, places, or things.

CAPITALIZE	DO NOT CAPITALIZE
Professor Monteverde	the instructor
Aunt Grace	my aunt
California	my home state
Cuba	an island
Business 101	a business course
Declaration of Independence	a treaty
Lake Michigan	a large lake
Father (used as a name)	my father
Fort Worth	a city
God (used as a name)	the gods
Loyola University	the university

Evergreen College	the college
the South	a southern state
Atlantic Ocean	the ocean
Main Street	the street
National Organization for Women	a women's organization
Old Globe Theater	the theater
Statue of Liberty	a statue
Revolutionary War	a war
I	the writer

2. Always capitalize names for religions, languages, races, and nationalities.

American   Hindu   English   Latino

3. Capitalize months, holidays, and days of the week; do not capitalize the seasons.

February   Memorial Day   Tuesday   spring

4. Capitalize brand names but not the type of product.

Hershey chocolate bar

Wisk detergent

Trojan condom

5. Capitalize the first, last, and all major words in titles and subtitles of works such as books, magazines, songs, poems, films, and articles.

The Guiness Book of World Records

Time

"The Star-Spangled Banner"

The Exorcist

6. Always capitalize the first word of a sentence. If the word group that follows a colon could stand alone as a complete sentence, you may capitalize the first word if you wish.

He decided at that point to return to college.

The instructor always begins his course with a practical joke: This semester, he gave a 500-page reading assignment for the first week.

APPLICATION ONE

Fill in the blanks using the proper capitalization.

EXAMPLE: <u>Canada</u> is the country directly north of the

United States.

1. My favorite season is _____.

2. Today is _____.

3. I was born in the month of _____.

4. _____ is the only U.S. state composed of islands.

5. The mother of one's parent is called a _____.

6. I live in (or near) the city of _____.

7. My family uses _____ dish soap.

8. My least favorite course this semester is _____.

9. The last movie I saw was _____.

10. My favorite holiday is _____.

APPLICATION TWO

The following sentences have been printed entirely in lowercase letters. Change the lowercase letters to capitals wherever necessary.

EXAMPLE: next thursday is my mother's birthday.

1. every summer my family goes to pittsburgh to visit grandma mareno.

2. everyone who wants a degree from torrance community college must pass english 101.

3. paul anka's first hit song "diana" was written about his baby-sitter.

4. the commercial says that tide detergent gets out hidden dirt; i'm not sure my mom would agree.

5. temple beth israel, the jewish synagogue on second street, was vandalized last sunday.

6. dr. jabra's waiting room is filled with ancient copies of *reader's digest*.

7. every veteran's day my dad puts an american flag in the front yard.

8. juli's little brother marc was afraid to ride his bike down elm street after he saw the movie *nightmare on elm street.*

9. mr. chiu and his family went to san francisco for the chinese new year celebration.

10. professor sanchez was born in cuernavaca, mexico, but she has lived in this country for most of her life.

▼ CHAPTER REVIEW

1. Capitalize **proper nouns;** proper nouns name *specific* people, places, or things. Do not capitalize common nouns; common nouns name types of people, places, or things.
2. Always capitalize names for **religions, languages, races,** and **nationalities.**
3. Capitalize **months, holidays,** and **days of the week;** do not capitalize the seasons.
4. Capitalize **brand names** but not the type of product.
5. Capitalize the **first, last, and all major words in titles and subtitles** of works such as books, magazines, songs, poems, films, and articles.
6. Capitalize the **first word of a sentence.** If the word group that follows a colon could stand alone as a complete sentence, you may capitalize the first word if you wish.

PRACTICE

Test your familiarity with the rules of capitalization by inserting capital letters wherever they are needed in the paragraph that follows.

italian in america

[1]between 1876 and 1924, over 4.5 million italians immigrated to the united states in search of a better life. [2]most of them came from rural southern italy, and they brought with them to america the cultural traditions of the italian countryside. [3]but they and their culture encountered considerable racism on the part of americans. [4]due to

their language and darker skin color, as well as to popular stereo-types about their catholic religion, italians were viewed as an inferior race. [5]e. a. ross, an influential writer of the time, for example, de-scribed italian immigrants as "low-browed, big-faced persons of obvi-ously low mentality." [6]further, italian immigrants were widely believed to have criminal tendencies or to have such limited mental capacities that they would work happily for low wages at undemand-ing jobs. [7]in fact, italian immigrants often competed for the most me-nial labor, labor which was set aside for "nonwhites"; in addition, numbers of italians were lynched during this period. [8]many italians, therefore, stayed within the safety of the "little italies," as the ghetto communities established by italian immigrants were called. [9]other italian immigrants simply gave up on american life. [10]recent histori-cal research reveals that more than half of the 4.5 million people who came from italy between 1876 and 1924 were so horrified by what they found in america that they returned to italy.

Using Quotation Marks

▼ CHAPTER PREVIEW

When you report the words of someone else, you can either tell about what the person said (or wrote) or use the person's exact words.

John told me that he is transferring in the fall.

John said, "I am transferring in the fall."

The information in the first sentence is an **indirect quotation;** John's words in the second sentence are called a **direct quotation.** Whenever you write down someone else's exact words, you need to use **quotation marks.**

In this chapter, you will practice **punctuating direct quotations,** and learn other uses for quotation marks.

A Professional Writer Uses Quotation Marks

About the Reading: Harry Mark Petrakis was born in St. Louis, Missouri, in 1923, but has spent most of his life in or near Chicago, Illinois. As a writer, Petrakis focuses on the experience of immigrants to America, especially on the people and events in Chicago's Greek community. The following selection from his autobiographical novel *Stelmark: A Family Recollection* (1970) details an exchange between the young Petrakis and Barba Nikos, a Greek shopkeeper. This exchange occurs when the remorseful boy returns to the shop after earlier insulting the grocer and stealing fruit from the old man.

As You Read: Quotation marks have been printed in bold. Notice how quotation marks function to indicate dialogue, and pay special attention to the way each quotation is capitalized and punctuated.

From *Stelmark*

[1]"You were the one," he said, finally, in a harsh voice.
[2]I nodded mutely.
[3]"Why did you come back**?**"
[4]I stood there unable to answer.
[5]"What's your name**?**"
[6]"Haralambos," I said, speaking to him in Greek.
[7]"You are Greek!" he cried. [8]"A Greek boy attacking a Greek grocer!" [9]He stood appalled at the immensity of my crime. [10]"All right," he said coldly. [11]"You are here because you wish to make amends." [12]His great mustache bristled in concentration. [13]"Four plums, two peaches," he said. [14]"That makes a total of 78 cents. [15]Call it 75. [16]Do you have 75 cents, boy**?**"
[17]I shook my head.
[18]"Then you will work it off," he said. [19]"Fifteen cents an hour into 75 cents makes"—he paused—"five hours of work. [20]Can you come here Saturday morning**?**"
[21]"Yes," I said.
[22]"Yes, Barba Nikos," he said sternly. [23]"Show respect."
[24]"Yes, Barba Nikos," I said.

After You Read: Refer to the reading selection to complete the following items:

1. Circle the answer that best describes why quotation marks are used in the reading selection.

   story title   dialogue or conversation   slang words

2. What mark of punctuation ends the quoted material in sentence 1? _____

3. What other marks of punctuation are used to end quoted material in the reading? _____

4. Are the marks of punctuation used to end quoted material placed inside or outside of the end quotation mark? _____

5. When a quotation is followed by words like "he said" or "he cried," is the word *he* capitalized? _____

6. In sentence 19, the quoted material is interrupted by the words "he paused" enclosed in dashes. Write the sentence as it would appear without this interruption. Include quotation marks.

   _____

   _____

7. Most of the lines in this short reading are indented. Can you figure out the rule Petrakis follows for indenting dialogue? Pay attention to who is speaking in each indented word group.

_____

_____

Quotation Marks

Use **quotation marks** around the **exact words of the speaker or writer.** Do not use quotation marks when you are reporting in your own words what someone said or wrote.

> Marta complained, "I hate multiple-choice exams!"

> Marta complained that she hated multiple-choice exams.
>   (Reported information often begins with the word *that.*)

Use quotation marks around the **titles of** newspaper and magazine **articles, poems, short stories, songs,** and **episodes of radio and television programs.**

> The *Time* article "Awaiting a Gringo Crumb" discusses the lack of Latinos on American television programs.

> Louise Erdrich won a prize for her short story "The World's Greatest Fishermen."

Use quotation marks around **slang words,** but don't overdo the use of slang.

> Jeff described himself as a former "gangbanger."

When you are recording **dialogue with more than one speaker,** indent to let the reader know you are changing from one speaker to another.

> "This is probably one of the hardest courses you will ever take," Professor Kellerman announced the first day.
>   "Can we take it for credit/no credit?" a rattled student immediately asked.
>   "Absolutely not!"

APPLICATION ONE

Insert quotation marks in the blanks as needed. Not all sentences will need quotation marks.

> EXAMPLE: Marvin yelled, __"__ Wait for me! __"__

1. Albert's mother was shocked when she heard the lyrics of _____ I Saw Your Mommy_____ coming from her son's CD player.

2. Vince told Samantha that _____ he wanted to quit his job. _____

3. _____ Does the college provide child care? _____ Ellie asked.

4. Young people nowadays use the term _____ homey _____ to apply to anyone in their group of friends, but it originally referred to someone from the same neighborhood.

5. Rita whispered, _____ I think there's someone in the house. _____

6. _____ Mommy, mommy! _____ wailed the lost child.

7. Rafael told Elaine that _____ there was a vacant apartment in his building. _____

8. Students are sometimes surprised to discover that e. e. cummings' poem _____ She Being Brand New _____ is, at the same time, about a ride in a new car and about a sexual encounter.

9. Professor Waylons said, _____ No late assignments will be accepted—for any reason. _____

10. _____ Please loan me ten dollars, _____ Ray begged.

APPLICATION TWO

Rewrite the following conversation using the proper indentation:

Molly said, "I'm not going to the concert tonight. I have too much studying to do." "But I paid fifty dollars apiece for front row tickets!" Eldon exclaimed in disbelief. "What's fifty dollars compared to having to take American history over again next semester or ruining my GPA?" Molly replied angrily. "I thought you would be more supportive about my going to school." "Well," Eldon shot back, "it would be a lot easier to be supportive if it didn't cost so much!"

_____

_____

_____

_____

_____

_____

_____

_____

_____

Punctuation and Capitalization

Quotations are often accompanied by statements that identify the speaker or writer of the quoted material, such as **he said** or **she said.** Statements commonly used with direct quotations include a name, title, or pronoun plus a verb.

> **He said,** "I will call you tomorrow."

> **Mario Stevens writes,** "The greatest threat to education is lack of funding."

> "Next time you park in a red zone, I'll ticket you," **the policeman warned.**

Verbs commonly used to introduce quoted material include the following: **said, writes, remarked, notes, points out, stated, asked.**

When a quotation begins with a statement like **he said** or **she said,** punctuate it like this example:

> He said, "I prefer a job with status."

1. Put **quotation marks** around the quoted words.
2. Put a **comma** after the **he said** statement.
3. **Capitalize** the first word of the quote.
4. Put an **end mark** inside the last quotation mark.

When the **he said** or **she said** statement comes at the end of the quotation, punctuate it like the following example:

"I prefer a job with status," he said.

1. Put **quotation marks** around the quoted words.
2. Put a **comma** (or an **!** or a **?**) inside the last quotation mark.
3. **Capitalize** the first word of the quotation.
4. Put a **period** after the ***he said*** statement.

When the ***he said/she said*** statement comes in the middle of a quotation, punctuate it like the following examples:

ONE-SENTENCE QUOTATION:

"I prefer a job," he said, "with status."

QUOTATION OF MORE THAN ONE SENTENCE:

"I prefer a job with status," he said. "A job as a dishwasher just will not do."

1. Put **quotation marks** around the quoted words.
2. When the ***he said*** statement comes in the middle of a quoted sentence, put a **comma** inside the first set of quotation marks and after the ***he said*** statement.
3. When the ***he said*** statement comes at the end of one quoted sentence, put a **comma** inside the first set of quotation marks and a **period** after the ***he said*** statement.
4. **Capitalize** the first word of each quoted sentence. (The quoted word that comes right after the ***he said*** statement in the first example is not capitalized because it is not the first word of a quoted sentence.)
5. Put an **end mark** inside the last quotation mark.

Don't use a comma at all if a quotation does not have a ***he said/she said*** statement.

The officers reported the crime was "the work of a professional arsonist."

Whenever you use an independent clause instead of a ***he said/she said*** statement to introduce a quotation, use a colon.

According to Chaka, graffiti is an art form: "The spray can is my brush, the concrete my canvas."

APPLICATION

Correct the following sentences, capitalizing and punctuating quoted material correctly.

EXAMPLE: Mom yelled, "Who ate the enchiladas for my party?"

1. She remarked I've never seen such a big dog before.

2. Your shirt is filthy said his date distastefully.

3. Because it is getting late Wanda said I have to go.

4. Muhammad Ali was particularly famous for one statement I float like a butterfly and sting like a bee.

5. The instructor stated three tardies will be treated as an absence.

6. Three tardies the instructor stated will be treated as an absence.

7. Roger yelled answer the door!

8. Dolly said I saw Sondra leave three hours ago.

9. It's still early she pointed out. let's go somewhere for a drink.

10. He asked are you taking an English class next semester?

Commas and End Marks

Always put commas and periods that come at the end of quoted material inside quotation marks.

> The woman with the gun hissed, "Give me all your money."
>
> "Give me all your money," she hissed, "or I'll shoot."

Put colons and semicolons outside quotation marks.

> The syllabus said, "Keep all of your returned papers"; however, Professor Ashley never returned half of the assignments.

Put exclamation points and question marks inside quotation marks unless they apply to the sentence as a whole instead of to the quoted material.

> Martin asked, "Would you like to go with me?"
> (Only the quoted material asks a question.)

> Did you hear the professor say, "It's due on Monday"?
> (The entire sentence asks the question; the professor's statement is not itself a question.)

Never use double punctuation, such as an exclamation mark with a period.

Incorrect: She kept saying, "I'm sorry!".

Correct: She kept saying, "I'm sorry!"

APPLICATION

Insert the proper punctuation into the following sentences:

> *EXAMPLE:*   Ferris asked, "How many people are going tomorrow night?"

1. "I have to read the whole book by Monday" he complained.
2. "Be careful moving that computer" Warren warned.
3. Stephanie said "I'm leaving town as soon as I finish my last exam"
4. "This calculator" said the clerk "is your free gift with purchase"
5. "Did Paulo make the team" Dave asked
6. Did Terrell say "The free tickets are only good Monday through Thursday"
7. "Hooray, we won" shouted the cheerleaders
8. In her letter, she wrote "Harrison can't be trusted"
9. The demonstrators shouted that they would get a "ten percent raise or strike"
10. "I will not pay my bill" Mr. Cheung stated "I refuse to pay for such poor service"

▼ CHAPTER REVIEW

- Use **quotation marks** around the **exact words of the speaker.**
- Use **quotation marks** around the **titles of** newspaper and magazine **articles, poems, short stories, songs,** and **episodes of television or radio programs.**
- Use **quotation marks** around **slang words.**
- **Indent dialogue** to indicate a **change of speaker.**
- Put **quotation marks around quoted words.**
- Use **commas to separate a** *he said/she said* **statement** from the quoted words.
- **Capitalize the first word of any quoted sentence.**
- Put an **end mark** or a **comma** inside the last quotation mark.
- Use a **colon** to introduce a quotation after an independent clause.
- Put **commas** and **periods that come at the end of quoted material inside quotation marks.**
- Put **colons** and **semicolons outside quotation marks.**
- Put **exclamation points and question marks inside quotation marks unless they apply to the sentence as a whole** instead of to the quoted material.

PRACTICE

To test your familiarity with quotation marks and their punctuation, read the following paragraph carefully and place quotation marks and appropriate punctuation around direct quotes. Quoted material has been printed in bold type.

American Dreams

[1]The Chicago writer Studs Terkel specializes in interviewing average Americans and encouraging them to tell their stories and to give their perspectives both on their lives and on life in America in general. [2]In preparing to write his 1980 book *American Dreams: Lost and Found*, Terkel traveled thousands of miles across the United States and asked hundreds of Americans what they thought of the idea of the American Dream. [3]Terkel finally selected 100 interviews to make up the book. [4]But Terkel also thanks those people whose stories he collected but did not include. [5]**Each was generous** he writes **in recounting a personal life and reflecting on a public dream.** [6]The stories that Terkel does use in the book reflect a wide variety of opinions about the topic, providing some fascinating insight into American life. [7]One of the stories that Terkel includes is that of William Gothard, a corporate attorney, who believes that very few people have found the American Dream. [8]Another interviewee, Stephen Cruz, reflects on what the American Dream means to him. [9]Cruz says **The American Dream, I see now, is governed not by education, opportunity, and hard work, but by power and fear.** [10]Peggy Terry seems to agree with Cruz. [11]In thinking about her childhood, Terry claims **I don't remember dreams when I was a child.** [12]**Our dream was to get through the week until payday.** [13]Vine De-

loria, a Native American, states **Maybe the American Dream is in the past. . . . Maybe this is a period of reflection.** [14]Another of Terkel's interviewees, Jill Robinson, the daughter of a Hollywood film producer, says **The American Dream, the idea of the happy ending, is an avoidance of responsibility and commitment.** [15]Some of the strongest beliefs in the American dream are expressed by immigrants. [16]One man who came to the United States from Latvia, Karlis Enins, says **America was something where everybody would like to be.** [17]Enins remembers landing in New York with his family. [18]**See** said his wife on their arrival **that's our dreamland.**

Editing Your Writing for Mechanics

▼ CHAPTER PREVIEW

In the previous chapters of this unit you have learned the rules for punctuation and capitalization. Referred to as "mechanics" in writing, these are the areas that a writer usually looks at last, once he or she has written a draft and revised it for content and style. So, only when you have made all other revisions, do you focus on editing. You might think of editing as the cleanup work after a construction job is finished; if you don't clean up, the job won't be complete and will look sloppy, but cleanup is left until the end—after the major work has been done.

In this chapter, you will have a chance to consider the advantages of using one mark of punctuation instead of another. Then you will be given a choice of writing assignments, followed by a sample student essay written on one of the topics. Finally, you will be asked to edit your own essay for mechanics.

Using Dashes for Emphasis

Commas, dashes, and parentheses can all be used to set off brief comments and bits of information, even lists, that are inserted into a sentence. The emphasis placed on these inserted items depends on which type of punctuation you use.

The incident occurred last week, not last month as the news story reported.

The incident occurred last week (not last month as the news story reported).

The incident occurred last week—not last month as the news story reported.

All of the punctuation marks in the examples physically set off the last part of the sentence, which contains the information about the incorrect report. The comma causes you to pause as you read the sentence but does not draw much extra attention to the incorrect report itself. The parentheses tend to make the part about the incorrect report seem like an afterthought that is informative but not too important. The dash both causes the reader to pause and makes the material about the incorrect report stand out by physically setting it off; as a result, the dash puts the most emphasis on the incorrect report information.

In your writing, try using a dash occasionally for variety and emphasis. If you tend to rely too much on parentheses for adding information, experiment with using a dash instead.

APPLICATION

Rewrite the following sentences, using dashes to set off and emphasize material:

> *EXAMPLE:*   His life sounds fast-paced, exciting, interesting, and incredibly lonely.
>
> **His life sounds fast-paced, exciting, interesting—and**
>
> **incredibly lonely.**

1. My best friend (or should I say former best friend) seduced my fiancé.

_____

_____

2. Though they are close together in age, separated by only two years, Andrea and Elvina could not be more different.

_____

_____

3. It was the perfect day for an outdoor concert (sunny but not too hot).

_____

_____

4. Kevin intercepted the pass, dribbled down the court, aimed for the basket, and tripped over his shoelace.

_____

_____

5. Doris swore (but who would believe her?) that she had meant to pay for the cosmetics in her purse.

_____

_____

Writing Assignments

Write on one of the following topics:

1. Describe a role you played in someone else's life. Perhaps you acted as big brother or sister to a niece or nephew, or maybe you were a role model for a younger person in school or a stand-in grandchild for an elderly person. In your essay, try to include at least a sentence or two of quoted dialogue.
2. Tell about a time that you influenced someone else's behavior or attitude. This influence may have been either positive or negative. Perhaps you take credit for talking a friend out of making a bad decision, or maybe you pressured someone into doing something wrong, like stealing or lying. In your essay, try to include at least a sentence or two of quoted dialogue.

To come up with a topic, you might begin by making a list of all of the people who have been close to you over the years. Then look back over this list to see if you played a significant role in the lives of any of the people on the list or if you influenced one of them to act in a certain way.

Once you have a topic, try brainstorming or freewriting to generate specific details for your essay. Then try to sum up your role or your influence in a single sentence, such as one of the following:

When I was fourteen, I talked my little brother into a stupid stunt that nearly got him killed.

I was more of a father to my niece than an uncle.

Luckily, I was able to talk my best friend out of making a decision that would have had a negative impact on the rest of her life.

A Student Responds to One of the Writing Assignments

About the Reading: Paul Browning, who wrote the essay that follows, is 27 years old. He works as a grounds supervisor and helps out part-time as an assistant softball coach. Browning is majoring in journalism, and, in his spare time, he likes to play golf.

Parents

In my mind, I see myself standing there, rocking back and forth. I'm trying to quiet my niece, Amanda, a nine and a half pound bundle of joy my sister had two weeks ago. Her glass-shattering, high-pitched cry has awakened me once again. Like before, my sister is lying next to where I am standing, fast asleep. She looks unaware of the noise that's going on in the tiny bed next to hers. The father, or bum, of the child, skipped town when news arrived of the positive pregnancy test. Because of the absence of a father, I believe that I have influenced Amanda's life a great deal.

Because of my love for children, Mandy and I hit it off right away. Even when she was an infant, I felt very comfortable holding, playing with, and baby-sitting my little niece. This is something I think a lot of men have trouble with. On the other hand, when it came to removing a diaper, I was out of the room like a bullet. It's hard to say what kind of influence I had on her in those early years, but later I know that my influence had an impact on her life.

When Amanda was three, Amanda and my sister still lived at home with my parents. Pam was a teenage mother, and living at home gave her the freedom to dump some of her motherly responsibilities on my parents as well as on me. I lived in an apartment that had a pool. So sometimes on warm days I would take Mandy swimming, teaching her how to kick, float, and blow bubbles. Even though she later took swimming lessons, I still personally take credit for teaching her how to swim.

A year later, when Mandy was four, a girlfriend of mine (who had a daughter of her own) and I took the two kids down to Rosarita Beach, Mexico for a day. We walked around window-shopping, ate fish tacos, and went horseback riding on the beach. Mandy had the time of her life. On the way home, Mandy fell asleep in the back of the car. To this day, she can still recall the trip and will often ask me to take her back someday.

My sister's youthful neglect and irresponsibility often left me to teach Mandy basic things, such as picking up her own clothes, putting her dishes in the sink, or even showing her how to throw something together when she felt hungry. It wasn't that Mandy went without food; it's just that kids are always hungry. I would often act as a father or mother to Amanda. I sometimes felt that she should call me "Uncle Dad" or "Mister Mom." My parents and I often took on the role of being parents. Mandy didn't seem to have grandparents or an uncle. To her we probably all seemed to be just parents.

On March 18, a month ago, my sister had her second baby. Unfortunately, the father situation is the same as before. Amanda is very helpful with the baby. She is always there to help change and feed her, and to rock her back to sleep when she wakes up screaming that all too familiar cry. I have this feeling that Amanda is going to grow up to be a much better

1

2

3

4

5

6

mother than my sister is. She is a very strong kid and I hope that my influence played a role in that. Yesterday at 4:00 A.M., I heard the baby cry. I then sat up in bed and got up to go and check on the baby. But before I reached the bedroom door, I heard Amanda singing softly to the baby as she tried to get her to go back to sleep. She had beaten me to this vocal alarm. So I hit the pillow and fell back asleep as quickly as I had awakened.

After You Read: Refer to the student essay to complete the following items:

1. This essay contains a one-sentence statement that sums up the writer's main point. Find this sentence in the first paragraph and copy it here:

   _____

   _____

2. Circle the letter of the items that you think best describes the order in which ideas are arranged in this essay.

   a. Space—left to right, top to bottom, front to back.

   b. Time—first to last, earliest to latest, most distant to most recent.

   c. Importance—least to most important, most to least important.

3. The essay begins with a description of the speaker rocking his baby niece. How does it end?

   _____

   _____

   How does the ending tie in with the beginning? _____

   _____

4. The following sentence from paragraph 4 needs an additional comma. Add the comma.

   A year later, when Mandy was four, a girlfriend of mine (who had a daughter of her own) and I took the two kids down to Rosarita Beach, Mexico for a day.

5. Rewrite the sentence in item 4 replacing the parentheses with dashes.

   _____

   _____

6. Add the needed comma to the following sentence from paragraph 6.

   She is a very strong kid and I hope my influence played a role in that.

Editing Your Essay for Mechanics

After you have written a draft of your essay and revised it to make sure it gets across the ideas you want to communicate, go back over it and check your use of capital letters and quotation marks (if any). Be sure you have included any necessary commas. Look especially for coordinating conjunctions that join two independent clauses, and for dependent clauses that begin a sentence. If you have included dates and place names, be sure they have any needed commas. If you have more than one or two items in parentheses, rewrite your sentences to avoid overusing parentheses. If you have used a semicolon to join ideas, make sure it separates two independent clauses.

Once you have checked over your essay for correct mechanics, find one sentence that contains information or a comment that you would like to emphasize. Rewrite the sentence, using dashes to set off this information.

▼ CHAPTER REVIEW

- In your writing, leave the **editing stage** until **after** you have completed **all major revisions.** Then check over the entire revised draft for correct mechanics.
- Use **dashes** occasionally to **emphasize material within a sentence.**

End Marks and Other Markers

- Use a **period,** a **question mark,** or an **exclamation point** to end a sentence.

    1. Use a **period** to end most sentences.
    2. Use a **question mark** to end a sentence that asks a direct question.
    3. Use an **exclamation point** to end a sentence that expresses strong feelings.

- Use a **semicolon** to join two closely related sentences into one sentence or to separate a series of items that already contain commas.
- Use a **colon** to direct attention to a quotation or a list, or to join two sentences when the second sentence explains or summarizes the first. Use a colon also after the salutation in some letter formats, between hours and minutes, and between a title and subtitle.
- Use **apostrophes** to form contractions and to show possession or ownership.
- Use **dashes** to set off brief comments inserted into a sentence or a word or words that rename a noun. Use a dash to set off a comment added to the end of a sentence or a series used to introduce a sentence.
- Use **parentheses** around extra information and brief comments inserted into a sentence, and use parentheses to indicate abbreviations.

Commas

- Use a comma **with a coordinating conjunction (*for, and, nor, but, or, yet, so*) to join two independent clauses that could stand alone as complete sentences.**
- Use a comma to **separate an introductory word group from the rest of the sentence.**
- Use commas to **separate items in a series.**
- Use commas to **separate items in an address. Do not, however, use a comma between a state and zip code.**
- Use commas to **separate items in a date.**
- Use a comma to **separate a one-word expression or a tag question from the rest of the sentence.**
- Use commas to **enclose words or phrases that are inserted into a sentence if the sentence meaning would be clear without the words or phrases.**
- Use commas to **enclose nonessential information.**
- Use commas to **enclose the name or title of a person you are speaking to directly.**

Capitalization

1. Capitalize **proper nouns;** proper nouns name *specific* people, places, or things. Do not capitalize common nouns; common nouns name types of people, places, or things.
2. Always capitalize names for **religions, languages, races,** and **nationalities.**
3. Capitalize **months, holidays,** and **days of the week;** do not capitalize the seasons.
4. Capitalize **brand names** but not the type of product.
5. Capitalize the **first, last, and all major words in titles and subtitles** of works such as books, magazines, songs, poems, films, and articles.
6. Capitalize the **first word of a sentence.** If the word group that follows a colon could stand alone as a complete sentence, you may capitalize the first word if you wish.

Quotation Marks

- Use quotation marks around the **exact words of the speaker.**
- Use quotation marks around the **titles of** newspaper and magazine **articles, poems, short stories, songs, and episodes of television or radio programs.**
- Use quotation marks around **slang words.**
- **Indent dialogue** to indicate a **change of speaker.**
- Put quotation marks **around quoted words.**
- Use **commas** to **separate a** *he said/she said* **statement** from the quoted words.
- **Capitalize the first word of any quoted sentence,** and put an **end mark** or a **comma inside the last quotation mark.**
- Use a **colon** to introduce a quotation after an independent clause.
- Put **commas** and **periods that come at the end of quoted material inside quotation marks.** Put **colons** and **semicolons outside quotation marks.**
- Put **exclamation points and question marks inside quotation marks unless they apply to the sentence as a whole** instead of only to the quoted material.

In Your Writing

- Leave the **editing stage** until **after all major revisions have been completed.** Then check over the entire revised draft for correct mechanics.

PRACTICE

Use the sentences that follow to test your mastery of the material in Unit 7. If you have difficulty, go back and review the information in Chapters 26–30.

A. Circle the letter of the sentence in each pair that is correctly punctuated.

EXAMPLE: a. Has Mrs. Chang found her lost cat.

(b.) Has Mrs. Chang found her lost cat?

1. a. The dietician told Henry never again to eat the following foods: cheese, eggs, butter, and red meat.

   b. The dietician told Henry never again to eat the following foods; cheese, eggs, butter, and red meat.

2. a. Hugh attends the University of Nevada, Las Vegas—UNLV.

   b. Hugh attends the University of Nevada, Las Vegas (UNLV).

3. a. "Her father shouted, Go out and get your own apartment!"

   b. Her father shouted, "Go out and get your own apartment!"

4. a. Aren't you going to work on your paper?

   b. Are'nt you going to work on your paper?

5. a. Phyllis wanted to change careers, consequently, she enrolled in courses at the local community college.

   b. Phyllis wanted to change careers; consequently, she enrolled in courses at the local community college.

6. a. The test was horrible—500 multiple-choice questions.

   b. The test was horrible; 500 multiple-choice questions.

7. a. I can't stand it anymore!

   b. I can't stand it anymore?

8. a. Jackie, Ray Lynn, and Martin—all are from my old neighborhood.

   b. Jackie, Ray Lynn, and Martin: all are from my old neighborhood.

9. a. The disappointing bonus gift consisted of: a paper bookmark, five coupons, and a tiny sample of hand lotion.

   b. The disappointing bonus gift consisted of a paper bookmark, five coupons, and a tiny sample of hand lotion.

10. a. At the baseball game, the line for the lady's room went all the way to the stairs.

    b. At the baseball game, the line for the ladies' room went all the way to the stairs.

B. Insert commas wherever needed in each sentence. Then, in the space provided, briefly summarize the rule that tells why you used a comma or commas.

EXAMPLE: Jumping out of bed, Ernie tripped over the cat.

separate introductory word group

1. Melanie was born on Tuesday July 18.

2. Cynthia did you use my hair dryer?

_____

3. We're moving to Portland Oregon in the fall.

_____

4. I wanted to raise my hand but I was afraid my answer might be wrong.

_____

_____

5. The test is on Friday isn't it?

_____

6. The tornado leveled the house the garage and the toolshed.

_____

7. My sister who is only seventeen years old is thinking about getting married.

_____

8. Sasha was determined nevertheless to get her revenge.

_____

9. As soon as Gary learned the winning lottery numbers he rushed to claim his prize.

_____

10. With a broom in her hand Grandma ran after the would-be burglar.

_____

C. The following sentences have been printed entirely in lowercase letters. Change the lowercase letters to capitals wherever necessary.

EXAMPLE: İ'm driving to Ťucson, Ärizona, next week.

1. mrs. meyer was raised a catholic, but she became an episcopalian when she married.

2. my friend teresa is always reading the _enquirer._

3. last sunday was father's day.

4. he ran by the minimart to pick up a pack of salem cigarettes and a six-pack of coors beer.

5. the miller family always goes to lake tahoe in the summer.

6. kim grew up speaking korean instead of english.

7. aunt carla is coming to dinner on saturday.

8. sarah enrolled in accounting 101 and japanese 2.

9. the congresswoman suggested that we write to governor forbes.

10. lonnie's favorite television show is *in living color.*

D. Place quotation marks wherever needed in the following sentences. Not all sentences will require quotation marks.

    EXAMPLE: "Do something about that cold," warned Alex.

1. My grandmother always asks me how I am doing at school.

2. I hate this book, the bored student complained.

3. It's important, said the counselor, to be at your counseling appointment on time.

4. The short story we had to read for today is called Everyday Use.

5. Martha said she would like to transfer to the state college.

6. Allen Ginsberg's poem Howl was a real shocker when it was first published.

7. You should avoid any products tested on animals, said the animal rights activist. It's the only way to stop this kind of testing for good.

8. Mr. Harrison concluded with the following statement: Every one of you, faculty and students alike, must work together to make the college the great institute it should be.

9. Justin remarked, Isn't that the dean of students necking with that young coed in the college van?

10. The professor urged us all to read his article Quantum Physics and the College Essay.

Editing for Correct Spelling

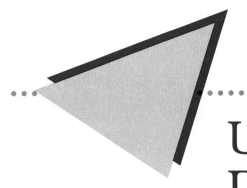

Using the Dictionary

▼ CHAPTER PREVIEW

If you know how to use it properly, a dictionary can be a powerful writer's tool. Not only does it give you the correct spelling of a word, but it also tells you how to pronounce a word and lets you know if a word does not follow the usual rules for adding endings.

In order to complete this chapter you will need an up-to-date desk dictionary. Several well-respected desk dictionaries are these:

The American Heritage Dictionary of the English Language

The Random House Webster's College Dictionary

Webster's New World Dictionary

Each dictionary has slightly different methods of showing information about a word, but all of them contain basically the same information. By the time you finish this chapter, you will have a good idea of what a dictionary can do for you.

A Dictionary Entry Gives Information about a Word

About the Entry: The sample entry below for the word ***profuse*** is taken from *The Random House Webster's College Dictionary*. This dictionary, just published in 1991, calls itself "The first dictionary for the 1990s!" It is particularly useful for today's college student because it includes new words that have come into the language, like *biochip* and *infomercial,* and multiple words that are used to mean one thing, like *ozone layer* and *mommy track.*

As You Read: Labels have been provided to show where different bits of information can be found in the entry. Pay close attention to the various items included in a single entry.

359

word
division   grammatical
     pronunciation   label
                                                       meanings
spelling——**pro·fuse** (prə fyōōs′), *adj.* 1. spending or giving freely, often to ex-
cess; extravagant (often fol. by *in*): *profuse in their praise.* 2. made or
done freely and abundantly: *profuse apologies.* 3. abundant; in great
amount. [1375–1425; late ME < L *profūsus*, ptp. of *profundere* to
pour out or forth. See PRO-¹, -FUSE-²] —**pro·fuse′ly,** *adv.*
—**pro·fuse′ness,** *n.*—**Syn.** See LAVISH.   word
                                                    other   origin
                                   synonym   forms

After You Read: Refer to the sample entry to complete the following
items:

1. The word division information in the entry tells where you can
   split a word if you come to the end of a line and the entire word
   won't fit. Wherever there is a dot, you can split a word. Between
   what two letters can you split the word ***profuse?***

   _____

2. Refer to the grammatical label and circle the part of speech that
   describes the word ***profuse.***

        adjective (adj.)   noun (n.)   adverb (adv.)

3. A **synonym** is a word that means the same as another word. Write
   in the blank a word that means the same as ***profuse.***

   _____

4. This entry gives three meanings for ***profuse.*** Which meaning
   makes sense in the following sentence:

   The paramedics were worried by the patient's profuse bleeding.

   _____

5. The accent symbol (′) in the pronunciation information indicates
   which syllable to stress when you say the word ***profuse.*** Underline the stressed syllable: PROFUSE.

6. According to the word origin information, between what dates is
   the word ***profuse*** thought to have entered the English language?

   _____

Spelling

The first bit of information in the dictionary, called the **main entry,**
is the correct spelling of a word. If you have some idea of how to spell

a word, but you are not completely sure of your spelling, you can look up the word in the dictionary. For example, if you are unsure whether **responsable** or **responsible** is the correct spelling, your dictionary would tell you that the second one, **responsible,** is the right one. A dictionary will also tell you if a word is commonly hyphenated, like the word **drip-dry.** Occasionally, you will find two spellings for the same word; while both spellings are correct, the first one given is the preferred spelling.

APPLICATION

Use your dictionary to find the correct spelling of each word, and circle the correctly spelled word. If your dictionary gives more than one correct spelling, circle the preferred spelling.

EXAMPLE: finaly   (finally)

1. progres   progress

2. practical   practicle

3. preventable   preventible

4. envalope   envelope

5. embarassment   embarrassment

6. persue   pursue

7. inspecter   inspector

8. fotographer   photographer

9. son in law   son-in-law

10. anniversary   anniversery

Word Division

In addition to showing you how a word is spelled, the dictionary also divides each word into its separate syllables. Each syllable is composed of one sound unit. A word like **no** has only one syllable; a word like **enter** has two syllables: **en** and **ter.** Most dictionaries use dots to show where one syllable ends and another begins.

APPLICATION

Use your dictionary to look up the syllable division of the following words. Use a vertical line to mark the divisions, and then indicate on the blank how many syllables are in each word.

EXAMPLE: b e|l i e v e   __2__ syllables

1. d i s p l e a s u r e   _____ syllables

2. r e s p o n s i b i l i t y   _____ syllables

3. p r o d i g i o u s   _____ syllables

4. k n o w l e d g e a b l e   _____ syllables

5. u n p r e c e d e n t e d   _____ syllables

Pronunciation

The pronunciation of a word is usually given in parentheses directly after the main entry. The pronunciation for the word **baggy** might look like (bag′ē). To decode pronunciation marks, look for key words at the bottom of the page or locate a pronunciation key at the beginning of your dictionary. The key will show common words containing the same symbols. For example, a key may give the word **act** to show what the **a** in **baggy** sounds like and use the first **e** in the word **even** to describe the **y** sound in **baggy.**

In all words of more than one syllable, one syllable is stressed more than the others. In pronouncing the word **student,** for example, you would emphasize the first syllable: **stu**dent. Some dictionaries label a stressed syllable with an accent mark (′) after the syllable to be emphasized, some put a stress mark (') before the syllable to be emphasized, and others place the stressed syllable in **bold type.** So, the accent mark in the pronunciation guide for **baggy,** (bag′ē), indicates that you stress the first syllable. Sometimes a word has more than one pronunciation. The first pronunciation listed in the dictionary is the more common or preferred one.

APPLICATION

Using your dictionary, copy down the complete pronunciation (all of the information in parentheses) for each word. Then, refer to the pronunciation key to pronounce each word aloud. If two pronunciations are given for a word, copy just the first one.

EXAMPLE: jettison **jet′-i-sŏn**

1. banal _____

2. indictment _____

3. indecorous _____

4. anarchy _____

  5. pedagogy _____

  6. schism _____

  7. harass _____

  8. catastrophic _____

  9. personify _____

10. frugivorous _____

Grammatical Labels

Just before the meanings are given for a word, the dictionary will indicate whether that word is a noun, verb, or other part of speech, and even, in some cases, whether a word is plural or singular. This information is abbreviated. To decode the abbreviations, look in the front of your dictionary. You will find, for example, that *n.* tells you a word is a noun.

Some words can be more than one part of speech, depending on how they are used. For example, the word *work* can be a noun, a verb, or an adjective. When you come across an unfamiliar word, be sure you look up the meaning that fits the way your word is being used.

APPLICATION

Look up the following symbols:

EXAMPLE: adj. ___**adjective**___

1. v. _____

2. prep. _____

3. pl. _____

4. adv. _____

5. sing. _____

Forms of Irregular Verbs and Nouns

Some dictionaries will list the **past tense and -ing** form for every verb; other dictionaries give this kind of information only for irregular verbs. For example, your dictionary should show you that the past tense of **keep** is **kept.**

The dictionary also tells you the **plural spellings for irregular nouns.** These are nouns, like **child** and *children,* that do not follow the rules for adding *-s* or *-es* to form the plural.

The dictionary will also indicate if a verb or noun that ends in **y changes the y to i before adding *-es.***

APPLICATION ONE

List all of the forms given in your dictionary for the following irregular verbs:

EXAMPLE: know _____**knew, known, knowing**_____

1. bring _____

2. sing _____

3. drink _____

4. do _____

5. freeze _____

APPLICATION TWO

Give the plural forms of the following nouns:

EXAMPLE: goose ____**geese**____

1. crisis _____

2. phenomenon _____

3. credo _____

4. library _____

5. alumnus _____

Word Meanings

When a word has more than one meaning, the meanings are numbered. When you look up an unfamiliar word in your reading or conversation, you need to find the one definition that fits the way the word is being used in this particular case. For example, the word *anxious* can mean either "worried" or "eager." Only the second definition would make sense in the following sentence:

He was *anxious* to get started on his vacation.

APPLICATION

In each sentence, one word is printed in italics. Look up that word in the dictionary and copy the *one* definition that explains the word's meaning in the sentence.

EXAMPLE: Pablo was not *compensated* for his overtime.

Definition: _____**paid a reasonable sum**_____

1. The dean would have to be pretty *credulous* to believe her story.

   Definition: _____

2. Derrick spent an *inordinate* amount of time styling his hair every morning.

   Definition: _____

3. The newsman announced that the weather would be *fair* over the weekend.

   Definition: _____

4. My father's *cardinal* rule is "Always tell the truth."

   Definition: _____

5. The mortgage form asked the couple to list all of their *assets*.

   Definition: _____

Usage Labels

The fact that you find a word in a dictionary does not guarantee that the word is acceptable as "standard" English. **Usage labels** tell you if a meaning is an old one that has gone out of use or if it is restricted to one subject area, like mathematics, or one geographic region, like Britain. A usage label will also tell you if a particular word, like **ain't,** is a slang word. These labels may be abbreviated, so if you see a label in italics, like **obs.** for **obsolete** (no longer used), look in your dictionary's list of abbreviations to find what the label means.

APPLICATION

Look up the italicized words and find the definition that fits the meaning of the word as it is used in the sentence. Copy down the label, if any, that your dictionary gives to this definition.

EXAMPLE: She brought home a *poke* of potatoes.

informal—bag or sack

1. Partner, there goes one fine *cayuse.* _____

_____

2. Don't get your *dander* up! _____

3. *Methinks* a dictionary is a marvelous thing. _____

4. Jack thought his friend's new motorcycle was *cool.* _____

_____

5. His parents threatened to send him to *bedlam* if he didn't stop act-

ing crazy. _____

Word Origin

Many words have come into English from other languages, such as Latin (L) or Greek (Gk). Most hardbound desk dictionaries, and some paperback dictionaries, include information about a word's history. This information is usually enclosed in brackets [ ], either before or after the word meanings. An up-to-date desk dictionary might tell you, for example, that the word **reggae** was first introduced in the 1968 song "Do the Reggay."

APPLICATION

Write down any information that your dictionary gives about the origins of the following words:

EXAMPLE: malapropism **Named after Mrs. Malaprop in Sheridan's**

play *The Rivals,* who got words confused.

1. cannibal _____

_____

2. wife _____

_____

3. taboo _____

_____

4. boycott _____

_____

5. bikini _____

_____

Synonyms

Sometimes dictionaries provide a list of words with the same or similar meanings to the entry word. These words, called **synonyms,** usually appear at the end of the entry. For example, if you look up the word ***bother,*** you might find the word ***annoy*** listed as a synonym. Use synonyms when you want to avoid repeating one word over and over in your writing.

APPLICATION

Use your dictionary to list the synonyms for each of the following words:

EXAMPLE: suggest **imply, hint, intimate, insinuate** _____

1. hate _____

2. old _____

3. follower _____

4. work (n.) _____

5. instrument _____

Other Information

Your dictionary can also give you information about a place name or a person's name, and tell you what a common foreign phrase means. For example, a dictionary could tell you that Inchon is a seaport in the western part of South Korea, or that Gogol was a Russian novelist and playwright who lived from 1809 to 1852. In some dictionaries, names of famous people are found in a separate section of Biographical Names, and place names are located in a section of Geographical Names. In other dictionaries, all information is given in the main section.

APPLICATION

Use your dictionary to look up the following people, places, and foreign phrases:

EXAMPLE: joie de vivre **carefree enjoyment of life** _____

1. carpe diem _____

2. Godard _____

3. in loco parentis _____

4. Stalin _____

5. Shanghai _____

▼ CHAPTER REVIEW

- Use a **desk style dictionary** to give you the following information about a word:

  1. spelling
  2. syllable divisions
  3. pronunciation
  4. grammatical labels
  5. irregular forms
  6. meanings
  7. usage
  8. origins
  9. synonyms

- Use a dictionary to find basic information about **famous people.**
- Use a dictionary to look up **place names.**
- Use a dictionary to find the **meanings of common foreign phrases.**

PRACTICE

To test your familiarity with the dictionary, use your dictionary to find the following information:

1. What's another word for ***prevent?*** _____

2. Who is Persephone? _____

_____

3. What is the meaning of ***caveat emptor?*** _____

4. What does the word **cause** mean in the following sentence?

   He often complained without *cause*. _____

5. What part of speech is **broadside** in the following sentence?

   The car hit the truck *broadside*. _____

6. What does the British term **gaol** mean? _____

7. What is the former name of Iran? _____

8. What is the plural form of the word **query?** _____

9. What does it mean to be *xenophobic*? _____

   _____

10. What is the meaning of the word **angst** and from what language

    did the term come into English? _____

    _____

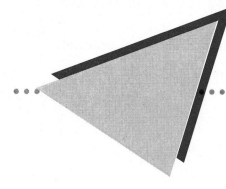

Improving Your Spelling

▼ CHAPTER PREVIEW

The best way to improve your spelling is to look over your corrected papers for misspelled words and keep a list of these words. This list should show the correct spelling and give the rule, if there is one, that this spelling follows. In this chapter, you will learn which letters are **vowels** and which letters are **consonants,** and you will become familiar with some of the **basic spelling rules.**

A Professional Writer Uses Correct Spelling

About the Reading: Raymond Carver, who was the son of a saw filer from Yakima, Washington, had his first writing instruction through a correspondence course. By the time of his death from lung cancer in 1989, Carver had been elected to the American Academy and Institute of Arts and Letters. He is best known for his realistic short stories about ordinary people. The selection that follows is taken from a story called "The Student's Wife," which appears in his tenth book, *Where I'm Calling From.*

As You Read: Words that illustrate the basic rules of spelling contained in this chapter have been printed in bold type. Pay close attention to the way some words change their spellings when endings like *-ing* or *-ed* are added to them.

From "The Student's Wife"

[1]When it began to be light outside, she got up. [2]She walked to the window. [3]The cloudless sky over the hills was **beginning** to

turn white. [4]The trees and the row of two-story apartment houses across the street were **beginning** to take shape as she watched. [5]The sky grew **whiter,** the light expanding rapidly up from behind the hills. [6]Except for the time she had been up with one or another of the children (which she did not count because she had never looked outside, only **hurried** back to bed or to the kitchen), she had seen few sunrises in her life and those when she was little. [7]She knew that none of them had been like this. [8]Not in pictures she had seen nor in any book she had read had she learned a sunrise was so terrible as this.

[9]She waited and then she moved over to the door and turned the lock and **stepped** out onto the porch. [10]She **closed** the robe at her throat. [11]The air was wet and cold. [12]By stages things were **becoming** very visible. [13]She let her eyes see everything until they fastened on the red winking light atop the radio tower atop the opposite hill.

After You Read: Refer to the reading selection to complete the following items:

1. In sentences 3 and 4, **begin** + **ing** is spelled how? _____

   To add **-ing,** what extra letter was added to **begin?** _____

2. In sentence 5, **white** + **er** is spelled how? _____ What letter was dropped from the end of **white** before **-er** was added? _____

3. In sentence 6, **hurry** + **ed** is spelled how? _____ To add **-ed,** the **y** in **hurry** changed to what letter? _____

4. In sentence 9, **step** + **ed** is spelled how? _____ To add **-ed,** what extra letter was added to **step?** _____

5. In sentence 10, **close** + **ed** is spelled how? _____ What letter was dropped from the end of **close** before **-ed** was added? _____

6. In sentence 12, **become** + **ing** is spelled how? _____ What letter was dropped from **become** before the **-ing** was added? _____

Vowels and Consonants

Before you can learn the basic spelling rules, you must know the difference between **vowels** and **consonants.** The letters **a, e, i, o,** and **u** are **vowels.** All of the other letters are **consonants.** The letter **y** can be either a vowel or a consonant, depending on the sound it makes. If it sounds like the **y** in **my** or **funny,** it is a vowel. If it sounds like the **y** in **yet,** it is a consonant.

APPLICATION

Above each letter in the following words, write **V** for vowel or **C** for consonant.

EXAMPLES:

$$\underbrace{\text{C C V V C}}_{\text{s t a i n}} \qquad \underbrace{\text{C V C C}}_{\text{y a r n}}$$

1. r e t i r e d

2. h a p p y

3. f o r m u l a

4. j a z z

5. q u i c k l y

6. y o u n g

7. l o c a t e

8. b r e a k

9. w o r t h y

10. v e x

Doubling the Final Consonant in One-Syllable Words

If a **one-syllable word** ends in the combination of consonant-vowel-consonant (CVC), double the final consonant whenever you add an ending that starts with a vowel (like **-ing, -est, -ed**). If a one-syllable word ends in something other than consonant-vowel-consonant, just add the ending.

$$\underset{\text{s w i m}}{\text{C V C}} + \text{ing} = \text{swimming} \qquad \underset{\text{t u r n}}{\text{V C C}} + \text{ing} = \text{turning}$$

$$\overset{\text{C V C}}{\text{f l i p}} + \text{ed} = \text{flipped} \qquad \overset{\text{V C C}}{\text{r i s k}} + \text{ed} = \text{risked}$$

$$\overset{\text{C V C}}{\text{w e t}} + \text{est} = \text{wettest} \qquad \overset{\text{V C C}}{\text{m e a n}} + \text{est} = \text{meanest}$$

APPLICATION

Decide whether each word ends in CVC, then add **-ed** and **-ing.** Double the final consonant if necessary.

	WORD	LAST THREE LETTERS	ADD **-ed**	ADD **-ing**
EXAMPLE:	spot	**CVC**	spotted	spotting
1.	rip			
2.	fish			
3.	train			
4.	grip			
5.	scan			
6.	sift			
7.	plug			
8.	mail			
9.	jell			
10.	skip			

Doubling the Final Consonant in Words of More Than One Syllable

Whenever you add an ending that starts with a vowel to a **word of more than one syllable,** double the final consonant if

1. the last three letters are CVC, and
2. the stress is on the **last** syllable.

To decide which syllable is stressed, say the word aloud and listen to which syllable gets the most emphasis. In the following words, the stressed syllable is printed in bold.

pat**rol**   ad**mit**   **vi**sit   re**port**

$$\overset{\text{C V C}}{\text{p a t r o l}} + \text{ed} = \text{patrolled} \qquad \overset{\text{C V C}}{\text{v i s i t}} + \text{ed} = \text{visited}$$

$$\overset{\text{C V C}}{\text{a d m i t}} + \text{ing} = \text{admitting} \qquad \overset{\text{C V C}}{\text{r e p o r t}} + \text{ing} = \text{reporting}$$

APPLICATION

Say each word aloud and underline the stressed syllable. Then check to see if the word ends in CVC. Finally, add the endings *-ed* and *-ing,* doubling the final consonant if you need to.

	WORD	LAST THREE LETTERS	*-ed*	*-ing*
EXAMPLE:	happen	CVC	happened	happening
1.	commit			
2.	travel			
3.	prefer			
4.	program			
5.	order			
6.	expel			
7.	repeat			
8.	occur			
9.	insist			
10.	control			

Keeping or Changing the Final *y*

Whenever you add an ending other than *-ing* to a word that ends in *-y,* change the *y* to *i* if the letter before the *y* is a consonant.

$$\overset{\text{C}}{\text{w o r r y}} + \text{ed} = \text{worried} \qquad \overset{\text{V}}{\text{s t a y}} + \text{ed} = \text{stayed}$$

$$\overset{\text{C}}{\text{w o r r y}} + \text{ing} = \text{worrying} \qquad \overset{\text{V}}{\text{s t a y}} + \text{ing} = \text{staying}$$

Be aware of the following exceptions:

day + ly = daily   pay + ed = paid
lay + ed = laid   say + ed = said

APPLICATION

Add the ending shown to each word.

EXAMPLE: apply + ed = __applied__

1. cry + ed = _____

2. mercy + ful = _____

3. juicy + est = _____

4. study + ed = _____

5. pay + ed = _____

6. angry + ly = _____

7. happy + ness = _____

8. buy + ing = _____

9. wealthy + er = _____

10. enjoy + able = _____

Keeping or Dropping the Final *e*

Whenever you add a new ending that begins with a vowel (like *-ing* or *-able*) to a word that ends in *e,* drop the final *e.* Whenever you add a new ending that begins with a consonant (like *-ly* or *-ment*), keep the final *e.*

like + able = likable   polite + ly = politely

Exceptions include **argument, awful, courageous, judgment, manageable, noticeable, seeing, truly.**

APPLICATION

Add the suffix shown to each word.

EXAMPLE: swipe + ed = __swiped__

1. write + ing = _____

2. advertise + ment = _____

3. love + able = _____

4. argue + ment = _____

5. complete + ing = _____

6. hope + ful = _____

7. time + ly = _____

8. shave + ed = _____

9. use + less = _____

10. use + able = _____

Adding -s or -es

Add **-es** instead of **-s** for

1. words ending in **ch, sh, ss, x,** or **z.**

crut**ch** + es = crutches   fi**x** + es = fixes

2. most words ending in **o.**

potat**o** + es = potatoes   g**o** + es = goes

(Exceptions include the words **pianos, radios,** and **solos.**)

3. words in which you have changed the final **y** to **i**

fly + es = fl**ies**   carry + es = carr**ies**

APPLICATION

Add **-s** or **-es** to each word.

EXAMPLE: match ____matches____

1. echo _____

2. radio _____

3. fizz _____

4. reply _____

5. catch _____

6. tomato _____

7. ash _____

8. boss _____

9. tax _____

10. hero _____

Using *ie* or *ei*

Use **i** before **e,** except after **c,** or when sounding like **ay** as in **neighbor** or **weigh.**

piece   receive   freight

When the **c** has a **sh** sound, however, use **ie** after **c.**

ancient   conscience

Exceptions to these rules include the following words: **either, neither, foreign, height, seize, society, their, weird.**

APPLICATION

Fill in the blanks with either **ie** or **ei.** Pronounce each word to see if the missing letters sound like **ay** or if the **c** sounds like **sh.**

EXAMPLE: conc __e__ __i__ ve

1. f __ __ ld

2. __ __ ght

3. rel __ __ ve

4. bel __ __ ve

5. soc __ __ ty

6. s __ __ ze

7. effic __ __ nt

8. gr __ __ f

9. th __ __ r

10. w __ __ rd

▼ CHAPTER REVIEW

- The letters **a, e, i, o,** and **u** are **vowels.** All of the other letters are **consonants.** The letter **y** can be either a vowel or a consonant.

Rule 1: Doubling the Final Consonant in a One-Syllable Word

If a **one-syllable word** ends in a combination of consonant-vowel-consonant (CVC), double the final consonant whenever you add an ending that starts with a vowel (like **-ing, -est, -ed**).

Rule 2: Doubling the Final Consonant in a Word of More Than One Syllable

Whenever you add an ending that starts with a vowel to a **word of more than one syllable,** double the final consonant if (1) the last three letters are CVC, and (2) the stress is on the **last** syllable.

Rule 3: Keeping or Changing the Final **y**

Whenever you add an ending other than **-ing** to a word that ends in **y,** change the **y** to **i** if the letter before the **y** is a consonant.

Rule 4: Keeping or Dropping the Final **e**

Whenever you add a new ending that begins with a vowel (like **-ing** or **-able**) to a word that ends in **e,** drop the final **e.** Whenever you add a new ending that begins with a consonant (like **-ly** or **-ment**), keep the final **e.**

Rule 5: Adding **-s** or **-es**

Add **-es** instead of **-s** for

1. words ending in **ch, sh, ss, x,** or **z.**
2. most words ending in **o.**
3. words in which you have changed the final **y** to **i**

Rule 6: Using **ie** or **ei**

Use **i** before **e,** except after **c,** or when sounding like **ay** as in **neighbor** or **weigh.** When the **c** has a **sh** sound, however, use **ie** after **c.**

PRACTICE

To test your knowledge of the spelling rules in this chapter, supply the correct spelling of each word in the blank.

A Woman's Work Is Never Done

[1]A term that is _____ to catch the attention of many
                      begin + ing

Americans, especially American women, is the "second shift." [2]This

term, which is _____ to women who are part of _____
                  apply + ed   work + ing

couples, refers to the fact that many women work a job outside of the

home and then come home to work another job. [3]In fact,

_____ women, especially mothers who also hold jobs outside
  work + ing

the home, _____ end up _____ what amounts to one
            real + ly   work + ing

extra month of twenty-four-hour days every year. [4]Over twelve years,

this figure adds up to an entire year of twenty-four-hour days. [5]R

search on the two-income American family _____ the
                                            discuss + es

_____ pace of life in today's world and the strain on family life
  hurry + ed

that results from the fact that many American _____ expect
                                                 family + es

more from themselves and from each other than they _____
                                                       use + ed

to. [6]But, researchers point out, the demands that family life places on

women who work outside the home are far _____ than the de-
                                           great + er

mands on men, _____ when the couple has children. [7]In
                 particular + ly

many American _____, women _____ take on far
                 family + es   routine + ly

more _____ and household chores than their male partners
       parent + ing

do because women feel more personal _____ for home and
                                       responsible + ity

children. [8]Women are more likely to arrange for playmates to visit, to keep track of doctors' and dentists' appointments, and to make sure

that children have costumes and gifts for birthday _____.
                                                    party + es

[9]Women are also more _____ to check in with the baby-sitter
                          like + ly

while they are at work. [10]Working the second shift does not always

make for a happy or _____ life. [11]Research shows that women
                       fulfill + ed

feel deeply torn between the demands of _____ work and
                                          their or thier

home lives. [12]_____ numbers of American women feel
                 Increase + ing

_____ at men who do not share the workload of the home.
 frustrate + ion

[13]Although researchers _____ that American _____
                          beleive or believe   family + es

are _____ rapidly, the fact remains that men and women will
     change + ing

have to change a lot more if they are to work together _____.
                                                         successful + ly

CHAPTER 33

Mastering Words Easily Confused

▼ CHAPTER PREVIEW

Many spelling errors occur either because different words sound or look alike, or because their meanings are similar. In this chapter, you will look at these troublesome words and learn how to tell them apart.

A Professional Writer Uses Words Easily Confused

About the Reading: Born in 1906 to Japanese immigrant parents, S. I. Hayakawa became a professor of English at the University of California at Berkeley, the president of San Francisco State College, and a U.S. senator from California. Hayakawa, who felt strongly that English should be the official language of the United States, was well known for his articles and books about language. The selection that follows is taken from *Language and Thought*, a book first published in 1939 and updated in its fifth edition in 1990 with the help of Hayakawa's son Alan. The part of the book from which this selection is taken looks at how television shapes the way we see the world.

As You Read: Words that sound like other words have been printed in bold type. Pay attention to the different spellings of the various words that sound alike.

From *Language and Thought*

[1]Even in news footage and other images that we tend to accept as "real," this distinction between on- and off-camera also exists. [2]An unwritten rule of both newspaper and television news photography is that the camera never shows evidence of **its** own presence—

381

no photographers, technicians, **or** other cameras, and only selected reporters, **are** to be depicted. [3]This rule is generally observed even though the presence of cameras and reporters may be exerting a major effect on the events being photographed. [4]As **an** example, public officials **and** reporters who work together regularly at **a** state capitol or **a** city hall may banter with each other before **a** press conference, but assume **an** entirely different demeanor when the lights come on **and** the cameras start rolling. [5]To a person present at a public hearing, cameras and lights may physically dominate the entire proceeding, but the televised report may exhibit little direct evidence of the presence of such apparatus.

[6]The narrow vision of the television camera also makes spaces and groups of people seem much larger. [7]After seeing one of the most familiar television rooms in America, the studio where "The Tonight Show" is filmed, visitors often say, "**It's** so small." [8]On "the tube," the studio seems boundless and the crowd huge because the camera seldom shows the space as a whole. [9]Many people who stage demonstrations and political rallies **know** this fact. [10]When the cameras arrive, chanting becomes louder and more unified, and organizers often try to get their people to crowd together in front of the lens to wave, cheer, or jeer so that they will appear to be a much bigger group than they **are.** [11]During the 1960s and 70s, some television and newspaper editors became so aware of this phenomenon and the extent to which it was exploited by various groups that they issued guidelines to **their** reporters and photographers on ways to avoid being manipulated into "creating" the news where **there** might otherwise be none.

After You Read: Refer to the reading to complete the following items:

1. In sentence 2, the words **or** and **are** sound very similar, yet they have different meanings. Which word is a verb? _____

2. Sentence 4 contains three words that sound similar: **a, an,** and **and.** Fill in each of these words in the appropriate blank in the following paragraph:

   _____ is a noun marker used before a word that begins with a vowel sound (**a, e, i, o, u**). _____ is a noun marker used before a word that begins with a sound other than a vowel sound. _____ is a coordinating conjunction used to connect words or word groups.

3. What two words in sentence 11 sound alike but have different spellings? _____ _____

4. The word *its* appears in sentence 2. The sound-alike word *it's* appears in sentence 7. Which one means "it is"? _____

5. The word *know* in sentence 9 is pronounced just like the word *no* in sentence 2. Which one means "not any"? _____

Words That Sound Alike

a, an, and

Use *a* before a word that begins with a consonant sound.

a toy, a pencil, a uniform (*u* has the sound of *y*)

Use *an* before a word that begins with a vowel sound.

an operator, an elephant, an honest man (*h* is silent)

Use *and* to join words or word groups.

Frankie and Johnny

accept, except

Use *accept* as a verb to mean "receive what is offered."

I accept your offer of a free lunch.

Use *except* to mean "but" or "excluding."

I finished everything except the last section.

affect, effect

Use *affect* as a verb to mean "influence."

The things we do today will affect future generations.

Use *effect* as a noun to mean "a result."

The punishment did not have the desired effect.

all ready, already

If you can leave out the word *all* and the sentence still makes sense, use *all ready.*

We were all ready to leave.

If you can't leave out the **all** and still have the sentence make sense, use **already.**

I already delivered those pizzas.

are, or, our

Use **are** as a verb.

They are going with us.

Use **or** to show two or more possibilities.

We plan to go tonight or tomorrow night.

Use **our** to show possession.

Our car was stolen.

brake, break

Use **brake** if you mean "to slow or stop" or if you are referring to a device that slows or stops motion.

He tried to brake his fall.

She slammed on the brakes to keep from hitting the dog.

Use **break** if you mean "to shatter" or "come apart," or if you are referring to a brief time out from an activity.

Be careful not to break that vase.

Let's take a ten-minute break.

coarse, course

Use **coarse** to describe rough texture or manners.

The blanket was woven from coarse yarn.

Use **course** for all other meanings.

He really enjoyed the computer course.

compliment, complement

Use **compliment** to mean "praise." To remember that the one spelled with **i** means praise, think of "**I** like compliments."

The professor complimented her on her excellent paper.

Use **complement** with an **e** to mean "completes something."

That tie certainly complements your outfit.

do, due

Use **do** as a verb: you **do** something.

I do sit-ups every night before bed.

Use **due** if you mean something is scheduled for a certain time.

The assignment is due on Monday.

fourth, forth

Use **fourth** if you are referring to the number four. (The word **fourth** contains the word **four**).

Hester was fourth in line.

Use **forth** if you do not mean a number.

He paced back and forth.

have, of

Use **have** as a verb. When you pronounce the contractions **could've** and **would've,** they may sound like they end in **of,** but they end in a shortened version of **have.**

I should have gone home earlier. (I should've gone.)

Use **of** only in a prepositional phrase.

He is a good friend of hers.

hear, here

Hear contains the word **ear.** Use **hear** to mean what you do with your ear.

I can hear you from across the campus.

Use **here** to tell where. The word **where** contains the word **here.**

He'll be here shortly.

its, it's

Use **its** if you want a possessive pronoun.

The dog chewed on its bone.

Use **it's** if you mean "it is" or "it has."

It's not easy finding a job these days.

APPLICATION

Circle the correct word in parentheses. If you are not sure which word to use, don't guess. Instead, go back over the definitions.

EXAMPLE: I did not mean to (break, brake) your VCR.

1. Everyone was at the reunion (accept, except) Dominick.
2. Is it time to take a (break, brake) (all ready, already)?
3. (Our, Or, Are) rent is (do, due) on the fifteenth.
4. The coat was made of a (course, coarse) material.
5. She received the ultimate (compliment, complement) on her new hair style.
6. I should (of, have) gotten (hear, here) earlier.
7. The catnip had a crazy (affect, effect) on the animal.
8. (A, An) small child often clings to (it's, its) mother.
9. He ventured (forth, fourth) in spite of the sleet and snow.
10. The company rehired every one of the laid-off workers (accept, except) Gordie.

More Words That Sound Alike

knew, new

Use **knew** when you mean the past tense of **know.**

I knew he wouldn't be on time.

Use **new** to mean "not old."

She was saving her money to buy a new car.

know, no

Use **know** when you mean having to do with knowledge. The word **knowledge** contains the word **know.**

He should know the answer.

Use **no** to mean "not any" or the opposite of **yes.**

I have no more money.

passed, past

Use **passed** when you mean the past tense of the verb **pass.**

I passed him in the hall.

Use *past* when it's not a verb.

He drove past the house.

She tried to hide her past.

peace, piece

Use *peace* when you mean the opposite of war.

The two countries had been at peace for forty years.

Use *piece* to mean a "portion" of something. To help you remember, think of "piece of pie"; the word *piece* begins with *pie.*

He wanted a piece of the action.

principle, principal

Use *principle* when you mean "rule." Both *principle* and *rule* end in *le.*

The first principle of safe driving is to watch out for the other guy.

Use *principal* to mean "main" or to refer to the head of a school. Remember the saying, "The principal is your pal"; the word *principal* ends in *pal.*

The principal is the main teacher in the school.

In banking terms, the principal is the main amount of money.

The principal problem has been solved.

right, write

Use *right* to mean "correct" or "proper."

He tried to do the right thing.

Use *write* to mean what you do with a pen.

We have to write eight papers for our English class.

stationary, stationery

Use *stationary* with an *a* when you mean "stays in one place" or "unchanging."

He exercised on a stationary bike.

Use *stationery* with an *e* when you mean "writing paper." *Stationery* and *paper* both have *er.*

She wrote him a note on scented stationery.

their, there, they're

Use **their** to mean "belonging to them."

Isn't that their car?

Use **there** to mean a place or to be a place holder in a sentence that begins with "There is" or "There are." **There** contains the word **here.**

I left it over there.

There is always someone who will work for less money.

Use **they're** to mean "they are."

She said they're going to come later.

threw, through

Use **threw** to mean the past tense of "throw."

The pitcher threw a curveball.

Use **through** if you don't mean "to throw something."

She's finally through with her essay.

He looked through the microscope.

to, too, two

Use **two** when you mean "the number two."

She has a son who is two years old.

Use **too** when you mean "also" or "more than enough."

He is too lenient with his teenage daughter.

Use **to** for all other meanings,

We took a bus to the ball game.

use, used

Use the word **use** to mean "function" or "make use of."

I have no use for liars. (noun that rhymes with **moose**)

Do you use a handbook? (verb that rhymes with **news**)

Use the word **used** to mean "in the habit of" or "secondhand," or as the past tense of the verb **use.**

We used to attend that church.

She bought a used car.

weather, whether

Use **weather** to refer to atmospheric conditions.

The weather is unseasonably cold.

Use **whether** to mean "if."

The boy asked his mother whether he could go.

who's, whose

Use **who's** to mean "who is" or "who has."

Who's supposed to buy the lottery tickets this week?

Use **whose** to show possession.

Whose truck is this?

you're, your

Use **you're** to mean "you are."

You're supposed to pay the cashier first.

Use **your** to mean "belonging to you."

Is that your dog?

APPLICATION

Circle the correct word in parentheses. If you are unsure, don't guess. Instead, look at the definition.

EXAMPLE: We had terrible (weather, whether) for our entire vacation.

1. He jogged (past, passed) Main Street and then sprinted (threw, through) the park.
2. For many years, world leaders have been trying to achieve (piece, peace) in the Middle East.
3. She tried to live off her interest and not touch the (principal, principle).
4. (Their, They're, There) asking (who's, whose) bike that is in the driveway.
5. Are you sure (your, you're) not (too, two, to) tired?
6. I (know, no) I should (right, write) more often.

7. Has anyone heard (whether, weather) tuition fees will be increased?

8. The college has (its, it's) own letterhead (stationary, stationery).

9. Will there be any (knew, new) course offerings in the fall?

10. Patty and Raymond (use, used) to go to the lake every summer.

Words That Look Alike

advise, advice

Use **advise** as a verb to mean "counsel." **Advise** rhymes with **wise.**

I would advise you not to go.

Use **advice** when it's not a verb. **Advice** rhymes with **nice.**

That was good advice he gave me.

choose, chose

Use **choose** to mean "select."

I will choose a major next semester.

Use **chose** when you want the past tense of **choose.**

Last semester I chose a major.

clothes, cloths

Use **clothes** to mean "wearing apparel." **Clothes** rhymes with **those.**

She has beautiful clothes.

Use **cloths** to mean "pieces of fabric." **Cloths** rhymes with **moths.**

The car wash attendants used soft cloths to dry the cars.

conscience, conscious

Use **conscience** when you are talking about right and wrong.

Let your conscience be your guide!

Use **conscious** to mean "aware."

I was not conscious of the pain.

dessert, desert

Use **dessert** to mean "something sweet after dinner." Remember that the one with two **s**'s is the one you want two helpings of.

He had cheesecake for dessert.

Use *desert* for all other meanings.

> The soldier was tempted to desert. (Stress is on the second syllable: de**sert.**)

> The cactus thrived in the desert. (Stress is on the first syllable: **de**sert.)

feel, fill

Use *feel* to describe your health or emotions, or to mean touch.

> I feel like I'm coming down with a cold.

> I feel good about the decision I made.

> She loves the feel of satin sheets.

Use *fill* to describe what you do with a glass.

> He went to fill his glass from the faucet.

loose, lose

Use *loose* when you mean "not tight." *Loose* rhymes with *moose.*

> The top of the jar was loose.

Use *lose* to mean "misplace" or the opposite of win. *Lose* rhymes with *cruise.*

> The team did not want to lose the playoff game.

> Did you lose your watch?

moral, morale

Use *moral* when you're talking about right and wrong. Stress the first syllable when you pronounce **mor**al.

> He has strong moral values.

Use *morale* to mean "the spirit of the individual or group." Stress the second syllable when you pronounce mor**ale**.

> Employee morale was at an all-time high.

personal, personnel

Use *personal* to mean "private" or "individual." Stress the first syllable when you pronounce **per**sonal.

> It was a very personal decision.

Use *personnel* when you mean "a group of workers." Stress the last syllable when you pronounce person**nel**.

> All personnel were expected to work during inventory.

quiet, quite

Use **quiet** to mean the opposite of loud. **Quiet** rhymes with **diet.**

Be quiet!

Use **quite** to mean "very." **Quite** rhymes with **bite.**

It was getting quite late.

than, then

Use **than** to compare two things. **Than** rhymes with **fan.**

He is shorter than I.

Use **then** to tell when. **Then** rhymes with **when.**

Then she decided to become an actress.

were, where

Use **were** when you want a past tense verb. **Were** rhymes with **her.**

We were fifteen miles from the nearest phone.

Use **where** to refer to a place. It contains the word **here. Where** rhymes with **hair.**

Where have you been?

woman, women

Use **woman** to mean *one* person.

That woman has been in here before.

Use **women** to mean more than one **woman.**

There were only two women in the class.

APPLICATION

Circle the correct word in parentheses. If you are unsure don't guess, but go back and check the definition.

EXAMPLE: I'll never forget my grandfather's (advise, advice).

1. Felicity is (quiet, quite) a dancer!
2. She asked where she might find the (personal, personnel) office.
3. If you are not in front of the library, (were, where) will I find you?
4. The (moral, morale) of the four (woman, women) on the debate team was low.

5. As I recall, in high school Dennis always (chose, choose) his (clothes, cloths) very carefully.

6. How does Aurora manage to (lose, loose) her notebook every semester?

7. Maria and Don (fill, feel) well prepared for the exam.

8. I will take your (advice, advise) and try the (desert, dessert).

9. Martina would rather follow her own (conscience, conscious) (then, than) do what others want her to do.

10. Dan enjoys riding his motorcycle in the (desert, dessert).

Words That Have Similar Meanings

among, between

Use **among** when you are talking about more than two things.

It was an agreement among friends.

Use **between** when you are talking about two things.

Let's keep this conversation just between you and me.

amount, number

Use **amount** to refer to things that cannot be counted.

She put just the right amount of sugar in his coffee.

Use **number** to refer to things that can be counted.

They needed to know the number of people that were coming.

disinterested, uninterested

Use **disinterested** to mean "impartial" or "neutral."

They brought their dispute before a disinterested third party.

Use **uninterested** to mean "not interested."

The lazy cat was uninterested in the mouse.

fewer, less

Use **fewer** to refer to things that can be counted.

She decided to take fewer classes in the spring.

Use **less** to refer to things that cannot be counted.

This brand of ice cream has less fat.

precede, proceed

Use **precede** when you mean "go before."

The maid of honor will precede the bride down the aisle.

Use **proceed** when you mean "go forward" or "go on."

If I'm late, please proceed without me.

rise, raise

Use **rise** when you mean "get up."

I try to rise early on school days.

Use **raise** when you mean "lift" or "increase," or to refer to an increase in salary.

They tried without success to raise the sunken ship.
The college planned to raise the tuition.
I was hoping my boss would give me a raise.

APPLICATION

Choose the correct word in parentheses and write it in the blank.

EXAMPLE: She and her sister split the inheritance

__**between**__ them. (among, between)

1. Harrison seems very _____ in school. (disinterested, uninterested)

2. There are always _____ students in the class at the end of the semester than there are at the beginning. (fewer, less)

3. Despite the poor turnout, they decided to _____ with the performance. (precede, proceed)

4. The _____ of Americans satisfied with their standard of living is constantly decreasing. (number, amount)

5. Biology 1 is designed to _____ Biology 2. (precede, proceed)

6. The gossip about the boss and his secretary spread quickly _____ the twelve employees. (among, between)

7. Today many products are available in brands that have

_____ calories. (fewer, less)

8. The commission was made up of seven _____ citizens.

(disinterested, uninterested)

9. He was unable to _____ from his bed without assistance.

(rise, raise)

10. The _____ of raffle tickets sold by the Women's Studies

Department was over 5,000. (amount, number)

▼ CHAPTER REVIEW

• A number of words are used incorrectly because they look or sound like other words, or because they are similar in meaning to other words. The following **words** are among the **most often confused:**

accept, except
Use **accept** as a verb to mean "receive what is offered." Use **except** to mean "but" or "excluding."

advise, advice
Use **advise** as a verb to mean "counsel." **Advise** rhymes with **wise.** Use **advice** when it's not a verb. **Advice** rhymes with **nice.**

affect, effect
Use **affect** as a verb to mean "influence." Use **effect** as a noun to mean "a result."

among, between
Use **among** when you are talking about more than two things. Use **between** when you are talking about two things.

amount, number
Use **amount** to refer to things that cannot be counted. Use **number** to refer to things that can be counted.

dessert, desert
Use **dessert** to mean "something sweet after dinner." Use **desert** for all other meanings.

disinterested, uninterested
Use **disinterested** to mean "impartial" or "neutral." Use **uninterested** to mean "not interested."

fewer, less

Use **fewer** to refer to things that can be counted. Use **less** to refer to things that cannot be counted.

have, of

Use **have** as a verb. Use **of** only in a prepositional phrase.

its, it's

Use **its** if you want a possessive pronoun. Use **it's** if you mean "it is" or "it has."

moral, morale

Use **moral** when you're talking about right and wrong. Use **morale** to mean "the spirit of the individual or group."

personal, personnel

Use **personal** to mean "private" or "individual." Use **personnel** when you mean "a group of workers."

principle, principal

Use **principle** when you mean "rule." Both **principle** and **rule** end in **le.** Use **principal** to mean "main" or to refer to the head of a school. Remember the saying, "The principal is your pal"; the word **principal** ends in **pal.**

rise, raise

Use **rise** when you mean "get up." Use **raise** when you mean "lift" or "increase," or to refer to an increase in salary.

stationary, stationery

Use **stationary** with an **a** when you mean "stays in one place" or "unchanging." Use **stationery** with an **e** when you mean "writing paper."

their, there, they're

Use **their** to mean "belonging to them." Use **there** to mean a place or to act as a place holder at the beginning of a sentence. Use **they're** to mean "they are."

to, too, two

Use **two** when you mean "the number two." Use **too** when you mean "also" or "more than enough." Use **to** for all other meanings.

use, used

Use the word **use** to mean "function" or "make use of." Use the word **used** to mean "in the habit of" or "secondhand."

woman, women

Use **woman** to mean *one* person. Use **women** to mean more than one **woman.**

who's, whose

Use **who's** to mean "who is" or "who has." Use **whose** to show possession.

you're, your

Use **you're** to mean "you are." Use **your** to mean "belonging to you."

PRACTICE

To test your knowledge of words easily confused, read the following paragraph carefully and circle the correct word in each word pair.

Deadwood Dick

[1]From the 1860s to the 1880s, America's attention was often focused on (its, it's) western frontiers. [2]These were the years of the great cattle drives, years in which the image of the cowboy had (all ready, already) become fixed in the American imagination. [3]Today, when most people think of the cowboys of the old West, they think of men who lived hard-riding, hard-drinking lives. [4]In fact, most cowboys were young men in (their, there) teens and twenties who, (due, do) to the fact that they had no other skills, worked for a year or two as cowpunchers and (than, then) pursued different livelihoods. [5]Cowpunching was young men's work; it involved long hours, pay of (no, know) more than $30 per month, and hazardous working conditions, which ranged from the danger of accidents on the trail to the danger posed by gangs of cattle thieves. [6]The (principal, principle) activity of these gangs was attacking cowboys in the (coarse, course) of the journey from southern Texas to Abilene, Kansas. [7]Of the 35,000 to 55,000 men who rode the (dessert, desert) trails in those days, nearly one-fifth were African-American

or Mexican. [8]Barred from many other trades, African-American cowboys enjoyed the freedom of life on the trail. [9]Many (were, where) ex-slaves or the sons of slaves who left for Kansas after the Civil War. [10]Several, especially Nat Love, became legends (through, threw) their accomplishments. [11]The son of Tennessee slaves, Love won prize money in roping and shooting contests and was (quiet, quite) famous—in fact, he was so famous that he was given a (new, knew) name—Deadwood Dick. [12]Between 1877 and 1885, thirty-three Deadwood Dick novels (were, where) published. [13]But, in order to please his readership, the author of these novels made Deadwood Dick a white man who dressed in black (cloths, clothes) and rode a black horse.

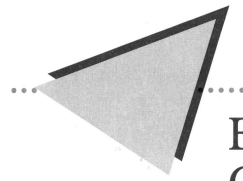

Copyright © 1994 Macmillan College Publishing Company

CHAPTER 34

Editing for Correct Spelling

▼ CHAPTER PREVIEW

In the preceding chapters of this unit, you have practiced using a dictionary, learned a few basic spelling rules, and looked at words easily confused. In this chapter, you will see how a personal spelling list can help you improve your own spelling. Then you will be given a choice of writing assignments, followed by a sample student essay on one of the topics. Finally, you will practice checking the spelling in your own essay, based on what you have learned in this unit.

Keeping a Personal Spelling Log

While you may have one or two spelling trouble spots, chances are that you do not have to learn every single spelling rule or memorize every pair of words that are easily confused. Keeping a spelling log for yourself, based on misspelled words in essays returned to you, can help you focus on the rules and words you need to learn to make you a better speller. Look at the following sample spelling log:

INCORRECT SPELLING	CORRECT SPELLING	RULE (OR MEMORY JOGGER)
recieve	receive	*i* before *e* **except** after *c*
enviromental	environmental	has the word *iron* in it
govenor	governor	has the word *govern* in it
beleive	believe	*i* before *e*
writting	writing	no CVC, drop *e* add *-ing*
arguement	argument	no *e,* exception to rule

Notice that two types of mistake are repeated. One mistake is the result of a pronunciation problem. If this student pronounces the words **environmental** and **governor** so that all the letters are heard, he or she will not have problems with spelling these words. The other spelling problem can be corrected by memorizing the *i* before *e* rule.

399

APPLICATION

In the space provided, make a spelling log for the misspelled words.

releive   worryed   writting   nieghbor   swiming

Writing Assignments

Choose one of the following topics to develop into an essay:

1. Describe a place that you visit regularly. Try to capture the feeling or mood of the place. Maybe you have a special place, such as a park, where you go to feel at peace, or perhaps you are struck by the sense of things being in disrepair when you visit your grandmother.
2. Describe a place that had or has had a strong impact on you, either positive or negative. Perhaps you visited a historical home that made you think about the way people lived in the past, or maybe you were frustrated after visiting a government office like the Department of Motor Vehicles.

To choose a topic, you might try one or both of the following:

1. List all of the places you have gone in the past month, including school, work, relatives' homes, shopping, and outings.
2. Freewrite to remember a place in the past that might have had an impact. If you get stuck, you can repeat a word like "offices" or a phrase like "weird places."

Once you have decided on a place, you might want to revisit the place (if possible) and record the details as though you are a camcorder panning the area. If you cannot revisit the place, try brainstorming or freewriting to recapture the details. Once you have your details and have thought about what you are going to write, compose a sentence that identifies the place and tells what kind of impact it had on you or what mood characterizes the place. Here are three examples:

The Department of Motor Vehicles office is designed to frustrate people.

My grandmother's attic is filled with ghosts of the past.

Anyone who enters my uncle's house can tell that a sports fanatic lives there.

A Student Responds to One of the Writing Assignments

About the Reading: Written by Kevin Glover, the essay that follows won first prize in a college essay competition for students in developmental writing classes. Thirty-three years old and the father of two children, Glover is a respiratory care major. When he finishes his education, he would like to go into the field of respiratory equipment sales. In addition to attending academic classes, Glover is enrolled in a construction training program, in which he works as a carpenter's apprentice. He also volunteers with the Red Cross in disaster relief work, as well as teaching CPR and first aid classes.

As You Read: Notice the way Glover organizes the details in his essay so that you feel as if you were moving into the building and looking at the waiting room yourself. Pay attention also to the language of this essay: almost every word is carefully chosen. Finally, be aware of the fact that all of the details work together to give you a particular sense of the place.

The Waiting Room

For most people, going to the Department of Public Social Services and applying for either General Relief or Aid to Families with Dependent Children can be an extremely trying experience. On average, an entire day can be squandered waiting for one's name to be called by a social worker in a lobby filled to overcapacity by individuals varying from despondent, dejected skid row "street people" to recently laid off aerospace workers. The "Welfare Office," as it is more commonly called, can be a crowded, dirty and difficult place to walk around in; however, I see the many adverse conditions as profound inspiration. **1**

The seemingly mile-long line, which in light of current economic downtrends establishes itself more consistently each morning outside the double doors of the Welfare Office, is an accurate indicator for predicting the sizable crowd of desperate, destitute people who will merge into the limited spaces. Gaining entrance into the building is not an easy feat. After all bags, briefcases and contents of pockets have been searched and examined by a metal detector, there are more lines to wait in. There is a lengthy line to acquire an application if a person is newly applying for aid. Also, there is a line for people with appointments but who must still register in order for a social worker to realize this particular person has kept his or her scheduled appointment. Perhaps the most challenging task following such lines is finding a vacant seat among the two hundred pea green and dull red stiff plastic chairs making up the bulk of the furnishings. **2**

Regardless of whether one is standing or sitting, the "awaitee" begins to look around the lobby only to discover the ugly **3** decor. Fading paint is chipping, and crumbling wall boards house outdated public service posters warning against the use of intravenous drugs. The "NO SMOKING" signs try to prohibit smokers who will no doubt test to see if the regulation is enforced by the overworked staff. By this time, however, the lobby is full, making discovery of the offensive smoker unlikely. Also, about this time, trash, in the form of newspapers, soda cans, fast-food wrappers, and incorrectly filled out state forms discarded by errant "awaitees," begins to accumulate on the badly stained tile floor and beneath chairs. Spilled liquids—coffee, water, the formula from an infant's bottle—are also constituents of this odoriferous waste.

At last the awaited moment comes when one's name is announced over a public address speaker, the volume of which is either just loud enough to be indistinct or so loud that the person speaking sounds garbled and unintelligible. At the recognition of his name, the anxious "awaitee" jumps to his feet and begins the slow struggle to free his entangled self from the many knees, ankles and feet of the other beleaguered "awaitees" seated around him. Although this is a seemingly easy task, the person who has been summoned may encounter a drunk sprawled across the floor between rows of chairs. **4**

Seeing firsthand what a truly homeless person looks like, and realizing that my own personal economic situation is far better than some other poor soul's, I have vowed to do my best, one hundred and ten percent of the time, within legal means, to keep from sinking below the poverty line. In spite of the conditions at the Department of Public Social Services, I have gained immense inspiration from frequent visits. **5**

After You Read: Refer to the student essay to complete the following items:

1. Copy the sentence in paragraph 1 that you think best sums up the essay.

   _____

   _____

   _____

2. Circle the letter of the item that best describes how the details in the essay are organized.

   a. Least to most upsetting things a person sees and does.

   b. First to last things a person does and notices.

   c. Left to right view of the waiting room.

3. This essay is filled with very specific details, including information about what is printed on signs, what kinds of materials make up

the overflowing trash, how the voice on the loudspeaker sounds. What two details work best to help you hear, smell, or see the scene? (Copy them exactly.)

_____

_____

_____

4. This essay has some words that may be unfamiliar to you. Use your dictionary to help you explain the meaning of the words in bold print as they are used in their sentence.
   A. The "Welfare Office," as it is more commonly called, can be a crowded, dirty and difficult place to walk around in; however, I see the many **adverse** conditions as profound inspiration.

   _____

   B. Also, about this time, trash, in the form of newspapers, soda cans, fast-food wrappers, and incorrectly filled out state forms discarded by **errant** "awaitees," begins to accumulate on the badly stained tile floor and beneath chairs.

   _____

   C. Spilled liquids—coffee, water, the formula from an infant's bottle—are also constituents of this **odoriferous** waste.

   _____

   D. At the recognition of his name, the anxious "awaitee" jumps to his feet and begins the slow struggle to free his entangled self from the many knees, ankles and feet of the other **beleaguered** "awaitees" seated around him.

   _____

5. Copy the sentence in the last paragraph that restates (says the same thing in different words) the final sentence of paragraph 1.

_____

_____

_____

Checking for Correct Spelling in Your Own Writing

If you have been keeping a spelling log, look over the types of words that give you difficulty. If you have not, look over returned papers and see which words are labeled as misspelled. Then proofread your essay focusing on these types of words. For example, if you have trouble deciding when to use *ie* and when to use *ei,* you can focus on words containing these two letters and look up any spellings you are unsure of. If you confuse words like ***are*** and ***our,*** check these words any time they appear in your paper to make sure you have used them correctly.

After you have checked your paper for correct spelling, look for one word that is used repeatedly. Use your dictionary to find an alternative word with the same or a similar meaning to use instead in one sentence.

▼ CHAPTER REVIEW

- Keep a **personal spelling log** to help you assess and correct your own spelling problems.

UNIT **8** *Highlights*

Using a Dictionary

- Use a dictionary to find basic information about **famous people.**
- Use a dictionary to look up **place names.**
- Use a dictionary to find the **meanings of common foreign phrases.**
- Use a **desk style dictionary** to give you the following information about a word:

1. **spelling**
2. **syllable divisions**
3. **pronunciation**
4. **grammatical labels**
5. **irregular forms**
6. **meanings**
7. **usage**
8. **origins**
9. **synonyms**

Basic Spelling Rules

The letters *a, e, i, o,* and *u* are **vowels.** All of the other letters are **consonants.** The letter *y* can be either a vowel or a consonant.

Rule 1:   Doubling the Final Consonant in a One-Syllable Word
If a **one-syllable word** ends in a combination of consonant-vowel-consonant (CVC), double the final consonant whenever you add an ending that starts with a vowel (like *-ing, -est, -ed*).

Rule 2:   Doubling the Final Consonant in a Word of More than One Syllable
Whenever you add an ending that starts with a vowel to a **word of more than one syllable,** double the final consonant if (1) the last three letters are CVC, and (2) the stress is on the last syllable.

Rule 3:   Keeping or Changing the Final **y**
Whenever you add an ending other than *-ing* to a word that ends in *y,* change the *y* to *i* if the letter before the *y* is a consonant.

Rule 4:   Keeping or Dropping the Final **e**
Whenever you add a new ending that begins with a vowel (like *-ing* or *-able*) to a word that ends in *e,* drop the final *e.* Whenever you add a new ending that begins with a consonant (like *-ly* or *-ment*), keep the final *e.*

Rule 5: Adding -s or -es
Add *-es* instead of *-s* for
1. words ending in **ch, sh, ss, x,** or **z.**
2. most words ending in **o.**
3. words in which you have changed the final **y** to **i.**

Rule 6: Using ie or ei
Use *i* before *e*, except after *c*, or when sounding like **ay** as in **neighbor** or **weigh.** When the *c* has a **sh** sound, however, use *ie* after *c*.

Words Most Commonly Confused

Many words are misspelled either because they look or because they sound like another word. Still other words are confused with one another because they have similar meanings. Look out for these commonly confused words:

accept, except

advise, advice

affect, effect

among, between

amount, number

dessert, desert

disinterested, uninterested

fewer, less

have, of

its, it's

moral, morale

personal, personnel

principle, principal

rise, raise

stationary, stationery

their, there, they're

to, too, two

use, used

woman, women

who's, whose

you're, your

Personal Spelling Log

Keep a **personal spelling log** to help you assess and correct your own spelling problems.

PRACTICE

Use the sentences that follow to test your mastery of the material in Unit 8. If you have difficulty, go back and review the information in Chapters 31–34.

A. Follow the basic spelling rules to combine the following words and endings:

EXAMPLE: swim + ing ___**swimming**___

1. control + ed _____

2. run + ing _____

3. ready + ness _____

4. penny + less _____

5. nerve + ous _____

6. debate + able _____

7. terrify + ing _____

8. write + ing _____

9. believe + able _____

10. care + ful _____

B. Circle the correctly spelled word in each pair.

EXAMPLE: (their)   thier

1. weigh   wiegh
2. beginner   beginer
3. dayly   daily
4. seize   sieze
5. judgment   judgement
6. prayed   praid
7. guesses   gueses
8. sliped   slipped

9. angryly   angrily
10. potatoes   potatos

C. Circle the correct word in parentheses.

EXAMPLE: They told me to stand over (here, hear).

1. (Accept, Except) for the fact that Jose wears glasses, he looks just like his twin, Jaime.
2. (There, They're) going to have a live band at the party.
3. The mechanic told her she needed new (breaks, brakes) on her car.
4. Mr. Johnson has been described as having a few screws (loose, lose).
5. "All right," Monroe demanded, "(who's, whose) car is blocking the driveway?"
6. I would (advice, advise) you not to (wear, where) the string bikini when you visit your boyfriend's parents.
7. There were (too, to, two) many rental movies to choose from.
8. (Its, It's) hard not to judge other people by (our, are) own values.
9. The politician walked quickly (past, passed) the dilapidated housing project.
10. My (principal, principle) aim is to find a job that pays enough to live on while I'm in school.

D. Use your dictionary to explain the meaning of the bold word as it is used in the sentence.

EXAMPLE: I appreciated the sales clerk's **candid** remark about the bathing suit.

honest, frank

1. My boss' Cadillac has a special **governor** that keeps the car from going over 55 miles per hour.

2. Her father **squelched** her enthusiasm for a car when he told her she would have to work to pay for the insurance.

3. The antique rocking chair was a real **find** for the bargain hunter.

4. They painted the child's room in **primary** colors.

_____

_____

5. Without his glasses, Ray was unable to **distinguish** distant objects.

_____

6. The woman in the news story had **milked** the unsuspecting old man for half a million dollars.

_____

7. The court issued a **gag** order in the case.

_____

8. It was his **practice** to jog five miles every day.

_____

9. They donated $500 to the earthquake **relief** fund.

_____

10. The woman described her husband to the therapist as someone who is very **remote**.

_____

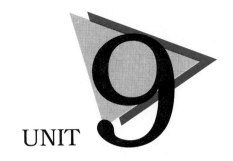

UNIT 9

Addressing Special Concerns of ESL Students

CHAPTER 35

Using Articles

▼ CHAPTER PREVIEW

If you have learned English as a second language, you may find that the proper use of articles is particularly difficult to master. In fact, a native speaker of English might be surprised at the complexity of the rules for using the **definite article** *the* and the **indefinite articles** *a* and *an.* In this chapter, you will learn these rules and have a chance to practice applying them.

A Professional Writer Uses Articles

About the Reading: Jon D. Hull has been a Los Angeles correspondent for *Time* magazine. He is currently the *Time* bureau chief in Jerusalem. Hull has written many articles about homelessness and about drugs. In order to research "Slow Descent into Hell," which first appeared in *Time* in February 1987, Hull spent a week in Philadelphia living with the homeless. In the excerpt from "Slow Descent into Hell" that follows, Hull describes the life of one of the homeless men with whom he lived.

As You Read: Articles have been printed in bold type. Pay special attention to the noun that comes after each article.

From "Slow Descent into Hell"

[1]**A** smooth bar of soap, wrapped neatly in **a** white handkerchief and tucked safely in **the** breast pocket of **a** faded leather jacket, is all that keeps George from losing himself to **the** streets. [2]When he wakes each morning from his makeshift bed of newspapers in **the** subway tunnels of Philadelphia, he heads for **the** rest room of **a** nearby bus station or McDonald's and begins **an** elaborate ritual of

washing off **the** dirt and smells of homelessness: first **the** hands and forearms, then **the** face and neck, and finally **the** fingernails and teeth. [3]Twice **a** week he takes off his worn Converse high tops and socks and washes his feet in **the** sink, ignoring **the** cold stares of well-dressed commuters.

....

After You Read: Refer to the reading selection to complete the following items:

1. In sentence 1, what articles appear before the following nouns:

   _____ bar, _____ handkerchief, _____ pocket

2. In sentence 2, what article does Hull use before "elaborate ritual"?

   _____ elaborate ritual

3. In sentence 2, what articles does Hull use before the following words? _____ hands and forearms, _____ face and neck, and _____ fingernails and teeth?

4. In sentence 3, what articles does Hull use before the following words? _____ sink, _____ cold stares

Noun Markers

The articles **a, an,** and **the** are sometimes described as noun markers because they signal that a noun is about to appear. (Refer to Chapter 9 for more information about various noun markers.) The noun may appear directly after the article, or other words may come in between.

> **the** rope, **the** frayed **rope**
>
> **a** picture, **a** beautifully painted **picture**
>
> **an** athlete, **an** outstanding **athlete**

Use **a** before a word that begins with a consonant sound, and use **an** before a word that begins with a vowel sound.

APPLICATION

In each sentence, circle the articles and draw an arrow from each article to the noun that follows it.

EXAMPLE: Elena sent a letter to the congressman.

1. He found a lizard on the bathroom wall.

2. The woman stumbled over a large crack in the sidewalk.

3. The man picked an apple from the tree.

4. Mrs. Petrowski bought a velvet painting of Elvis Presley.

5. Manuel discovered a large hole in the backyard.

6. Kito gave the money to the cashier behind the counter.

7. He was an incredibly conscientious student.

8. She was taking an awful risk by investing in the poorly rated bonds.

9. Tricia came to the costume party dressed as a vampire.

10. He locked the front door but forgot to close the bedroom window.

Count and Noncount Nouns

The decision whether to use a definite or indefinite article depends, in many cases, on the type of noun it marks. Nouns can be divided into two categories: **count nouns** and **noncount nouns. Count nouns** refer to people, places, or things that can be counted.

three **sisters**   one pepperoni **pizza**   five **dollars**

Noncount nouns refer to things that cannot be counted.

furniture   water   assistance   freedom   love

APPLICATION

Each item contains both a count noun and a noncount noun. Label each noun as either **C** for "count" or **NC** for "noncount."

EXAMPLES: eggs ___**C**___

milk ___**NC**___

1. snow _____   6. personality _____

   rocks _____   ears _____

2. chemistry _____   7. grammar _____

   courses _____   nouns _____

3. tea _____   8. sleepwear _____

   cookie _____   gown _____

4. bronze _____   9. equipment _____

   coins _____   pencils _____

5. jewelry _____   10. filth _____

   bracelet _____   stains _____

Indefinite Articles

1. Use **a** or **an** with singular count nouns whose specific identity is not known to the reader.

   a woman

   a job

   a city in the Midwest

2. Do not use **a** or **an** with plural or noncount nouns.

water	oil	truth
bread	pasta	bacon
information	happiness	candies
concrete	oranges	anger
men	cereal	cups

   Sometimes, you will see a noncount noun used with a quantity word that indicates an amount or unit.

   one **quart** of ice cream

   two **gallons** of white wine

   five **pounds** of sugar

   a single **blade** of grass

   Even though the noun cannot be counted, the quantity can. A quantity word, like **quart** or **pound,** is always countable.

APPLICATION

Place correct indefinite articles in the following sentences if they are needed. If they are not, leave the space blank.

> *EXAMPLE:*   She needed _____ time to herself.
> (No article is needed because time is a noncount noun.)

1. Because her grandmother watches soap operas for at least four hours every day, Dianne always asks her for _____ advice about men.

2. Her brother's dog loves to drink _____ beer and eat _____ ice cream.

3. Lily's older brother has two important qualities—_____ intelligence and _____ wealth.

4. Maida went shopping for _____ celery, _____ oil, and _____ air conditioner.

5. My grandmother always told me that when _____ poverty comes in the door, _____ love flies out the window.

6. Ryan and Alex have been looking for _____ apartment near the park.

7. After they got engaged, Denisha and Michael decided to save the money they would have spent on a big wedding and buy _____ new furniture instead.

8. Leo's next-door neighbor asked him to pick up _____ milk at the grocery store; Leo didn't know how much his neighbor wanted, so he bought _____ gallon.

9. Completing his research essay gave him a feeling of _____ great satisfaction.

10. A day at the amusement park with my niece was really _____

fun.

Definite Articles

There is only one definite article in English—**_the._** Use **_the_** with most nouns whose specific identity is known. There are several ways to decide whether to use a definite or an indefinite article, but the real problem is determining whether or not the noun has been specifically identified. Usually, the identity of the noun is clear for one of these reasons:

1. The noun has been mentioned previously.

> A man carrying his small child sat across from Clarice. When **the** man smiled, Clarice smiled back.
> (**_the_** describes the man who had already been mentioned.)

2. The phrase or clause following the noun makes its identity clear.

> **The** book on the second shelf was very useful for my research project.
> (**"on the second shelf"** identifies the specific book that was useful for the research project.)

3. The situation makes the noun's identity clear.

> Please help me open **the** car door.
> (Both the person speaking and the person being spoken to would know which door is being referred to.)

4. A superlative (such as **_greatest_** or **_most beautiful_**) makes the identity of the noun clear.

> Of all my cousins, Dash has **the** best personality.
> (The superlative **_best_** makes the identity clear.)

5. The noun describes a unique person, place, or thing.

> I feel romantic whenever I look at **the** moon.
> (There is only one moon, so the identity of the noun is clear.)

In general, do **not** use **_the_** with most singular proper nouns. Do **not** use **_the_** with names of persons, streets, parks, cities, states, countries, continents, lakes, bays, mountains, and islands (Mr. Suarez, Tracy Hendersen, Marina Street, MacArthur Park, St. Louis, New Jersey, Argentina, Lake Isabella, San Francisco Bay, Mount St. Michel, Merritt Island).
    Exceptions to this rule include names of large regions (**the** West Coast), and names of oceans, seas, gulfs, canals, and rivers (**the** At-

lantic, **the** Caspian Sea, **the** Gulf of Mexico, **the** Suez Canal, **the** Mississippi River). Remember, however, that ***the*** is used to mark plural proper nouns: **the** United States, **the** Appalachians, **the** Poconos.

Do **not** use ***the*** with plural or noncount nouns meaning "in general" or "all."

> In Mexican cooking, **beans** are an important source of protein.
> (***beans*** in general are a source of protein.)

But:

> **The beans** in the cupboard are for dinner tonight.
> (Only these specific ***beans*** are for dinner.)

APPLICATION

Add the article ***the*** in the space wherever it is needed.

> *EXAMPLE:*   Her uncle makes ___the___ best burritos I've ever tasted.

1. _____ Pamela Walker is _____ tallest person in her family.

2. My sister is planning to go on vacation to _____ Paris, France, after she saves enough money.

3. Before they came to _____ United States, they lived in _____ Bahamas.

4. _____ Boston is my favorite city on _____ East Coast.

5. In _____ Ireland, people eat _____ potatoes on a daily basis.

6. Many years ago, _____ Ms. Gardiner traveled through _____ Philippines.

7. After visiting _____ Persian Gulf, Loretta was glad to see _____ New York Harbor.

8. Belva had always wanted to cross _____ Andes on a mule.

9. Before the class studied _____ Italy, they learned about _____ ancient Rome.

10. _____ beach is _____ best place to relax.

▼ CHAPTER REVIEW

- The **articles a, an,** and **the** are also called **noun markers** because they are always followed by a noun. They may be followed directly by a noun, or several words may come in between.
- **A** and **an** are **indefinite articles; the** is a **definite article.**
- Use **a** before a word that begins with a consonant sound, and use **an** before a word that begins with a vowel sound (**a, e, i, o, u**).
- Nouns can be divided into two categories: **count nouns** and **noncount nouns.** If a quantity word is used with a noncount noun, the quantity *can* be counted.
- Use **indefinite articles** (**a, an**) with singular count nouns if the specific identity of the nouns is unknown. Do not use indefinite pronouns with plural or noncount nouns.
- Use the **definite article** (**the**) with most nouns whose specific identity is known. In most instances, do not use **the** with singular proper nouns, except the names of large regions and bodies of water, or with plural or noncount nouns meaning "all" or "in general."

PRACTICE

To test your understanding of articles, add the appropriate articles in the spaces provided. If no article is needed, leave the space blank.

Women's Suffrage

[1]_____ women's suffrage movement arose in _____ decade after _____ Civil War. [2]Early suffragists wanted _____ right to vote as _____ means to gain _____ equality with men. [3]By challenging _____ male authority, these women threatened traditional values and roles; as a result, they had trouble attracting support. [4]There were also numerous divisions among _____ suffragists themselves. [5]Some tried to find allies among people seeking to obtain _____ equal rights for African-Americans. [6]Other suffragists were concerned only with women's issues. [7]In _____ 1872 election, _____ Susan B. Anthony and two other suffragists tried to cast ballots, but without _____ success, and _____ Ms. Anthony was convicted of illegal voting. [8]By the end of _____ century, women

had gained many of _____ opportunities sought by early women's rights advocates: _____ woman had access to higher education and the professions, and many states had granted married women rights to property as well as to guardianship of children. [9]But _____ right to vote was denied to _____ American women until after _____ World War I.

Using Verbs Correctly

▼ CHAPTER PREVIEW

Because English is a complicated language, many people who speak English as their native language have some problems with English verbs. But there are also some things about English verbs that present special difficulties to speakers of English as a second language. In this chapter, you will look at common problems that ESL students encounter when using verbs and learn how to avoid these problems.

A Professional Writer Uses Verbs Correctly

About the Reading: Sucheng Chan, who was born in China, contracted polio at the age of four. She was not expected to live, and her partial recovery was slow and painful. While she was still a child, Chan's family left China, moving to Hong Kong and Malaysia before coming to the United States. Chan received her PhD from the University of California, Berkeley, where she taught for ten years and received an award for distinguished teaching. Now wheelchair-bound, Chan teaches history at the University of California, Santa Barbara.

As You Read: Although English is not Chan's native language, this piece shows her ability to express herself fluently and with emotional power. Watch especially how she moves from one verb tense to another; verbs appear in bold type.

From "You're Short, Besides"

[1]I**'ve** often **wondered** if I **would have been** a different person **had** I not **been** handicapped. [2]I really **do**n't **know,** though there is no question that being handicapped **has marked** me. [3]But at the same time I usually **do** not **feel** handicapped—and consequently I **do** not **act** handicapped. [4]People **are** therefore less likely to treat me as a

handicapped person. ⁵There **is** no doubt, however, that the lives of my parents, sister, husband, other family members and some close friends **have been affected** by my physical condition. ⁶They **have had** to learn not to hide me away at home, not to feel embarrassed by how I **look** or react to people who **say** silly things to me, and not to resent me for the extra demands my condition **makes** on them.

···

After You Read: Refer to the reading to answer the following questions:

1. List   the   three   verbs   that   appear   in   the   first   sentence:

   _____ , _____ , _____ .

2. Write the three verbs in the reading that begin with the helping verb **do.**

   _____ , _____ , _____

3. Circle the letter of the following item that best describes the use of the helping verb **do** in the complete verbs listed in question 2.

   a. To ask a question.

   b. To express a negative meaning with the adverb **not.**

   c. To emphasize a main verb in a positive sense.

4. **Is** and **are** are both forms of the verb _____ .

Helping Verbs + Base Forms

Remember that **helping verbs *always* appear before main verbs.**

      HV   MV
We **will look** for him when we finish lunch.

   HV   MV
Do you **have** any idea where he was last seen?

But, in English, you cannot put just any helping verb together with any main verb—only certain combinations of helping verbs and main verbs make sense.

There are many helping verbs in English. However, nine of them can *only* be helping verbs: ***can, could, may, might, must, shall, should, will,*** and ***would.*** After these helping verbs, always use the base form of the verb as the main verb. The **base form** is the verb form used after the word ***to*** (to **see**, to **go**).

<table>
<tr><td>can see</td><td>can go</td></tr>
<tr><td>could see</td><td>could go</td></tr>
<tr><td>may see</td><td>may go</td></tr>
<tr><td>might see</td><td>might go</td></tr>
</table>

must see   must go
shall see   shall go
should see   should go
will see   will go
would see   would go

Remember that adverbs can sometimes come between the helping verbs and the main verb:

I **can** always **tell** when Joe is hungry.
(***always*** is an adverb, not a main verb)

APPLICATION

Circle the helping verb(s) and underline the base verb(s) in each of the following sentences:

EXAMPLE: Katrine would appreciate a letter from you.

1. I must telephone her if I should get to New York.
2. If you could see him now, you would not know him.
3. Lyle and Kerrie will do the dishes.
4. Children really must learn their telephone numbers.
5. If Uncle Gene would help us, we could calculate our taxes.
6. Before he will tell us anything, we must buy him several cups of coffee.
7. Robert may move to South Texas, but, then again, maybe he will remain in Virginia for a few more years.
8. I would give you my last dime.
9. You should know why your brother is the way he is.
10. My grandmother can tell wonderful stories about growing up in Brazil.

Do, Does, or *Did* + Base Form

You can use the helping verbs ***do, does,*** and ***did*** in three ways:

1. To express a negative meaning with the adverbs ***not*** or ***never.***

   They **do not** know what happened.

   He **does not** know why he was fired.

   She **never did** find out his name.

2. To ask a question.

   Do you have any idea where I left my car keys?

Does she have the answer key?

Did he find his book?

3. To emphasize a main verb in a positive sense.

I **do** intend to sign up for the course.

I **did** hope you would think about my offer.

She **does** want to get together soon.

APPLICATION

In the space before each of the following sentences, write the number of the rule that best describes the function of the helping verb *do, does,* or *did:*

EXAMPLE: 2   Don't you ever think about the future?

_____ 1. I don't know where you get your strange ideas.

_____ 2. Does your friend know what time it is?

_____ 3. They do indeed belong here.

_____ 4. Do you know where the Student Services Building is located?

_____ 5. He did help her with the housework when she was going to school.

_____ 6. Staci did belong to a health club, but she canceled her membership.

_____ 7. Although Ivan promised to write, he didn't really mean it.

_____ 8. Does the entire Watson family have to be invited?

_____ 9. I did intend to mow the lawn after lunch.

_____ 10. Janis didn't remember to pick up the dry cleaning.

Have, Has, or *Had* + Past Participle

After helping verbs that are a form of *have* (*have, has, had*), use a past participle to form one of the perfect tenses. Past participles usually end in *-ed, -d, -en, -n,* or *-t.*

have looked	have chosen	have spent
has looked	has chosen	has spent
had looked	had chosen	had spent

APPLICATION

Write in the blank the correct past participle form of the verb in parentheses.

> *EXAMPLE:*   Annemarie has ____**decided**____ (decide, decided) to become a chemist.

1. Kenzo had _____ (learned, learn) English as a child.

2. My sister's parrots have _____ (eaten, eat) all of her plants.

3. Before he came to the United States he had _____ (live, lived) in several other countries.

4. She has always _____ (wanted, want) to dance professionally.

5. The plane flight had _____ (ended, end) before they finished their card game.

6. He had always _____ (believe, believed) in love.

7. Jessamyn and Howard have already _____ (bought, buy) tickets for the concert.

8. When the police questioned her, she admitted that she had _____ (ignored, ignore) several previous warnings about her noisy parties.

9. For as long as I can remember, my Aunt Angela has _____ (loved, love) chocolate in any form.

10. They have _____ (move, moved) to a new, less expensive apartment.

Be + *-ing* Words

After the helping verbs **be, am, is, are, was, were,** or **been,** you can express a continuing action by using a helping verb or verbs with an **-ing** word.

HELPING VERBS	-ING WORD
am, is, are	watching, waiting
was, were	watching, waiting
can **be**, could **be**	watching, waiting
may **be**, might **be**, must **be**	watching, waiting
shall **be**, should **be**	watching, waiting
will **be**, would **be**	watching, waiting
has **been**, had **been**	watching, waiting
may have **been**, could have **been**	watching, waiting
might have **been**, must have **been**	watching, waiting
should have **been**	watching, waiting
would have **been**	watching, waiting

In verbs ending in **-ing,** notice that the helping verbs **be** and **been** must be preceded by other helping verbs.

Ariel **has been watching** television for the last three hours.

Caution: Some English verbs are not normally used in the **-ing** form. In general, these are verbs that express a state of being or a mental or sensory activity instead of an action. Some examples of this kind of verb include **seem, taste, feel, believe, think, understand, contain, like, need, see, appear, have, hear,** and **want.**

Some of these verbs have special uses in which **-ing** forms are normal. Because there is no rule to cover these special uses, you will need to make a note of the exceptions as you experience them.

APPLICATION

In the blank, write the correct **be** + **-ing** form of the verb in parentheses.

> *EXAMPLE:*   She _____is going_____ to the library tomorrow. (go)

1. When I saw her last week, Annette _____ a new dress for

   herself. (make)

2. They _____ dinner together after class all semester. (eat)

3. I hear that Walter _____ a new car as soon as he saves a

   little more money. (buy)

4. His brother _____ the Marines as soon as he finishes

   high school. (join)

5. We _____ to see that new movie, but the lines were too

   long. (hope)

6. Dean should have _____ this year, but he did not complete his English requirement. (graduate)

7. My uncle says he _____ for the right time to sell his house. (wait)

8. Before I enrolled in college, I _____ as a dishwasher. (work)

9. Marco _____ to four major universities for acceptance as a communications major. (apply)

10. While she works on her degree, George's cousin _____ as a literacy tutor. (volunteer)

Verb + *to* + Base Verb

You can use certain verbs either with an **-ing** form or with the **to + verb** form to mean essentially the same thing. These verbs include **begin, love, hate, like, continue,** and **start.**

> He loves **eating.**
> He loves **to eat.**
>
> The children began **to play.**
> The children began **playing.**
>
> The couple continued **to argue.**
> The couple continued **arguing.**

With some verbs, though, such as **forget, remember, stop,** and **try,** you need to be careful when deciding to use the **-ing** form or the **to + verb** form, because the meaning of the verb changes depending on the form you choose:

> She stopped **speaking** to her daughter's boyfriend.
> (She would no longer talk to her daughter's boyfriend.)
>
> She stopped **to speak** to her daughter's boyfriend.
> (She stopped what she was doing so that she could talk to her daughter's boyfriend.)

APPLICATION

Circle the expression in parentheses that would make sense in the sentence. In some cases, either expression would make sense in the sentence; in others, only one expression is appropriate to the sentence meaning.

EXAMPLE: The baby loves (playing, to play) with the family dog.

1. Despite her anxiety attacks, she continued (drinking, to drink) caffeinated coffee.
2. He tried unsuccessfully (giving up, to give up) cigarettes.
3. Tammy's boyfriend forgot (to renew, renewing) his driver's license, so it expired.
4. Virginia can't help (to remember, remembering) the time she fell down the stairs.
5. James forgot (to register, registering) for the class, so he'll have to take it next semester.
6. The couple next door like (to go, going) square dancing on Friday nights.
7. His mother-in-law tried (to speak, speaking) to the police officer, but the officer ignored her.
8. The woman stopped (to look, looking) for a job when she signed up for classes.
9. Harold hated (to write, writing) letters home.
10. His doctor told him to stop (to eat, eating) twelve hours before his blood test.

Verb + Noun or Pronoun + *to* + Base Verb

Use certain **verbs** with a **noun or pronoun followed by *to* + verb.** The noun or pronoun usually names a person who is affected by the action of the verb. Verbs that follow this rule include

advise	warn	have	tell
allow	cause	command	convince
encourage	have	instruct	order
persuade	remind	require	

Marji **asked** me **to warn** you about that restaurant.

The safety inspector **encouraged** Lou **to remind** his landlord about installing a fire alarm.

In the cases of a few verbs, you will sometimes include the noun or pronoun and other times leave it out.

> ask expect need want would like

Elmer **asked to speak** to the store manager.

Elmer **asked the store manager to speak** to the rude salesperson.

In some cases you omit the word **to**: verb + **noun or pronoun** + (**to**) + **verb.**

have (meaning "cause")

let (meaning "allow")

make (meaning "force")

Having children **makes** people **be** more flexible.
(Having children **forces** people **to be** more flexible).

After all you've done for me, **let** me **buy** you dinner.
(After all you've done for me, **allow** me **to buy** you dinner).

APPLICATION

Circle the correct form in parentheses.

> *EXAMPLE:* We plan (to visiting, (to visit)) the Empire State Build-
> ing while we are in New York.

1. Sondra and her sister both (enjoy, to enjoy) playing soccer.
2. They urged the child (play, to play) with his birthday gifts.
3. I still have (deciding, to decide) which classes to take next semester.
4. She asked (speak, to speak) to the head cashier.
5. Angie and Nate convinced me (to try out, try out) for a role in the annual musical.
6. I'd like (pay, to pay) for these books now.
7. The Students' Union invited the Marxist historian (give, to give) a lecture to the student body.
8. Luciano (loving, loves) to ski.
9. Please let me (to buy, buy) lunch for you today.
10. The college (requires, to require) all students to take a World Civilizations course.

Two-Word Main Verbs

As you learned in Chapter 2, a number of English verbs are composed of two words, a verb followed by a preposition or an adverb.

These verbs often express **idiomatic** ideas that cannot be understood in a literal way. Two-word verbs are especially common in informal English, and only experience will help you to become familiar with them.

> I **looked over** my notes before the test.
> (In this case, the two-word verb means "reviewed.")

> My sister **dropped in** on my Aunt Maggie.
> (In this case, the two-word verb means "paid a short visit.")

In some cases, the preposition or adverb can follow the verb immediately, or it can be separated from the verb by other words.

> Kendall **called off** the graduation party.

> Kendall **called** the graduation party **off.**

In each example, the words *the graduation party* are needed to complete the meaning of the sentence, but they can be placed either in the middle of the two-word verb or after the two-word verb. However, if the word that completes the meaning of a verb is a **pronoun,** always put it between the verb and the preposition or adverb.

> Kendall **called** it **off.**

Some two-word verbs are never separated by other words.

Always: The dean will **look into** her complaint.

Never: The dean will **look** her complaint **into.**

You probably already know some of the most common **inseparable** two-word verbs:

call on	catch up	check into
come across	drop out	get along
go over	grow up	look after
look into	look like	look out
pass away	run into	run across
take after		

APPLICATION

Use the cue in parentheses to supply an appropriate two-word verb for each of the following sentences:

> *EXAMPLE:*   (Came to adulthood) My parents _____**grew up**_____ in New Mexico.

1. (Resembles) Everyone tells me that my son _____ me.

2. (Demolish) Giorgio heard that the city is going to _____ that old building.

3. (Discover information) They were looking at the newspaper and trying to _____ what time *The Rocky Horror Picture Show* is playing on Saturday.

4. (Submit an assignment) All of the instructor's classes _____ their research papers on the same day.

5. (Free oneself) As soon as she _____ of debt, she plans to buy a new car.

6. (Force someone to leave) Did he really get _____ of another apartment?

7. (Put on clothing to see if it fits) When I _____ the jacket, I realized that I had gained several pounds too many.

8. (Finish a supply) While watching yet another sad love story, my grandmother _____ a whole box of tissues.

9. (Exist satisfactorily) Sara just cannot _____ with her roommate.

10. (Gain admittance) Jack hoped that he could _____ the class even though he wasn't on the roster.

▼ CHAPTER REVIEW

- **Only certain combinations of helping verbs and main verbs make sense in English.**
- **Helping verbs always come before main verbs.**
- Use the **base form** of the verb with the helping verbs *can, could, may, might, must, shall, should, will, would, do, does,* and *did.*
- Use the **helping verbs** *do, does,* and *did* in three ways: **to express a negative meaning with the adverbs** *not* or *never,* **to ask a question,** and **to emphasize a main verb used in a positive sense.**

- To form one of the **perfect tenses,** use *have, has,* or *had* followed by the *-ing* form of the verb.
- To **express an action in progress,** use *am, is, are, was, were, be,* or *been,* followed by the *-ing* form of the verb.
- Some **verbs** may be **followed by an *-ing* word or *to* + verb** with little or no difference in meaning; in other cases, the meaning changes substantially.
- Use some **verbs** with a **noun or pronoun followed by *to* + verb.** After some verbs, you may leave out the noun or pronoun, or omit the word *to.*
- Be careful to use **two-word** verbs correctly. In some cases the two parts of the verb may be separated by other words.

PRACTICE

Use your knowledge of verbs to underline the correct item in parentheses. If both items would be correct, underline either one of them.

Red Emma

[1]Named by law-enforcement officials of her day "the most dangerous woman in America," Emma Goldman (born, was born) in Lithuania in June 1869. [2]In 1885, sixteen-year-old Goldman and her older sister boarded a ship bound for New York. [3]Goldman quickly found work as a seamstress in a Rochester factory, but she soon began (feeling, to feel) that her life in the New World might be no better than the life she had (leave, left). [4]In 1889, her disappointment (caused Goldman to, caused to Goldman) pack up her sewing machine and move to New York's Lower East Side, the center of political labor activism for Eastern European immigrants. [5]Soon, Goldman was deeply (involve, involved) in the struggle for social and labor reform. She declared herself a feminist and an anarchist, and she advocated free speech, free love, and birth control. [6]As a lecturer, Goldman would (electrified, electrify) her listeners; she traveled across the country to bring her political messages to audiences

across the United States. [7]Goldman (was imprison, was imprisoned) many times for the contents of her speeches, yet she continued (to speak, speaking) out for her political beliefs. [8]Because of her beliefs, Goldman (was label, was labeled) "Red Emma." [9]Ultimately, Goldman (was deported, was deport) from the United States, and she died in exile in Canada. [10]After her death, however, her body (was return, was returned) to the United States. [11]Her grave is in Chicago; the monument (was erected, erected) to her carries her own words: [12]"Liberty will not (descend, descending) to a people. [13]A people must (to raise, raise) themselves to liberty."

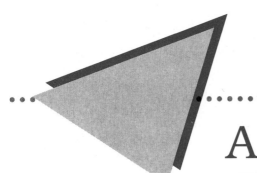

Addressing Other ESL Concerns

▼ CHAPTER PREVIEW

Even native speakers sometimes have problems with the complexity of rules for the correct use of English. If you are a nonnative English speaker, some aspects of English may give you difficulty even after you have become fluent in the language.

This chapter addresses **aspects of English** that tend to cause some problems even for nonnative speakers who can communicate well in English. Some of them may serve as a review of information, while others address issues that are not covered anywhere else in the text.

A Professional Writer Models English for ESL Students

About the Reading: Elizabeth Wong's essay "The Struggle to Be an All-American Girl" first appeared in the *Los Angeles Times.* In her essay, Wong recalls her childhood rejection of Chinese culture and her resistance to learning Chinese, a language that she considered a source of embarrassment. But, as her essay ultimately reveals, by the age of twenty, she had a different attitude toward the importance of her culture. In the excerpt that follows, Wong describes how her mother enforced the children's attendance at Chinese school.

As You Read: Watch carefully how Wong uses adverbs and adjectives. Pay particular attention to the series of adjectives in the second paragraph that are printed in bold type.

From "The Struggle to Be an All-American Girl"

[1]Every day at 5 P.M., instead of playing with our fourth- and fifth-grade friends or sneaking out to the empty lot to hunt ghosts and animal bones, my brother and I had to go to Chinese school. [2]No amount of kicking, screaming, or pleading could dissuade my mother, who was solidly determined to have us learn the language of our heritage.

[3]Forcibly, she walked us the **seven long hilly** blocks from our home to school, depositing **our defiant tearful** faces before the stern principal. [4]My only memory of him is that he swayed on his heels like a palm tree, and he always clasped **his impatient twitching** hands behind his back. [5]I recognized him as **a repressed maniacal** child-killer, and knew that if we ever saw his hands we'd be in trouble.

After You Read: Refer to the reading selection to complete the following questions:

1. Identify the -*ly* adverbs that appear in the final sentence of the first paragraph and the first line of the second: _____ and

   _____ .

2. In each sentence in the second paragraph, Wong uses several adjectives to modify a single noun. Identify each of the nouns:

   a. seven long hilly _____

   b. defiant tearful _____

   c. impatient twitching _____

   d. a repressed maniacal _____

Using Subjects and Verbs Correctly

The English language requires a subject for all sentences except commands, sentences in which the subject *you* is understood ("Sit down"). If you speak a language that allows you to omit the subject, remember that English does not.

When the subject does not come before the verb—its usual position in English—English sometimes requires *there* or *it* at the beginning of the sentence or clause.

There are some suspicious-looking people in that car.

(The subject **people** follows the verb **are,** so **there** is needed at the beginning of the sentence.)

It is healthier to eat a salad instead of a steak.
(The subject **to eat a salad** follows the verb **is,** so **it** is needed at the beginning of the sentence.)

The word **it** is also used to start a sentence describing the weather. When you use **it** in this way, **it** is the subject of the sentence.

You may speak a language that allows you to leave out the verb when the meaning of the sentence is clear without it. Remember that English language rules do not allow you to leave out verbs.

Incorrect: Nadia in the backyard.

Correct: Nadia **is** in the backyard.

Except for questions, sentences in English **cannot** begin with **is, are, was,** or **were.**

Incorrect: **Is** already in his seat.

Correct: Adam **is** already in his seat.

APPLICATION

Complete the following sentences by supplying an appropriate word in each blank:

     EXAMPLE: _____**Tricia**_____ has a large collection of beer cans.

1. If _____ fly nonstop, _____ can reach São Paolo

   in twelve hours.

2. _____ are several gas stations down the street.

3. _____ is usually muggy in New York in August.

4. Jamey _____ exceptionally busy right now.

5. _____ is better to fly than drive across country.

6. _____ have great interest in martial arts.

7. _____ is a great day today.

8. _____ loves to go to baseball games.

9. _____ is a large community of Samoans in this area.

10. Whenever _____ are ready, _____ can leave.

Avoiding Needless Repetition

In some languages words are repeated later in the sentence. In English, however, such repetitions are not allowed, so be careful not to add a word that merely repeats another word in the sentence. The following rules will help you remember what you should not repeat:

1. Use pronouns only when they are substituting for a noun or another pronoun and not in addition to the noun or other pronoun.

   Incorrect: The boy **he** was hit by the ball.
   (The pronoun **he** needlessly repeats the noun **boy**.)

   The truck barely missed the car that we were riding in **it**.
   (The pronoun **it** needlessly repeats the noun **car**.)

   Correct: The boy was hit by the bus.
   The truck barely missed the car that we were riding in.

2. Do not add the word **there** to a sentence unnecessarily.

   Incorrect: The place where I like to eat lunch **there** is closed today.
   (The word **there** serves no purpose in the sentence.)

   Correct: The place where I like to eat lunch is closed today.

APPLICATION

Rewrite the sentences that follow in order to eliminate unnecessary repetition:

   EXAMPLE: Casey he is a good friend.

   Casey is a good friend.

1. My father he lives in Korea.

   _____

   _____

2. The cat that lives next door it had kittens last week.

   _____

   _____

3. The man ran after the bus that we were riding in it.

   _____

   _____

4. My cousins they own a small computer business.

   _____

   _____

5. The thief ran into the video store we were standing in it.

   _____

   _____

6. The place where I like to go in the summer that is Portland.

   _____

   _____

7. The car that was wrecked it was only six months old.

   _____

   _____

8. The job I liked best it was in a clothing store.

   _____

   _____

9. The people who saw the accident they were in shock.

   _____

   _____

10. The place where I live there is thirty minutes from the college.

   _____

   _____

Placing Adjectives

Adjectives describe nouns or pronouns. Even native speakers of English often have trouble with the use of adjectives, so, if English is not your native language, you may have some problems deciding where to place adjectives.

You have already learned that in English adjectives usually come before the nouns they describe. You have also learned that adjectives may appear after linking verbs. In both of the following sentences, the adjective **new** describes the noun **dress.** In the first example, the adjective precedes the noun; in the second example, the adjective follows the linking verb **was.**

Marisa wore a **new** dress.

Marisa's dress was **new.**

When several adjectives come in front of a noun, however, you may have trouble deciding how to arrange them. If the adjectives are separated by commas, you may place them in any order. If they are not separated by commas, they are usually arranged in a particular order.

Incorrect: Maria was wearing a **blue silk beautiful** dress.

Correct: Maria was wearing a **beautiful blue silk** dress.

A general guide to follow when you use a series of unseparated adjectives before a noun follows. But because this list is a general guide, be prepared to find exceptions.

USUAL ORDER OF UNSEPARATED ADJECTIVES

1. **Article or other noun marker**

   a, an, the, his, Jeri's, six, a few, much

2. **Evaluative word**

   delicious, trustworthy, good-looking, horrible

3. **Size**

   tiny, gigantic, large, little

4. **Length or shape**

   circular, square, long, short

5. **Age**

   old, new, antique, aged

6. **Color**

   violet, green, black, gold

7. **Nationality**

   Irish, Korean, Brazilian, Italian

8. **Religion**

   Jewish, Muslim, Protestant, Catholic

9. **Material**

   paper, fur, wool, metal

10. **Noun used as an adjective**

    dog (as in dog house), *bedroom* (as in bedroom wall)

11. **Noun being described**

    child, cat, garage, coat, typewriter

Because long lists of unseparated adjectives are awkward, as a general rule, you should use no more than *two or three* unseparated adjectives between the article or other noun marker and the noun that the adjectives are describing.

Look carefully at these examples using unseparated adjectives:

a beautiful old silver ring
    (article, evaluative word, age, material, noun)

some small green bottles
    (noun marker, size, color, noun)

the rectangular wooden bookshelf
    (article, shape, material, noun)

APPLICATION
....

Using information about the usual order of unseparated adjectives, arrange the following words in the correct order:

    EXAMPLE: many, chairs, antique, leather, comfortable

                 many comfortable antique leather chairs

1. Italian, cozy, restaurant, a

2. red, some, roses, long-stemmed

_____

3. junkyard, dog, snarling, the

_____

4. antique, a, black, Rolls Royce

_____

5. oval, table, large, claw-footed, a

_____

6. new, sweater, purple, cotton, her

_____

7. an, energetic, boy, Irish

_____

8. apartment, high-rise, spacious, Ed's

_____

9. quilt, brightly colored, American, patchwork, the

_____

10. pie, tasty, apple, deep-dish, a

_____

Placing Adverbs

Adverbs that modify verbs appear in various positions. You can place them at the beginning or end of a sentence, before or after the verb, or between a helping verb and a main verb.

Quickly, we ran for shelter.

Georgianna picked up her mother's antique bowl **carefully.**

Martina **always** wins when we play cards.

Albert is **usually** at work on time.

Be careful, however, not to place an adverb between the verb and any words needed to complete the meaning of the verb.

Incorrect: He tossed **carelessly** the book onto the desk.
(The adverb *carelessly* comes between the verb *tossed* and the word *book,* which tells what he tossed.)

Correct: He **carelessly** tossed the book onto the desk.
(Now the words that tell what he did *carelessly* are all together.)

APPLICATION

Place the adverb in parentheses in a correct position within the sentence.

EXAMPLE: LaToya drinks coffee in the mornings. (always)

LaToya always drinks coffee in the morning.

1. Matt doodles instead of taking notes. (often)

    _____

    _____

2. Lucien and Francisco play basketball every Saturday morning. (usually)

    _____

    _____

3. Chris calls Rebecca every night. (usually)

    _____

    _____

4. Camilo enrolled in a karate class last week. (eagerly)

    _____

    _____

5. Emery walks to work. (occasionally)

    _____

    _____

6. I hate to cook, but I'm glad to do it for you. (generally)

_____

_____

7. After the child received her good conduct award, she jumped up and down. (happily)

_____

_____

8. She screamed at the arresting officer. (hysterically)

_____

_____

9. Corina unwrapped the package. (carefully)

_____

_____

10. Vinh's younger brother pulled the car into the driveway. (slowly)

_____

_____

Adjectives

In English, you can use both **-*ing* words** and **past participles** as **adjectives.** You can easily identify past participles because they usually end in **-*ed, -d, -en, -n,*** or **-*t.***

-*ing* words:	bor**ing**	confus**ing**
past participles:	bor**ed**	confus**ed**

When you use -*ing* words or past participles as adjectives, they can precede the nouns they modify. They can also follow linking verbs; if they follow linking verbs, they will describe the subject of the sentence.

Patrice was a **terrified** viewer.
    (**terrified** describes the noun ***viewer***)

The movie was **terrifying.**
    (***terrifying*** describes the subject ***movie***)

An -**ing word** should **describe a person or thing that causes an experience or feeling.**

Although the speaker received a lot of publicity, she was **boring.**
(The speaker is *causing* boredom, not experiencing it.)

Listening to her, the students were **bored** to tears.
(The students are *experiencing* boredom, not causing it.)

If you have learned English as a second language, the following -*ing* words and past participles may cause you trouble:

annoying/annoyed   exhausting/exhausted
boring/bored   fascinating/fascinated
confusing/confused   frightening/frightened
depressing/depressed   satisfying/satisfied
exciting/excited   surprising/surprised

APPLICATION

Using the word in parentheses, supply the correct -*ing* form or **past participle** for the sentence.

EXAMPLE: My mother was very ___annoyed___ the first time I stayed out all night. (annoy)

1. The exhibit about African-American life in the 1930s was _____. (fascinate)

2. Tara was _____ after working a fourteen-hour shift. (exhaust)

3. Jasmine was pleasantly _____ when she realized that her friends were taking her to dinner to celebrate her birthday. (surprise)

4. The employees found the company's offer of compensation _____. (insult)

5. My Aunt Velma finds the level of violence in children's cartoon shows _____. (disgust)

6. Terence's lab partner is a perfectionist; she is never _____ with his work. (satisfy)

7. The small child was _____ by the rattlesnake. (frighten)

8. When Helene saw the amount of reading she was expected to do for her American History course, she immediately felt _____. (depress)

9. While discussing their upcoming Hawaiian vacation, Leslie and Danielle became extremely _____. (excite)

10. I felt completely _____ when I arrived at JFK airport for the first time. (confuse)

▼ CHAPTER REVIEW

- **English requires a subject for all sentences except commands.**
- When the subject does not come before the verb, **English sometimes requires the word *there* or *it* at the beginning of the sentence or clause.**
- *It* **can be used to start a sentence describing the weather.** When you use *it* in this way, *it* is the subject of the sentence.
- **Except for questions, sentences in English cannot begin with *is*, *are*, *was*, or *were*.**
- **Do not repeat the subject of a sentence.**
- **In English, adjectives usually precede the nouns they modify; they may also appear following linking verbs.**
- **The usual order of unseparated adjectives is article or other noun marker, evaluative word, size, length or shape, age, color, nationality, religion, material, noun used as an adjective, the noun modified.**
- In English -***ing*** **words and past participles can act as adjectives.** Past participles usually end in *-ed*, *-d*, *-en*, *-n*, or *-t*.

PRACTICE

To test your mastery of the material in this chapter, read the paragraph that follows, and circle each correct item in parentheses.

Frontier Schools

[1]When nineteenth-century Americans embarked on the westward migration in search of land and new lives, those who came to live on the (untamed American, American untamed) frontier faced

particular challenges. [2](It was, Was) a great challenge for pioneer families to educate their children. [3]When settlers first moved into an area, there were no schools of any kind, so (pioneer women, pioneer women they) first taught their children at home. [4]As more families began to move into an area, neighbors banded together to construct their own (small wooden or sod, wooden or sod small) schoolhouses, which often also served as churches on Sundays. [5]Building a school was not difficult. [6]A major difficulty, however, was finding equipment. [7]Some (early frontier, frontier early) schools had no educational equipment of any kind; children learned through memorization. [8]And, while many pioneer children were (excited, exiting) at the prospect of learning to read and write, the children's curriculum was limited to whatever reading material they could bring from home, whether a dictionary or a family Bible. [9]Because pioneer (families they, families) needed the labor of each family member, children attended school only as their chores and the weather allowed. [10]In addition, due both to low pay and (harsh working, working harsh) conditions, frontier schools had difficulty finding and keeping good teachers.

Highlights

Articles

- Use **a** or **an** with singular count nouns whose specific identity is not known to the reader.
- Do not use **a** or **an** with plural or noncount nouns.
- Use **the** with most nouns whose specific identity is known to the reader.
- Do not use **the** with plural or noncount nouns meaning "all" or "in general"; do not use **the** with most singular proper nouns.

Verbs

Match helping verbs and main verbs appropriately:

- After the helping verbs **can, could, may, might, must, shall, should, will,** and **would,** use the **base form of the verb.**

- After helping verbs that are a form of **do,** use the **base form of the verb.**

- To form one of the perfect tenses, use **have, has,** or **had** followed by a past participle (usually ending in **-ed, -d, -en, -n,** or **-t**).

- To express an action in progress, use **am, is, are, was, were, be,** or **been** followed by a **present participle** (the **-ing** form of the verb).

- Some verbs may be followed by an **-ing** word or **to** + **verb** with little or no difference in meaning; in other cases, the meaning changes substantially.
- Use some verbs with a noun or pronoun followed by **to** + **verb.** In certain cases, you will sometimes include the noun or pronoun and other times leave it out. After some verbs with nouns or pronouns, omit the word **to.**
- Be aware of verbs composed of two words, a verb followed by a preposition or an adverb; in some cases the second word may be separated from the first by other words. Two-word verbs often express an idiomatic meaning that cannot be understood literally.

Other ESL Concerns

- Do not omit subjects or the beginning word **there** or **it.**
- Avoid needless repetition. Use pronouns only when they are substituting for a noun or another pronoun, and do not add the word **there** to a sentence unnecessarily.

448

- Place **adjectives** carefully. In general, place adjectives before the word they describe or after a linking verb. Be sure to place a series of unseparated adjectives in the proper order.
- Be careful not to place an **adverb** between the verb and any words needed to complete the meaning of the verb.

PRACTICE

Use the sentences that follow to test your mastery of the material in Unit 9. If you have difficulty, go back and review the information in Chapters 35–37.

A. Follow the rules for definite and indefinite articles to complete each sentence. If no article is needed, write **NA** for "no article."

> *EXAMPLE:*   Nestor took _____**the**_____ advice of his counselor.

1. The children ride _____ 8:00 school bus every morning.

2. His country is plagued with _____ poverty.

3. The drought-stricken countryside was badly in need of _____ rain.

4. To celebrate her college graduation, Belinda ordered _____ bottle of wine with dinner.

5. Sometimes it's hard to get _____ information about course prerequisites.

6. _____ beauty of the plan is its simplicity.

7. A fox ate _____ chickens.

8. Marjorie moved to _____ United States from Canada.

9. Be sure to put _____ soap on the grocery list.

10. Wally was always munching on _____ piece of fruit.

B. Write the helping verb that correctly completes the following sentences:

> *EXAMPLE:*   We _____**will**_____ go on vacation next May.

1. Regina _____ not spoken to her father for two years.

2. I _____ heard of that book, but I have never read it.

3. Owen _____ not have the repair manual last week.

4. The last time I saw him, he _____ working downtown.

5. Dracula _____ always been one of my heroes.

6. _____ he really pierce his nose in three places?

7. Sometimes Carole seems to _____ lost her mind.

8. Last week I noticed that my history professor _____ begun to eat compulsively during lectures.

9. By next week the child _____ have read ten books.

10. Raymond _____ look for the CD when he gets home.

C. Underline the correct item in parentheses. If both items could be correct, underline them both.

EXAMPLE: She began (to speak, speaking) in an abusive tone.

1. The woman finally gave up and stopped (to search, searching) for her missing necklace.

2. The principal (expected see, expected to see) an improvement in student test scores.

3. She allowed her son (walk, to walk) to the nearby park.

4. Corey tried unsuccessfully (make, to make) his dog behave.

5. Mr. Edwards went straight to the library and checked (the book out, out the book).

6. I came (across the word, the word across) in two of my assignments last night.

7. Lorenzo will drop (off it, it off) on his way home.

8. The child certainly (takes after her father, takes her father after).

9. Please let me (get, to get) you some coffee.

10. Antonio still has not (decided, to decide) which university to attend.

D. Supply two or three unseparated adjectives for each of the following sentences; place them in the correct order between the noun marker and the noun that they will modify.

EXAMPLE: The ___elderly Lebanese___ man sat in the dark.

1. A _____ table sat in the center of the room.

2. Sally's _____ car was in the repair shop.

3. The _____ children played in the yard.

4. Some _____ students were hanging around the

   college library.

5. An _____ potted plant was delivered to his office.

6. Two _____ snakes slithered across his shoulder.

7. His _____ apartment was fumigated last week.

8. Our _____ uncle came to visit for a month.

9. Some _____ bottles decorated the shelf.

10. She wore a _____ flower in her hair.

E. Rewrite each sentence correcting any errors. Look for needless
repetition, misplacement of adjectives or adverbs, and incorrect
use of subjects and verbs. If a sentence is correct as written, put a
C on the line.

    EXAMPLE: Are too many people in my history class.

        There are too many people in my history class.

1. Is not healthy to be under too much stress.

   _____

   _____

2. The airport exceptionally busy around Thanksgiving.

   _____

   _____

3. The salesman he was very helpful.

   _____

   _____

4. The train that we were waiting for was almost two hours late.

   _____

   _____

5. The market where I like to shop there gives double coupons.

    _____

    _____

6. Maria's aunt and uncle they live in El Salvador.

    _____

    _____

7. Tristan's black new leather sofa cost more than $1,000.

    _____

    _____

8. He opened carefully the door to the cage.

    _____

    _____

9. Jenna often takes the subway home from work.

    _____

    _____

10. Is a beautiful night for a walk in the moonlight.

    _____

    _____

UNIT **10**

Writing Paragraphs

CHAPTER 38

Writing Effective Paragraphs

▼ CHAPTER PREVIEW

In its most basic form, a paragraph is a group of sentences that are related to each other. On occasion, a paragraph can even be a single sentence. Most of the time, the start of a new paragraph is signaled by indenting the first line of the paragraph five spaces. You may have noticed, however, that in some documents, paragraphs are separated from one another by double spacing instead of indenting; this practice has become common in business writing. You may also have noticed that paragraphs can have different purposes and that paragraphs can be either self-contained or part of a much larger work, such as an essay, a letter, a textbook chapter, or a short story.

Some paragraphs are used to introduce or conclude a piece of writing, to provide a transition between two ideas, or to record dialogue between characters. But most paragraphs in college writing develop a main idea. This chapter focuses on paragraphs that state and develop a main idea. In addition to becoming familiar with this type of paragraph, you will learn various techniques for making paragraphs clear and effective.

Main Idea Paragraphs

In most college writing, paragraphs that develop an idea contain three basic elements: (1) a statement of the main idea, called a **topic sentence,** (2) **specific support** to back up, explain, or illustrate the main idea, and (3) a **restated topic sentence** to conclude the paragraph. A **topic sentence** states the **topic** and gives a **controlling idea** for the paragraph. The controlling idea tells what point the writer will make about the topic. The **specific support** consists of examples, reasons, or facts that make the point stated in the topic sentence. The **restated topic sentence** reminds the reader of the topic and controlling idea of the paragraph.

455

Look at the sample paragraph that follows. The topic sentence, specific supports, and restated topic sentence in the sample paragraph have been diagrammed for you at the end of the paragraph. Before you look at the diagram, however, see if you can identify these three elements yourself.

Aunt Trudy

[1]Aunt Trudy is well known in our family for being stingy. [2]When her son left for college on a scholarship, she gave him a new toothbrush as a going-away gift. [3]When her 1941 Buick finally broke down, she decided to buy a bus pass instead of "wasting good money" on another car. [4]And, when her only daughter, Nora, got married, Aunt Trudy bought her a slightly stained $5.00 wedding dress at the Thrift Shop. [5]Even though my aunt could afford to live comfortably, she is, without a doubt, the cheapest person I know.

Topic sentence: Aunt Trudy is well known in our family for being stingy. (topic = Aunt Trudy, controlling idea = stingy)

Specific support: Gift to son

Specific support: Refused to replace car

Specific support: $5.00 Thrift Shop dress for daughter

Restated topic sentence: Even though my aunt could afford to live comfortably, she is, without a doubt, the cheapest person I know. (topic = Aunt Trudy, controlling idea = cheapest)

APPLICATION

To practice identifying the elements of a main idea paragraph, read the following paragraph and locate the topic sentence, specific supports, and restated topic sentence. Write these elements in the diagram that follows the paragraph.

Disadvantages of Studenthood

[1]While everyone says that going to college is a good idea, being a college student has its disadvantages. [2]For one thing, after paying registration fees and buying books, even if you work, you never have any extra money for things like clothes or concert tickets. [3]And, when all your nonstudent friends are having a fantastic time at one of the greatest parties of the century, you are usually in the library researching some boring topic you could not care less about. [4]Finally, it is almost impossible to have a relationship with someone else when

that person is talking about things like commitment and expressing feelings and all you can think about are things like that math test that's coming up on Monday or the fact that you really ought to be reading that 800-page novel your English teacher assigned a month ago. [5]Even though you know that going to college is the best thing you could be doing, it does have its drawbacks.

Topic sentence: _____

_____

Specific support: _____

_____

Specific support: _____

_____

Specific support: _____

_____

Restated topic sentence: _____

_____

Topic Sentences

The most important part of a good paragraph is its **main idea.** In college writing, the **topic sentence,** the sentence that states the main idea, serves as a guide to the entire paragraph. Because it acts as a guide for the paragraph, the topic sentence comes first in the paragraph.

Remember, a topic sentence is made up of two parts:

1. **Your topic**—the subject of your essay, presented in a key word or phrase.
2. **Your controlling idea**—your attitude, opinion, or judgment about your topic.

In the following topic sentences (TS), the topic and controlling idea (CI) have been labeled:

Topic   CI

Anthropology I is an **interesting** class.
> (The **topic,** "Anthropology I," tells what the paragraph will be about. The **controlling idea,** "interesting," is the writer's opinion about the topic.)

Topic   CI

Going to the mall in December is **like entering a battle zone.**
> (The **topic,** "going to the mall in December," tells what the paragraph will be about. The **controlling idea,** "like entering a battle zone," is the writer's attitude toward the topic.)

Announcing what you will discuss, your **topic,** and what point you will make in your paragraph, your **controlling idea,** lets the reader know what to expect and keeps you focused on making your point.

APPLICATION

In each of the topic sentences that follow, identify both the topic of the sentence and the controlling idea (CI):

EXAMPLE: Linda is a terrible gossip.

Topic: _____Linda_____   CI: ___terrible gossip___

1. Duncan's bedroom looks like a bomb hit it.

   Topic: _____   CI: _____

2. That statistics class was a nightmare.

   Topic: _____   CI: _____

3. Their vacation to New Orleans was the best ever.

   Topic: _____   CI: _____

4. Her stepson is noisy and rude.

   Topic: _____   CI: _____

5. Learning a new language can be fun.

   Topic: _____   CI: _____

6. Marina's cousin dresses like Morticia Addams.

   Topic: _____   CI: _____

7. Paintballing is Teddy's favorite sport.

   Topic: _____   CI: _____

8. Erwin's greatest talent is bragging.

   Topic: _____   CI: _____

9. My all-time favorite movie is *The Fugitive.*

   Topic: _____   CI: _____

10. When I eat Indian food, hotter is better.

Topic: _____   CI: _____

Writing Workable Topic Sentences

There are several things to remember about writing a good topic sentence. First, the topic sentence can never be a statement of fact. Instead, a topic sentence must contain an **opinion.** The following sentences would not be good topic sentences because they each express a fact rather than an opinion that can be supported or proven:

Gerard's bedroom contains a bed and a sound system.

My parents went to the Poconos for their honeymoon.

There is no idea in these sentences that the writer can develop into a paragraph. But, by adding an opinion, each sentence can be revised so that it can be an effective topic sentence.

Gerard's bedroom reflects his personality.

The highlight of my parents' life was their honeymoon in the Poconos.

In addition to expressing an opinion, an effective topic sentence must be limited enough to be supported convincingly in one paragraph. The sentences that follow would not make good topic sentences because the ideas they introduce are too broad or too general to support effectively:

All lawyers are crooks.

The laser disc is the most important invention of the twentieth century.

In the first sentence, the topic "All lawyers" is a broad generalization that cannot be proven, and in the second sentence, the controlling idea "the most important invention of the twentieth century" is too broad to be convincingly supported, especially in one paragraph. In order to be used as topic sentences, both of these statements would have to be limited.

The lawyer I hired after my car accident turned out to be a crook.
(The topic "all lawyers" has been limited to a particular lawyer.)

The laser disc is an important invention for film fans.
(The controlling idea "the most important invention of the twentieth century" has been limited to "important invention for film fans.")

APPLICATION ONE

Working with a partner, read the sentences that follow and decide which are effective topic sentences. Indicate workable topic sentences by writing **TS** in the space provided. Mark sentences that are too broad or that are statements of fact with an **X.**

EXAMPLE: _____**X**_____ Denise has one hazel eye and one blue eye.

_____ 1. Bettina's younger brothers are Nintendo addicts.

_____ 2. John Lennon was murdered by a fan.

_____ 3. Ancient World History is an interesting class.

_____ 4. Everyone at Bay City College is friendly.

_____ 5. Jason Brown is the best swimmer on the team.

_____ 6. Cara's dog tore up the laundry room floor.

_____ 7. Even though she is only eight years old, my niece is wise beyond her years.

_____ 8. Michael Bolton is the best singer of all time.

_____ 9. Although he is only forty, Ralph acts like an old man.

_____ 10. Eating fast food can be bad for you.

APPLICATION TWO

For each of the following general subjects, devise a topic sentence. To be sure each of your topic sentences has a topic and a controlling idea, circle the topic and underline the controlling idea.

EXAMPLE: Subject: your doctor

Topic sentence: (My doctor) has a terrible bedside

manner.

1. Subject: one of your professors

Topic sentence: _____

_____

2. Subject: a neighbor's dog

    Topic sentence: _____

    _____

3. Subject: a certain type of music

    Topic sentence: _____

    _____

4. Subject: a particular fast-food restaurant

    Topic sentence: _____

    _____

5. Subject: a particular television show

    Topic sentence: _____

    _____

6. Subject: a relative of yours

    Topic sentence: _____

    _____

7. Subject: your bedroom

    Topic sentence: _____

    _____

8. Subject: a friend's personality trait

    Topic sentence: _____

    _____

9. Subject: a freshman's first day of college

    Topic sentence: _____

    _____

10. Subject: your least favorite task

    Topic sentence: _____

    _____

Unity

Once you have decided on a topic and a controlling idea, you need to be sure that all of the supporting material in your paragraph sticks to your topic and clearly relates to your controlling idea. If all of your supporting material is clearly related to the topic sentence, your paragraph will have **unity.** In effect, your topic sentence promises your reader what you will talk about and what point you will make. If your paragraph is not unified with the topic sentence, you are breaking that promise.

Read the following paragraph. Notice how the sentences in bold type do not directly relate to the **controlling idea—happiest day of my life.**

Day of Freedom

[1]The happiest day of my life was the day I had my husband served with divorce papers. [2]**It took me years of therapy to get to that point.** [3]I felt elated when I saw the process server hand him that large manila envelope. [4]In addition, I had a deep sense of satisfaction when I realized that never again would my husband's obnoxious sister march into my home, rummage through every drawer and closet, and help herself to my clothes. [5]**She is an administrative secretary who is married to an engineer and she can certainly afford her own clothes.** [7]Finally, I literally jumped with joy when I realized that I never had to talk to my mother-in-law again. [7]**She never did like me, and she constantly told me so.** [8]All in all, the day I finally began to free myself from a bad marriage was the happiest and most important day of my life.

Look carefully at the sentences in bold type. In each case, the sentence does not directly relate to the topic sentence: "The happiest day of my life was the day I had my husband served with divorce papers." Sentence 2 tells about the writer's therapy, not about the happiest day of her life. Sentence 5 tells about her sister-in-law's economic position, not about the writer's happiness. And sentence 7 describes her mother-in-law's attitude, not the writer's happiness.

APPLICATION ONE

In the space provided, write the controlling idea (**CI**) of the topic sentence of each paragraph. Then, circle the number of any sentence in the paragraph that does not clearly relate to the topic sentence.

EXAMPLE: [1]My cat, Liz, is smarter than some people. [2]She always seems to know in advance when an earthquake is about to strike. ³She can climb a tree in the twinkling of an eye. ⁴She eats only food that is good for her and never touches alcohol. ⁵Most intelligent of all is the way she completely ignores the television; whenever she sees a game show on, she just curls up and goes to sleep. ⁶Without a doubt, Liz proves every day that she has more brains than some people.

CI _____**smarter than some people**_____

1.   ¹Attending Dr. Miramar's art history class was the most boring experience of my life. ²Before every class, I had to drink several large cups of coffee so that I could stay awake during her long-winded explanations. ³However, I usually began to doze off after the first five minutes, especially when I heard gentle snores coming from every corner of the lecture hall. ⁴She always wore long dangly earrings that sounded like little bells. ⁵When the lights went out so that she could show slides, my only source of entertainment was calculating how long it would be before I heard a head hit a desk, or, even better, a body hit the floor. ⁶I spent most of my time in that class waiting for the semester to end.

CI _____

2.   ¹My Aunt Kay is the worst busybody I know. ²She spends most of her time on the telephone trying to get information out of friends and relatives and then telling terrible stories about people's children. ³I'll never forget the time she got stranded in a phone booth. ⁴She loves watching *Lifestyles of the Rich and Famous* and reading fan magazines so that she has juicy star stories to pass along. ⁵She's never happier than when she has a new piece of information, and she has no hesitations about sharing it with everyone. ⁶Basically, telling your troubles to Aunt Kay is the equivalent of advertising them in a national newspaper.

CI _____

3.   ¹My career as a high school football player was the best time of my life. ²I do, however, have permanent problems as a result of knee surgeries. ³I was always excused from homework before a big game and after a big win. ⁴The local pizza place also had a "Free Pizza for Players" policy. ⁵And as a football hero, I never lacked for dates. ⁶My senior year we even won the Championship, and I was named to the All-County First Team. ⁶Overall, I felt really good about myself and my accomplishments as a football player.

CI _____

4.   ¹The day my wife gave birth to our twins was a nightmare. ²First of all, our brakes went out on the way to the hospital, and we had to flag down a taxi. ³When the driver realized my wife was

in labor, he informed us that he was unlicensed and had no insurance. [4]We begged him to let us out at the nearest phone booth, where I dialed 911 while my wife moaned in pain. [5]The dispatcher told me he would send an ambulance, but when it didn't arrive, I called again. [6]This time, he told me that the ambulance had been involved in an accident but that help was on the way. [7]When we finally got to the hospital, one baby was born in the elevator and the other in a hallway. [8]Even though I love my daughters, I always think of the day they were born as one of the worst days of my entire life.

CI _____

5.   [1]Working at a fast-food restaurant was the worst job I ever had. [2]The pay was so terrible that I began to feel I was working for free, especially when I found out that a "meal allowance" was being deducted from my paycheck, whether or not I ate during my shift. [3]In addition, my work hours kept changing, so much so that I had a hard time going to classes on a regular basis. [4]A few regular customers who were really nice to me were the only positive element of that job. [5]My supervisor, a middle-aged man who was obviously unhappy with his life, thought that college students had things too easy and went out of his way to see that I experienced his version of the "real world." [6]This meant, of course, that he made sure that I was assigned to the worst jobs and the worst shifts. [7]Without a doubt, the fast-food business was my worst-ever job experience.

CI _____

APPLICATION TWO

Read the following paragraph and underline the controlling idea in the topic sentence. Circle the number of each sentence that is not unified with the rest of the paragraph.

Little Monsters

[1]Even though they are related to me, I think that my sister's three children are the most horrible kids ever born. [2]Besides screaming constantly, they have no respect for anyone or anything. [3]Once in a while they look cute when they're asleep. [4]They have no table manners, they want everything they see in every store, and they make life miserable for anyone unfortunate enough to have to spend time with or near them. [5]I've seen them fight over toys like wild animals. [6]In fact, they hit, bite, and scratch each other at every opportunity. [7]Every time my sister asks me to baby-sit I try desperately to

think of excuses, but she whines about how exhausted she is and how she needs to get out for a few hours and begs me until I give in. [8]Once when I was having dinner at my sister's house, the oldest child wanted his sister's ice cream, so he threw her down a flight of stairs. [9]Another time, in a fight over who could hold the family cat, the youngest child screamed so much that she turned blue and had to be rushed to the emergency room. [10]The cat is incredibly nervous. [11]But the worst episode of all was the time that they got into a three-way battle over who should get to sit on the department store Santa Claus' lap. [12]I'll never forget the blood, the ruined holiday outfits, and the horrified stares of passing shoppers. [13]My sister smoked yet another cigarette. [14]I tried to pull them off each other. [15]As they screamed obscenities at me for interfering, I realized that my sister's children truly are little monsters who will probably end up in a triple-seater electric chair somewhere. [16]My mother thinks they all have food allergies.

Coherence

In writing, the term **coherence** refers to the relationship between individual elements in a composition. A paragraph is coherent if all of its parts clearly relate not only to the topic and controlling idea but also to one another. To make your paragraphs coherent, you need to include information to help the reader move smoothly from one idea to another.

In the sample paragraphs that follow, you can see how the following devices contribute to paragraph coherence:

1. Explanations of support
2. Repetition of terms referring to the topic
3. Reminders of the controlling idea
4. Transitions
5. Logical order

The paragraph that follows has a topic sentence, provides details to support the topic sentence, and even includes a restated topic sentence, yet it still lacks coherence.

Paragraph 1

My roommate, Vito, is a jinx. The bathtub in the apartment directly above us overflowed, and water leaked into our living room, leaving stains on the sofa my parents had just given me. At his brother's wedding, a rainstorm collapsed the caterer's tent, soaked the guests, and ruined the bride's gown. The bride's mother was knocked out by a large hailstone that hit her directly on the head. The geology instructor was injured by a falling boulder the day before school started, and the class had to be canceled. Wherever Vito goes, disaster seems to follow.

While a number of details about unfortunate occurrences are provided in this paragraph, it is not clear just how they relate to the topic sentence and to each other. What is Vito's connection to the leaky bathtub? What does the wedding incident have to do with Vito? Was he even there? What is Vito's relation to the geology instructor? The paragraph lacks coherence because these questions are left unanswered.

In Paragraph 2, which follows, Paragraph 1 has been revised to provide information that tells how the specific supports relate to the topic sentence. **Terms that refer to the topic (*Vito, he*)** are repeated, and **modifiers telling who, how, when, where, why, and under what circumstances** have been added. Added material is italicized.

Paragraph 2

My roommate, Vito, is a jinx. *The day he moved into the apartment,* the bathtub in the apartment directly above us overflowed, and water leaked into our living room, leaving stains on the sofa my parents had just given me. *When Vito was acting as best man at his brother's wedding,* a rainstorm collapsed the caterer's canopies, soaked the guests, and ruined the bride's gown. The bride's mother was knocked out by a large hailstone that hit her directly on the head. *After Vito decided at the last minute to sign up for Geology I last semester,* the geology instructor was injured by a falling boulder *in an accident* the day before school started, and the class had to be canceled. Wherever Vito goes, disaster seems to follow.

In Paragraph 2, you can clearly see how the items in the specific supports are related to the topic, Vito. In the following paragraph, **details** have been added to Paragraph 2 **to remind you of the controlling idea.** Notice how the italicized words in Paragraph 3 emphasize disaster and bad luck.

Paragraph 3

My roommate, Vito, is a jinx. The day he moved into the apartment, the bathtub in the apartment directly above us overflowed, and *murky* water leaked into our living room, leaving *nasty-looking brown* stains on the *new white* sofa my parents had just given me. When Vito was acting as best man at his brother's *garden* wedding, an *unpredicted* rainstorm collapsed the caterer's canopies, soaked the *frantic* guests, and ruined the *hysterical* bride's *designer* gown. *To everyone's horror,* the bride's mother was knocked out by a large hailstone that hit her directly on the head. After Vito decided at the last minute to sign up for Geology I last semester, the geology instructor was injured by a falling boulder in a *freak* accident the day before school started, and the class had to be canceled. Wherever Vito goes, disaster seems to follow.

The specific support in Paragraph 3 is now clearly related to the topic and the controlling idea in the topic sentence. In Paragraph 4, **transitions** have been added to help you move more smoothly from one specific support to the next. Transitions also help to stress the **logical order** of ideas in the paragraph.

Paragraph 4

My roommate, Vito, is a jinx. *For example,* the day he moved into the apartment, the bathtub in the apartment directly above us overflowed, and murky water leaked into our living room, leaving nasty-looking brown stains on the new white sofa my parents had just given me. *Even worse,* when Vito was acting as best man at his brother's garden wedding, an unpredicted rainstorm collapsed the caterer's canopies, soaked the frantic guests, and ruined the hysterical bride's designer gown. *And,* to everyone's horror, the bride's mother was knocked out by a large hailstone that hit her directly on the head. *Perhaps worst of all,* after Vito decided at the last minute to sign up for Geology I last semester, the geology instructor was injured by a falling boulder in a freak accident the day before school started, and the class had to be canceled. *Yes,* wherever Vito goes, disaster seems to follow.

In Paragraph 4, the transition *for example* tells you that a specific support will follow, and the word *and* indicates that an additional detail will follow. Words like *worse* and *worst* let you know that the supporting details have been arranged in the order of bad to worst. Other common arrangements are least to most important, left to right or front to back, and first to last. The word *yes* at the beginning of the last sentence signals the conclusion of the paragraph.

The following transitions are often used to help readers move from one idea to another.

COMMON TRANSITIONS

To add an idea: also, and, another, equally important, finally, furthermore, in addition, last, likewise, moreover, most important, next, second, third

To give an example: for example, for instance, namely, thus, evidently

To make a contrast: and yet, but, however, instead, nevertheless, on the contrary, on the other hand, still

To begin a conclusion: as a result, clearly, hence, in conclusion, no wonder, obviously, then, therefore, thus, yes

APPLICATION

In the following paragraph, underline transitions and circle words that remind you of the controlling idea in the topic sentence.

Hernando's Security

[1]Hernando's German shepherd, Loco, is a frightening guard dog. [2]For example, if anyone even walks near Hernando's yard, Loco begins to growl menacingly and curl back his lips in an intimidating sneer. [3]If someone should actually step up to the front gate, Loco makes a horrible noise like a crazed baboon protecting its territory; at the same time, he rips furiously at his shredded toy football as if to show what he would like to do to the person's head. [4]And, if a hand touches the handle at the top of the gate, it is likely to be met with ice-pick-sharp fangs as Loco hurls himself through the air like a deadly heat-seeking missile after his fleshy target. [5]Rodney Miller, the only person who has ever gotten inside the gate besides Hernando himself, still wears Loco's teeth marks on his left leg; moreover, Rodney has a puffy scar from the six-inch gash in his head where it hit the walkway after the 125-pound Loco pounced on him and crumpled him to the ground before he could reach the front door. [6]With his fearsome demeanor and intimidating reputation, Loco is better protection than a home security system.

▼ CHAPTER REVIEW

- A **paragraph** that develops an idea contains three basic elements:

  1. A statement of the main idea, called a **topic sentence.**
  2. **Specific support** to back up, explain, or illustrate the main idea.
  3. A **restated topic sentence** to conclude the paragraph.

- A **topic sentence** is made up of two parts:

  1. **Your topic**—the subject of your essay, presented in a key word or phrase.
  2. **Your controlling idea**—your attitude, opinion, or judgment about your topic.

- A **workable topic sentence** is an opinion that can be convincingly supported in one paragraph. Do not use a fact or an unsupportable opinion as a topic sentence.
- Your paragraph has **unity** if all of the supporting details clearly relate to the topic sentence.
- Use the following devices to contribute to paragraph **coherence:**

  1. Explanations of support
  2. Repetition of terms referring to the topic
  3. Reminders of the controlling idea
  4. Transitions
  5. Logical order

Developing Paragraphs

▼ CHAPTER PREVIEW

In the previous chapter you learned about the basic features of a main idea paragraph. Depending on your reason for writing—to explain how to do something, to give information, to tell what something looks like—you will use different methods for developing your paragraphs. This chapter will show you four common methods for developing paragraphs: description, process, exemplification, and comparison/contrast.

Description

A **descriptive paragraph** gives the reader a picture of a person, place, or thing. When you write a description of a person, you may want to focus either on physical appearance or on personality, or you can combine both. For example, if you are writing about a family member who inspired you, you might wish to include a paragraph enabling the reader to picture the person you are discussing, as well as a paragraph highlighting personality traits of this person.

When you describe a place or a thing, you may want to give your reader a picture of the physical features of the site or object, or you may wish to share a particular emotional or sensory response it evokes, depending on your reason for writing. If your art history instructor asks you to describe a particular feature of Byzantine architecture, for example, she probably wants a straight physical description rather than an emotional response with words like *majestic* or *awe-inspiring.*

The following sample paragraph focuses on the sense of hearing to describe a college cafeteria. Read the paragraph carefully and then complete the items that follow it.

No Place to Study

[1]The college cafeteria is no place to go for some quiet studying, as I found out when I went there to study for my first big math test. [2]As soon as I found a deserted table and spread out my books, the three muscled giants at the table next to me began arguing vigorously over some botched football play from last Friday's game. [3]Then, as I opened my algebra book, I was suddenly startled by the crash of forty plastic trays being tossed onto a wooden holder by a student worker. [4]Awakened by the crash, an infant stashed somewhere in the room began to scream with fright. [5]After the screams died down, I tried desperately to focus my attention on the equations I had to know for the exam, but my mind was continuously distracted by the disgusting thunk and splosh of uneaten food and drinks shoved into the half-filled trash container near my table. [6]Finally, I gave up on the noisy cafeteria and decided to look for a quiet spot in the library.

1. Look carefully at the topic sentence. What is the topic?

   _____ What is the controlling idea? _____

   _____

2. List the specific supporting details in the order they appear:

   a. _____

   b. _____

   c. _____

   d. _____

3. List at least five words in the paragraph that remind you of the

   controlling idea: _____

   _____

4. Circle the letter of the item that best describes the logical order of the paragraph:

   a. Least to most noisy.

   b. First to last disturbance.

   c. Front to back of the cafeteria.

Writing Your Own Descriptive Paragraph

Write a paragraph on **one** of the following topics:

1. Describe a scene, emphasizing a mood or a sense. For example, you may wish to describe a peaceful place, such as an area in a park near a stream, or a busy, crowded place, like a supermarket on Sunday afternoon. Or, you may wish to focus on the sensory impression that seems to dominate a scene, such as a *noisy* rock concert or an *aromatic* perfume counter in a department store.

Before You Write: Observe or mentally recreate the scene and jot down as many details as you can. Then choose the single sense (hearing, sight, smell) or the mood you want to use as the controlling idea of your paragraph.

Writing the First Draft: Write a topic sentence that identifies where you are and the sense or mood you will focus on. You may have to write several topic sentences before you can capture the dominant feeling or sense. Once you are satisfied with your topic sentence, select from your list of impressions all of the details that reinforce the mood or deal with the sense in your topic sentence. Then, decide on a logical order for presenting these details—left to right, least to most, first to last. Finally, concentrate on presenting your details in complete sentences.

Revising: Once you have written a draft of your paragraph, check for unity and coherence, making sure that you have included only those details that support your controlling idea and that you have included transitions and reminders of the topic and controlling idea wherever appropriate. Then, check your sentences for correct grammar and mechanics.

2. Describe a person, focusing on one personality trait or characteristic. For example, you could show that your cousin is a flashy dresser or that a friend is obsessively neat or habitually sloppy.

Before You Write: Choose as your subject someone who exhibits a strong personal characteristic or habitual behavior. List all of the details you can think of that illustrate this characteristic or behavior, such as actions, looks, hairstyle, speech, and so on.

Writing the First Draft: Write a topic sentence that identifies the person you will describe and tells what character trait will be the controlling idea for your paragraph. Once you are satisfied with your topic sentence, look over your list of details and decide on a logical order for presenting these details—first to last, top to bottom, or least to most (lazy, messy, rude, kind, etc.). Finally, concentrate on presenting your details in complete sentences.

Revising: Once you have written a draft of your paragraph, check for unity and coherence, making sure that you have included only those details that support your controlling idea and that you have included transitions and reminders of the topic and controlling idea wherever appropriate. Then, check your sentences for correct grammar and mechanics.

Process

A **process paragraph** can either give instructions for completing a process (tells how to do something) or describe how a process works (tells how something is done). The type of process paragraph you choose depends on your purpose in writing. For a chemistry lab, for example, you might need to write a paragraph describing the result of an experiment. Or, in a child development course, you might need to devise instructions telling a child how to complete a simple task. The following sample paragraph gives instructions for performing a process.

Crashing a Class

¹Your chances of adding—or "crashing"—a class in which you are not already enrolled can be greatly enhanced by following several simple steps. ²First, before classes begin, go to the bookstore and buy all of the books for the course. ³Then, on the first day of school, arrive at the classroom early to show you are eager to learn and to get a seat in the front of the room. ⁴After you find your seat, stack all of your textbooks on top of your desk to demonstrate how well prepared you are. ⁵When the instructor arrives, be sure to make eye contact with her, and respond appropriately to any preliminary remarks she makes; for example, you should smile at any of her attempts at humor and nod wisely at any of her serious statements. ⁶This way, by the time the instructor takes roll and finds out that you—now her favorite student—are not enrolled in the course, she will be inclined to accept you as a late add. ⁷Finally, if your worst fears are realized and the instructor announces that the class is filled to capacity, wait until after the class period ends and humbly request that the instructor allow you the privilege of attending the course even without being enrolled—just in case someone else who doesn't appreciate this wonderful learning opportunity should drop out. ⁸If you follow these simple steps, your efforts at crashing a class are almost guaranteed to be successful.

---

1. Look carefully at the topic sentence. What is the topic? _____

_____

What is the controlling idea?

_____

2. In brief form, list the steps given in the instructions. The first one has been listed for you.

   Step one: buy books

   Step two: _____

   Step three: _____

   Step four: _____

   Step five: _____

   Step six: _____

3. List three transition words that appear at the beginning of a sentence. _____

4. Circle the letter of the item that best describes the logical order of the paragraph.

   a. Least to most effective.

   b. First step to last step.

   c. Least to most difficult.

Writing Your Own Process Paragraph

Write a paragraph on **one** of the following topics:

1. Tell your reader how to accomplish a *simple* task that requires no more than ten steps to complete.

Before You Write: To help you choose a topic, try listing simple tasks that you perform regularly or that you are very familiar with, such as cleaning a fishbowl, changing a tire, or preparing a food item. After you have picked a process, break it down into simple steps and number the steps in order.

Writing the First Draft: Write a topic sentence that names your process and has a controlling idea containing a word like ***easy, simple,*** or ***successful.*** Then write your steps in complete sentences and arrange them in the order the reader should follow to perform the task.

Revising: Look over the draft of your paragraph to make sure that you haven't left out any necessary steps and that all of the steps are arranged in sequence. For coherence, add any necessary transitions and combine steps into a single sentence wherever appropriate. Then, check your sentences for correct grammar and mechanics.

2. Write a paragraph that describes a process. You might tell how a simple piece of machinery operates or tell how something is made.

Before You Write: To select a topic, brainstorm simple processes that you observe frequently. If you work in addition to attending college, think of the processes you see on the job, such as the preparation of a fast-food item, formation of a document, or mixing of a can of custom paint. Once you have chosen a process, break it down into steps and number the steps in order.

Writing the First Draft: Write a topic sentence that names the process you will describe and contains a controlling idea. If you have difficulty coming up with a controlling idea, you might use the number of steps involved. Then, write your steps in complete sentences in the order that they occur.

Revising: Look over the draft of your paragraph to make sure that you haven't left out any necessary steps and that all of the steps are arranged in sequence. For coherence, add any necessary transitions and combine steps into a single sentence wherever appropriate. Then check your sentences for correct grammar and mechanics.

Exemplification

An **exemplification paragraph** uses examples or reasons to develop the point made in the topic sentence. The point of the paragraph may be illustrated by a number of examples or by a single extended example, or it may be backed up by a number of reasons. On a psychology exam, for instance, you might illustrate your understanding of a behavior by giving several examples of ways people might exhibit this behavior or by using by one long example about a particular individual who typifies this behavior. Or, in an essay for political science, you might give your opinion of a candidate's political stance and support your opinion with reasons based on facts and observations.

The following paragraph is developed using numerous examples.

Easy Living

[1]With all the home gadgets available today, life is becoming easier and more hassle-free than ever before. [2]No more do you have to get drenched getting out of your car to open the garage door on a rainy day. [3]Now all you have to do is push a button on your automatic garage door opener and let it do the work for you. [4]Nor do you have to worry about missing that important phone call if you step out for a while; all you need is a phone-answering machine. [5]Best of all, you no longer have to make sure you're home in time to catch your favorite television program; all you have to do is tell your voice-activated remote control to program your VCR to tape the show for you. [6]Today, from the moment you wake up to the aroma of just-

brewed coffee courtesy of your timer-controlled coffee maker, to the time you clap your hands to turn off the lights when you're ready to go to sleep, your day is made easier by advances in home technology.

....

1. Look carefully at the topic sentence. What is the topic? _____

   _____

   What is the controlling idea? _____

   _____

2. List the specific examples used to support the topic sentence.

   a. _____

   b. _____

   c. _____

   d. _____

   e. _____

3. Circle the letter of the item that best describes the pattern of development in the paragraph:

   a. One extended example.

   b. Numerous short examples.

4. List three additional examples that could be used to develop the topic sentence in this paragraph.

   a. _____

   b. _____

   c. _____

Writing Your Own
Exemplification Paragraph

Write a paragraph on **one** of the following topics:

1. Explain why you enjoy a particular hobby or activity, such as collecting sports cards, going to rock concerts, or doing a craft.

Before You Write: To help you select a topic, make a list of the things you enjoy doing when you have time off from studying. Once you have chosen a topic, try brainstorming to find examples of all the things that make your hobby or activity enjoyable. Once you have selected the examples you will use, number them in order with the most enjoyable last.

Writing the First Draft: Write a topic sentence that names the hobby or activity and has a controlling idea that captures your feeling about your activity (enjoyable, exciting, relaxing, etc.). Then write your examples in complete sentences. Try to make your examples as specific as possible; in some cases you may want to use more than one sentence to present one example.

Revising: Look over the draft of your paragraph to make sure that your examples are as specific as possible and that all of them support the controlling idea. For coherence, add transitions wherever necessary. Common transitions in exemplification paragraphs include *for instance, for example, in addition,* and *also.* Finally, check your sentences for correct grammar and mechanics.

2. Write about a pet peeve—something that irritates you. Perhaps inconsiderate drivers get you fuming, or maybe you find yourself complaining to friends about unfriendly salesclerks or hard-to-open product packaging—these would qualify as pet peeves.

Before You Write: Make a list of all the things that gripe you—not major life problems, just minor irritations. Then look over your list to choose a topic for your paragraph. Once you have chosen a topic, write the topic at the top of a blank sheet of paper and freewrite about it to come up with specific examples explaining why you find it irritating or telling about different occasions on which it has irritated you.

Writing the First Draft: Write a topic sentence that describes your pet peeve; be sure to include a controlling idea that reflects your irritation. Then use complete sentences to portray the examples from your freewriting. Be sure to be as specific as possible and arrange your examples in order from least to most irritating.

Revising: Look over the draft of your paragraph to make sure that your examples are as specific as possible and that all of them support the controlling idea. For coherence, include reminders of the controlling idea and add transitions wherever necessary. Common transitions you may wish to use are *for instance, for example, moreover,* and *furthermore.* Finally, check your sentences for correct grammar and mechanics.

Comparison/Contrast

A **paragraph that compares** two subjects shows how they are alike; a **paragraph that contrasts** two subjects shows how they are different. In responding to a question on a history exam about the Civil War, for example, you might need to include a paragraph showing differences in the leadership styles of Grant and Lee. If you were writing a review of a comedy act for your college newspaper, you might have a paragraph showing similarities between an unknown comedian and a comedian with whom your readers would be familiar.

A comparison/contrast paragraph can be **patterned in two ways: subject by subject** or **point by point.** The paragraphs that follow include the same basic information, but the first one uses the point-by-point pattern, and the second uses the subject-by-subject pattern.

Two Professors
(Point by Point)

[1]My chemistry professor, Dr. Gates, and my English literature professor, Mr. Moreno, have teaching styles that are completely different. [2]Dr. Gates always arrives a few minutes before class begins so that she can organize her detailed lecture notes and get her seating chart prepared for taking roll. [3]In contrast, Mr. Moreno usually saunters into the classroom about five minutes late clutching a tattered old copy of some novel with his scribbled notes in the margins; he hasn't taken roll since the first day of class. [4]Standing at the podium, Dr. Gates begins lecturing over the assigned material precisely on the hour. [5]Mr. Moreno leans against a table in the front of the room and spends about ten minutes talking about something he's read that may or may not have anything to do with the assigned material. [6]During class, Dr. Gates takes questions from the students only during the last part of the period when she has finished lecturing; the format of Mr. Moreno's class is an informal discussion, so students can ask questions at any time. [7]Dr. Gates' formal style of teaching could not be more different from Mr. Moreno's casual approach.

Two Professors
(Subject by Subject)

[1]My chemistry professor, Dr. Gates, and my English literature professor, Mr. Moreno, have teaching styles that are completely different. [2]Dr. Gates always arrives a few minutes before class begins so that she can organize her detailed lecture notes and get her seating chart prepared for taking roll. [3]Standing at the podium, Dr. Gates begins lecturing over the assigned material precisely on the hour. [4]During class, Dr. Gates takes questions from the students only during the last part of the period when she has finished lecturing. [5]In contrast, Mr. Moreno usually saunters into the classroom about five minutes late clutching a tattered old copy of some novel with his scribbled notes in the margins; he hasn't taken roll since the first day of class. [6]Mr. Moreno leans against a table in the front of the room and spends about ten minutes talking about something he's read that may or may not have anything to do with the assigned material. [7]The format of Mr.

Moreno's class is an informal discussion, so students can ask questions at any time. [8]Dr. Gates' formal style of teaching could not be more different from Mr. Moreno's casual approach.

....

1. The topic sentences in both paragraphs are the same. What is the topic? _____ What is the controlling idea? _____

2. Refer to the point-by-point version of the paragraph to fill in the missing elements in the following diagram:

   Topic and CI: _____

   _____

   Arrival: Gates and Moreno

   Beginning of class: Gates and Moreno

   During class: _____

   Restated topic sentence: _____

   _____

3. Refer to the subject-by-subject version of the paragraph to fill in the missing elements in the following diagram:

   Topic and CI: _____

   _____

   Gates: Arrival

              Beginning of class

              _____

   Moreno: Arrival

              _____

              During class

   Restated topic sentence: _____

   _____

Writing Your Own Comparison/ Contrast Paragraph

Write a paragraph on **one** of the following topics:

1. Use either the point-by-point method or the subject-by-subject method of organization to compare or contrast two places where you have lived. Perhaps you have lived in two big cities that have a lot of similarities, or perhaps you have moved to a small town from a large city.

Before You Write: Once you have chosen the two places, decide whether you will compare them (show how they are alike) or contrast them (show how they are different). You will also need to choose three or four areas on which to focus, such as size, population, climate, or economic base. Then, decide whether you will organize your paragraph using the point-by-point method or the subject-by-subject method.

Writing the First Draft: Write a topic sentence that names both places and indicates whether you will focus on similarities or differences. Whichever pattern of organization you have chosen, be sure that for every aspect of place A you include, you mention that same aspect of place B. For example, if you discuss the physical appearance of place A, then be sure to discuss the physical appearance of place B.

Revising: Look over the draft of your paragraph to make sure that you have stuck to the controlling idea: if you are showing how two places are alike, for instance, make sure you have not mentioned differences. For coherence, add any necessary transitions, such as *similarly, in contrast, however,* and *likewise.* Then check your sentences for correct grammar and mechanics.

2. Contrast two of the following: radio stations (two rock stations, two talk stations, etc.), sports teams (same sport), schools (same level—secondary, community college, university, etc.), people you have dated, or professors. Be sure that the things or people have enough differences to develop a paragraph.

Before You Write: After you have chosen your general subject, limit your topic by listing or brainstorming about your subject (radio stations, teams, etc.) to find the two specific things or individuals you will write about. Then, decide whether you will organize your paragraph using the point-by-point method or the subject-by-subject method and choose three or four bases for your contrast. For instance, if you are writing about ratio stations, you might focus on differences in type of music, disc jockeys, and listener interaction.

Writing the First Draft: Write a topic sentence that names the two things or people you will discuss and indicates that you will focus on their differences. Whichever pattern of organization you have chosen, be sure that for every aspect of A you include, you mention that same aspect of B. For example, if you discuss the management style of baseball team A, then be sure to discuss the management style of baseball team B.

Revising: Look over the draft of your paragraph to make sure that you have stuck to the controlling idea of difference. For coherence, add any necessary transitions, such as *in contrast, however,* and *on the other hand.* Then check your sentences for correct grammar and mechanics.

▼ CHAPTER REVIEW

- Four common **methods of paragraph development** are

  1. description
  2. process
  3. exemplification
  4. comparison/contrast.

- A **descriptive paragraph** gives the reader a picture of a person, place, or thing.
- A **process paragraph** can either give instructions for completing a process or describe how a process works.
- An **exemplification paragraph** uses examples or reasons to illustrate a point.
- A **comparison paragraph** shows how things are alike; a **contrast paragraph** shows how they are different.
- In your college assignments outside an English class, whatever method you choose will be determined by your purpose in writing.

Index